First Workshop on Knowledge Extraction and Integration for Deep Learning Architectures (DeeLIO 2020)

Deep Learning Inside Out

Online
19 November 2020

ISBN: 978-1-7138-1994-3

EMNLP 2020

Deep Learning Inside Out (DeeLIO):
The First Workshop on Knowledge Extraction and Integration for Deep Learning Architectures

Proceedings of the Workshop

November 19 2020

Introduction

Welcome to the inaugural **Workshop on Knowledge Extraction and Integration for Deep Learning Architectures (DeeLIO)**! The DeeLIO workshop aims to bring together the knowledge interpretation, extraction and integration lines of research in deep learning, and cover the area in between. We hope that the DeeLIO workshop will become a regular forum for the exchange of ideas and will contribute to foster collaboration within these research fields.

This volume includes the 11 papers presented at the workshop. DeeLIO was co-located with the 2020 Conference on Empirical Methods in Natural Language Processing (EMNLP 2020) and was held on November 19, 2020 as an online workshop, following the exceptional "new normal" circumstances of 2020.

For the first edition of the workshop, we received 21 paper submissions. We accepted 11 papers (acceptance rate 52.4%) which were presented at the workshop. The accepted papers cover both thematic aspects of DeeLIO: the extraction of linguistic knowledge from deep neural models and the integration of knowledge from external resources, for different languages and applications. In addition to the regular workshop papers, the first edition of DeeLIO also included presentations of several papers from the EMNLP companion volume 'Findings of EMNLP' which were thematically relevant to the workshop goals. There was no distinction between oral and poster presentations this year, and all presentations involved pre-recorded talks accompanied with individual live Q&A sessions.

We take this opportunity to thank the DeeLIO program committee for their thorough reviews. We also thank the authors who presented their work at DeeLIO, and the workshop participants for the valuable feedback and discussions. Finally, we are honored to have two excellent invited talks from our invited speakers Ellie Pavlick and Eduard Hovy.

The DeeLIO workshop organizers,
Eneko Agirre, Marianna Apidianaki, and Ivan Vulić

Organizers:

Eneko Agirre (University of the Basque Country)
Marianna Apidianaki (University of Helsinki)
Ivan Vulić (University of Cambridge)

Invited Speakers:

Eduard Hovy (Carnegie Mellon University)
Ellie Pavlick (Brown University)

Program Committee:

Mikel Artetxe (Facebook AI)
Yonatan Belinkov (Harvard University)
Gemma Boleda (University Pompeu Fabra)
Jose Camacho-Collados (University of Cardiff)
Grzegorz Chrupała (Tilburg University)
Luis Espinosa-Anke (University of Cardiff)
John William Hewitt (Stanford University)
Goran Glavaš (University of Mannheim)
Aishwarya Kamath (New York University)
Gorka Labaka (University of the Basque Country)
Olga Majewska (University of Cambridge)
Prodromos Malakasiotis (Athens University of Economics and Business)
Tal Linzen (Johns Hopkins University)
Roberto Navigli (Sapienza University)
Kim-Anh Nguyen (University of Stuttgart)
Sebastian Padó (University of Stuttgart)
Valeria de Paiva (Samsung Research)
Jonas Pfeiffer (TU Darmstadt)
Edoardo Maria Ponti (University of Cambridge)
Simone Paolo Ponzetto (University of Mannheim)
Alessandro Raganato (University of Helsinki)
Marek Rei (Imperial College London)
Roi Reichart (Technion, IIT)
Steven Schockaert (University of Cardiff)
Sabine Schulte im Walde (University of Stuttgart)
Aitor Soroa (University of the Basque Country)
Daniil Sorokin (Amazon)
Lena Voita (University of Edinburgh)
Yogarshi Vyas (University of Maryland)
John Wieting (Carnegie Mellon University)
Deyi Xiong (Tianjin University)

Table of Contents

Correcting the Misuse: A Method for the Chinese Idiom Cloze Test

Xinyu Wang[1], Hongsheng Zhao[2], Tan Yang[2], Hongbo Wang[1]
[1]State Key Laboratory of Networking and Switching Technology,
Beijing University of Posts and Telecommunications
[2]School of Computer Science (National Pilot Software Engineering School),
Beijing University of Posts and Telecommunications
[1,2]{xinyu.wang, zhaohs, tyang, hbwang}@bupt.edu.cn

Abstract

The cloze test for Chinese idioms is a new challenge in machine reading comprehension: given a sentence with a blank, choosing a candidate Chinese idiom which matches the context. Chinese idiom is a type of Chinese idiomatic expression. The common misuse of Chinese idioms leads to error in corpus and causes error in the learned semantic representation of Chinese idioms. In this paper, we introduce the definition written by Chinese experts to correct the misuse. We propose a model for the Chinese idiom cloze test integrating various information effectively. We propose an attention mechanism called Attribute Attention to balance the weight of different attributes among different descriptions of the Chinese idiom. Besides the given candidates of every blank, we also try to choose the answer from all Chinese idioms that appear in the dataset as the extra loss due to the uniqueness and specificity of Chinese idioms. In experiments, our model outperforms the state-of-the-art model.

1 Introduction

The Chinese idiom comprehension requires the ability to understand Chinese idioms. Chinese idiom, which is called "成语" (*chengyu*) in Chinese, consists of four characters. Chinese idioms are mostly derived from stories in ancient literature from Chinese history, and often reflect the moral behind the stories. To measure the ability of understanding Chinese idioms, the Chinese idiom cloze test dataset was proposed (Zheng et al., 2019): given a sentence with a blank, an examinee is required to choose an idiom which best matches the context surrounding the blank. Table 1 shows an example of the Chinese idiom cloze test.

The misuse of Chinese idioms is prevalent among Chinese native speakers who did not receive a professional Chinese education. Due to the metaphorical meaning of Chinese idioms, even Chinese native speakers who do not major in Chinese would use a Chinese idiom with its literal meaning, which causes misuse. Table 2 shows some common misuses of Chinese idioms. The misuse meaning is often related to the literal meaning.

The misuse of Chinese idiom appears in various social media and text such as Weibo and Zhihu. The Chinese word embeddings and Chinese language models are pretrained on these corpora that contain the misuse of Chinese idioms and learn the incorrect meaning of Chinese idioms. For example, in Table 3, we use Google Translate to translate Chinese idioms finding that some results are incorrect, and the incorrect meanings happen to be the common misuses of these Chinese idioms. In this paper, we introduce the definition of Chinese idiom, which is written by the Chinese experts, to correct the misuse. The complete definition describes the accurate interpretation and usage of Chinese idioms. Besides, because the misuse often comes from the literal meaning of the Chinese idiom, we propose an attention mechanism called Attribute Attention that extracts the relationships between the character-level and word-level representations.

Moreover, using the definition to correct the misuse does not mean that the non-misuse part would be dropped. Take 七月流火 in Table 2 as an example. The common misuse of 七月流火 is not totally incorrect. 七月流火 referring to the weather is correct, but the weather turning hot is incorrect. Therefore, we propose Attribute Attention to make use of other representations of 七月流火 even if they contain incorrect information.

In addition, Chinese idioms are derived from stories in ancient literature and contain abundant information. Chinese idioms contain more information so they are more likely to be used in a more specific context than common words. For example, 美 means "beautiful", 轮 means "wheel",

Proceedings of Deep Learning Inside Out (DeeLIO):
The First Workshop on Knowledge Extraction and Integration for Deep Learning Architectures, pages 1–10
Online, November 19, 2020. ©2020 Association for Computational Linguistics

Sentence with a blank	他们希望能＿＿再进一步 They hope that they can ___ and achieve greater success.
A candidate idiom	百尺竿头 Literal translation: at the top of a hundred-foot pole. Free translation: make still further progress.
Definition	比喻到了极高的境地，仍须继续努力，求更大的进步。 When one has achieved great success, one should continue to work hard to make greater progress.

Table 1: An example of the Chinese idiom cloze test that contains a sentence, one of the candidate idioms, and the definition of the idiom.

Chinese idiom	**Literal meaning**	**Misuse meaning**	**Correct meaning**
翻云覆雨	A huge change for clouds and rain	Magnificent	Skillful
七月流火	Fire in July	The weather turned hot	The weather turned cold
三人成虎	Three persons become a tiger	Cooperation lead to great strength	Spread rumors

Table 2: Some common misuses of Chinese idioms.

and 奂 means "magnificent". The Chinese idiom 美轮美奂 means "a building is beautiful". 美轮美奂 can be used only when describing a building, whereas those four characters are not related to building. When those four characters are combined, the meaning becomes narrow. It is more difficult to find two similar Chinese idioms than normal words. In this paper, besides choosing the answer from the given candidates, our model tries to choose the answer from the whole vocabulary of candidate Chinese idioms that appear in the dataset and calculate its loss as a part of the final loss. In this way, relationships between much more idioms can be captured every time. It costs very few extra computing resources but provides significant improvement.

In experiments, our model outperforms the state-of-the-art model. Our main contributions are summarized as follows:

- We introduce the definition and propose Attribute Attention to balance the importance of different representations of the Chinese idiom.

- We add an extra loss obtained by choosing the answer from all Chinese idioms that appear in the dataset, which costs very few extra computing resources but provides significant improvement.

2 Related Work

The cloze test is a classic task of reading comprehension and many methods were proposed (Hermann et al., 2015; Chen et al., 2016; Wang et al., 2018; Zhang et al., 2018; Fu et al., 2019; Fu and Zhang, 2019). The Chinese idiom cloze test is more challenging because Chinese idioms convey the metaphorical meaning and are misused sometimes. Most works related to idioms focused on English idioms identification (Gedigian et al., 2006; Katz and Giesbrecht, 2006; Fazly et al., 2009; Shutova et al., 2010; Salton et al., 2016; Do Dinh et al., 2018b; Flor and Beigman Klebanov, 2018; Do Dinh et al., 2018a; Liu and Hwa, 2018). Some works have tried to use definitions: Spasic et al. (2017) analyzed the sentiment of definitions; Fathima Shirin and Raseek (2018) used the similarity between different definitions. However, these methods introduced definitions but did not try to understand them. Liu et al. (2017) used CharLSTM to encode the meaning of idioms, which has a similar idea to (Jiang et al., 2018). Only a few works have been done with Chinese idioms such as building Chinese emotion lexicons (Xu et al., 2010) and improving Chinese word segmentation (Chan and Chong, 2008; Sun and Xu, 2011; Wang and Xu, 2017). Chengyu Reader (CR) (Jiang et al., 2018) is proposed for the Chinese idiom cloze test, which used the def-

Chinese idiom	Common misuse meaning	Google Translate	Correct translation
空穴来风	Groundless	Groundless	Grounded and justified
危言危行	Dangerous words and behavior	Dangerous words	Upright words and behavior
差强人意	Unsatisfactory	Unsatisfactory	Generally satisfactory

Table 3: Some incorrect translations of Chinese idioms form Google Translate.

initions and the attention mechanism of Attentive Reader (AR) (Hermann et al., 2015; Chen et al., 2016).

3 Approach

Formally, the Chinese idiom cloze test requires the model to choose the correct answer from a number of the candidate idioms given a sentence with a blank. The sentence is defined as a sequence of characters with a blank, which is also called context in the following. The candidate Chinese idiom is defined as a sequence of four characters, which is called idiom in the following. The definition is defined as a sequence of characters interpreting the corresponding idiom. In this paper, the term "BERT" refers to the BERT-like models (Devlin et al., 2019; Liu et al., 2019; Lan et al., 2019; Sanh et al., 2019), because any one of them and even the new BERT-like model in the future can be used in our model. Figure 1 is an overview of our model. The following sections will introduce every part of our model one by one.

3.1 Integrating Context and Definition

The definition is not the next sentence of the context. The context and definition do not belong to the same document. It is inappropriate to set the context as the first sentence and set the definition as the second sentence separated by [SEP] for BERT. In this section, as shown in Figure 2, we propose a way to integrate the context and definition with BERT, which lets the model "know" that the definition is mainly related to the idiom.

We input the context, the candidate idiom, and definition together. For example, we input the context "他们希望能＿＿再进一步 *(they hope they can ＿＿ and achieve greater success)*", the candidate idiom "百尺竿头 *(make still further progress)*", and the definition "比喻高的成就 *(an outstanding achievement)*" together as "他们希望能 [MASK] 再进一步 [SEP] 百尺竿头:比喻高的成就 [SEP]". The context is defined as v. The candidate idiom and the definition are defined as d

here.

The Multi-Head Attention is applied to the context and definition in different ways. Formally, the Multi-Head Attention for the context is:

$$v_i^{(l)} = \text{MultiHeadAttention}(m^{(l-1)}, v_1^{(l-1)}, v_2^{(l-1)}, \ldots, v_{|v|}^{(l-1)}) \quad (1)$$

where $v_i^{(l)}$ denotes the i-th character of the context at the l-th layer, and $m^{(l)}$ denotes the [MASK] token at the l-th layer; $|v|$ denotes the number of characters of the context. The context only can "see" itself and the [MASK].

The Multi-Head Attention for the definition is:

$$d_i^{(l)} = \text{MultiHeadAttention}(m^{(l-1)}, v_{[SEP]}^{(l-1)}, d_1^{(l-1)}, d_2^{(l-1)}, \ldots, d_{|d|}^{(l-1)}) \quad (2)$$

where $d_i^{(l)}$ denotes the i-th character of the definition d at the l-th layer, and $v_{[SEP]}^{(l-1)}$ denotes the first [SEP] token at the l-th layer; $|d|$ denotes the number of characters of the definition. The definition is inaccessible to the context, which avoids that the BERT regards the definition as the next sentence of the context.

The Multi-Head Attention for the [MASK] is:

$$m^{(l)} = \text{MultiHeadAttention}(m^{(l-1)}, v_1^{(l-1)}, v_2^{(l-1)}, \ldots, v_{|v|}^{(l-1)}, d_1^{(l-1)}, d_2^{(l-1)}, \ldots, d_{|d|}^{(l-1)}) \quad (3)$$

The [MASK] can pay attention to the characters of both the context and definition. On the one hand, [MASK] "knows" what kind of idiom could match the context as the correct answer. On the other hand, [MASK] "knows" the candidate idiom definition. [MASK] integrates the information from context v definition and d in the character-level.

In this way, the relation between the context and the definition is built through the [MASK]. The output of the [MASK] is defined as h_m.

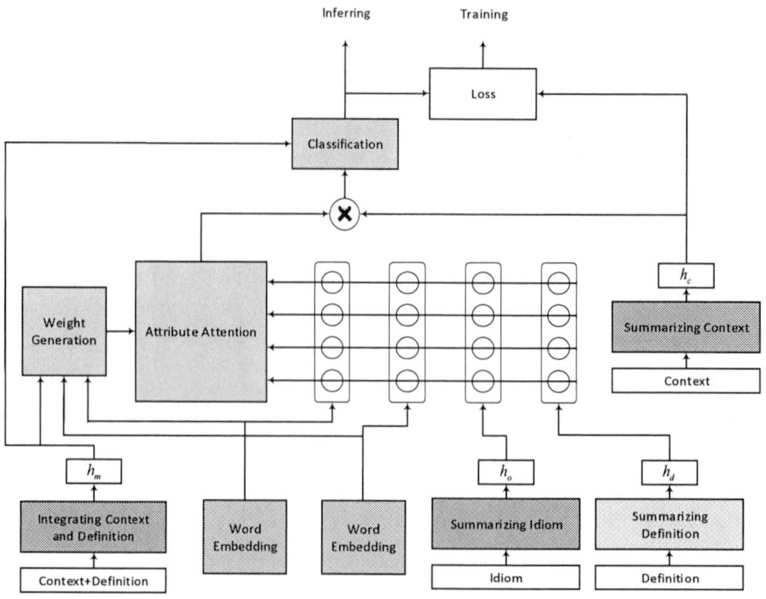

Figure 1: Architecture of our model.

3.2 Attribute Attention

This section is about how to do Attribute Attention and the preparations. In the beginning, we extract the summaries of the context, idiom, and definition. Then we calculate the weight of Attribute Attention with h_m from Section 3.1. After that, Attribute Attention will be done with these summaries and the weight.

3.2.1 Summarizing Context

Summarizing context is to predict what kind of idiom would be the correct answer for the blank based on the contextual information. For example, in Figure 3a, the sentence is "他们希望能___再进一步 *(they hope they can ___ and achieve greater success)*". The input is "他们希望能[MASK]再进一步". The output of [MASK] is defined as h_c as shown in Figure 3a.

3.2.2 Summarizing Idiom

We use BERT to extract and summary character-level information of Chinese idiom. The output is defined as h_o, as shown in Figure 3b.

The context and candidate idioms are from the same corpus and share a similar contextual representation. Besides, the [CLS] is not used when summarizing context. Therefore, we use one BERT to model both the context and idiom and use the [CLS] to summarize idioms. In the example

of Figure 3b, the candidate idiom is "百尺竿头 *(achieve great achievement)*". The input is "[CLS]百尺竿头"

3.2.3 Summarizing Definition

Introducing the definitions can correct the misuse of idioms. We use [CLS] to summary definition. In the example of Figure 3c, the definition is "比喻高的成就 *(an outstanding achievement)*". The input is "[CLS]比喻高的成就". The output of [CLS] is defined as h_d.

3.2.4 Word Embedding of Idiom

We use word embeddings to extract word-level information in this section. To utilize more information from various corpora, more than one word embedding can be introduced. Different attributes of different word embeddings will be assigned different weights in Attribute Attention. The word embeddings from different sources of one idiom are defined as $\{e_i\}_{i=1}^{|e|}$, where $|e|$ is the number of word embeddings.

3.2.5 Weight Generation

As shown in Figure 1, this section is about generating the weight with h_m and $\{e_i\}_{i=1}^{|e|}$. For the standard attention mechanism, the attention weight is a series of scalars, whereas the attention weight is a series of vectors in Attribute Attention.

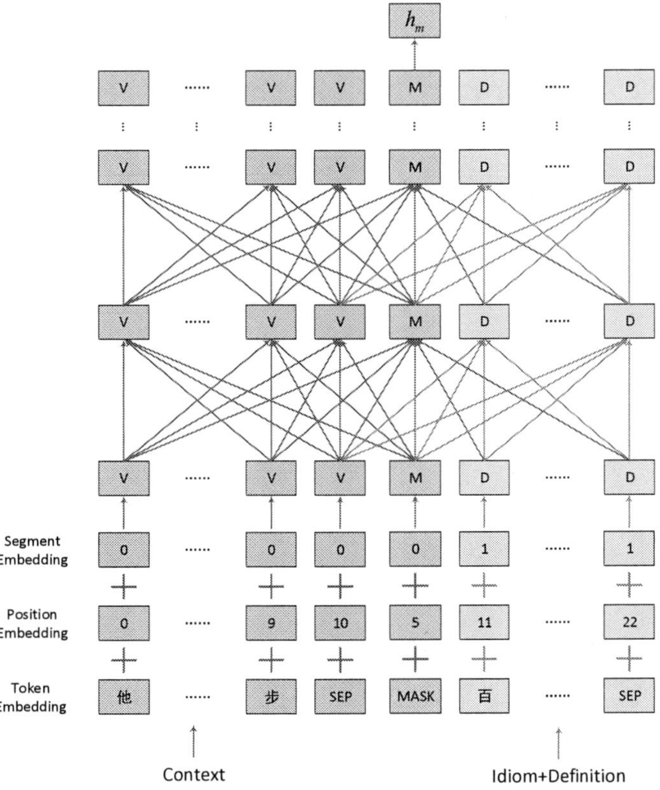

Figure 2: Integrating the context and definition with BERT, where "V" denotes the context, "D" denotes the idiom and definition, and "M" denotes [MASK]. The Multi-Head Attention is applied to the context, definition, and [MASK] in different ways. The input is "他们希望能 [MASK] 再进一步 [SEP] 百尺竿头:比喻高的成就 [SEP]".

h_m contains information about the context and idiom. A Chinese idiom may not be misused in all contexts. h_m can tell the importance of different attributes of an idiom under a certain context. The attention weight vectors for h_m are defined as $\{a_m^{<i>}\}_{i=1}^{|e|+2}$:

$$a_m^{<i>} = W_m^{<i>} h_m \qquad (4)$$

where $W_m^{<i>} \in \mathbb{R}^{m \times b}$ is a learnable parameter; m denotes the hidden size of attention, and b denotes the hidden size of BERT such as 768 or 1024.

h_m generates the weight based on the context, which is more accurate but also more likely to overfit. The weight $\{a_m^{<i>}\}_{i=1}^{|e|+2}$ may "remember" every context-idiom pair in the training set. $|e|$ is the number of word embeddings. In this case, we also introduce word embeddings here. The word embedding cannot provide context information but will have stronger generalization ability because it is hard to overfit the training set unless an idiom only

appears several times. The attention weight vectors for word embeddings are defined as $\{a_e^{<i>}\}_{i=1}^{|e|+2}$:

$$a_e^{<i>} = \frac{1}{|e|} \sum_{j}^{|e|} W_{ej}^{<i>} e_j \qquad (5)$$

where $W_{ej}^{<i>} \in \mathbb{R}^{m \times d}$ is a learnable parameter; d denotes the size of word embedding such as 300.

$a_m^{<i>} \in \mathbb{R}^m$ gives more accurate weight but may overfit, whereas $a_e^{<i>} \in \mathbb{R}^m$ is more generalized but lacks the context. We add them up to get the final weight $\{a^{<i>}\}_{i=1}^{|e|+2}$:

$$a^{<i>} = a_m^{<i>} + a_e^{<i>} \qquad (6)$$

where $a^{<i>} \in \mathbb{R}^m$. In this way, we can have accuracy and generalization from the two weights.

3.2.6 Attention Calculation

We define $a_j^{<i>}$ as the j-th element of $a^{<i>}$. In other words $a_j^{<i>}$ is the j-th element of the i-th

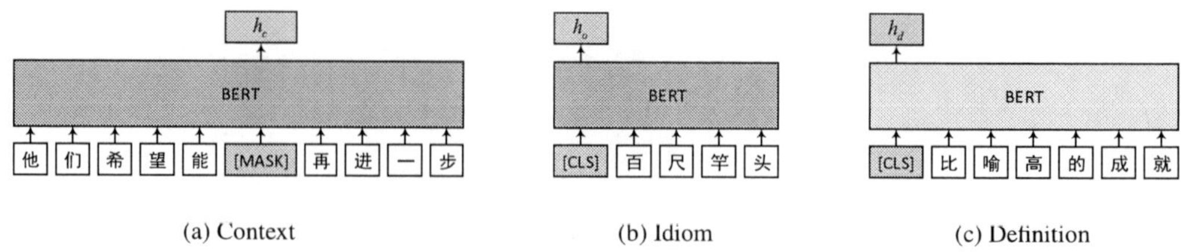

Figure 3: Summarizing the context, idiom, and definition.

vector of $\{a^{<i>}\}_{i=1}^{|e|+2}$. Then the softmax function is applied as:

$$\overline{a}_j^{<i>} = \frac{e^{a_j^{<i>}}}{\sum_{k=1}^{|e|+2} e^{a_j^{<k>}}} \qquad (7)$$

After that, before applying the attention:

$$\begin{aligned}
\boldsymbol{h}_o &\leftarrow \boldsymbol{W}_{ao}\boldsymbol{h}_o \\
\boldsymbol{h}_d &\leftarrow \boldsymbol{W}_{ad}\boldsymbol{h}_d \\
\boldsymbol{e}_i &\leftarrow \boldsymbol{W}_{ae_i}\boldsymbol{e}_i
\end{aligned} \qquad (8)$$

where $\boldsymbol{W}_{ao} \in \mathbb{R}^{m \times b}$, $\boldsymbol{W}_{ad} \in \mathbb{R}^{m \times b}$, and $\boldsymbol{W}_{ae_i} \in \mathbb{R}^{m \times d}$ are learnable parameters; m denotes the hidden size of attention, b denotes the hidden size of BERT, d denotes the size of word embedding.

As shown in Figure 1, the attention goes through as:

$$\overline{h}_j = \overline{a}_j^{<|e|+1>} h_{o_j} + \overline{a}_j^{<|e|+2>} h_{d_j} + \sum_{i=1}^{|e|} \overline{a}_j^{<i>} e_{i_j} \qquad (9)$$

where $\overline{h}_j$ is the j-th element of the output which is defined as $\overline{\boldsymbol{h}} \in \mathbb{R}^m$; h_{o_j} is the j-th element of $\boldsymbol{h}_o$, h_{d_j} is the j-th element of $\boldsymbol{h}_d$, and e_{i_j} is the j-th element of $\boldsymbol{e}_i$;

$\overline{\boldsymbol{h}}$ contains an accurate and correct description of an idiom under a certain context by choosing information from the idiom, definition, and word embeddings. The correct and important part of every representation remains, and the incorrect and unimportant part is dropped.

The final output of Attribute Attention is:

$$u_a = \overline{\boldsymbol{h}}^T \boldsymbol{W}_{ua} \boldsymbol{h}_c \qquad (10)$$

where $\boldsymbol{W}_{ua} \in \mathbb{R}^{m \times b}$ is a learnable parameter. $u_a \in \mathbb{R}^1$ is the score to describe whether a candidate idiom is the correct answer.

3.3 Classification

This section will introduce the classification part in Figure 1. One reason for Attribute Attention summarizing the context and definition is to make use of word embedding. Using $\boldsymbol{h}_m$ for classification can provide more details about the relationship between characters of the context and characters of the definition.

Formally, the classification for $\boldsymbol{h}_m$ is:

$$u_m = \boldsymbol{W}_{cm}\boldsymbol{h}_m + b_{cm} \qquad (11)$$

where $\boldsymbol{W}_{cm} \in \mathbb{R}^{1 \times b}$ and $b_{cm} \in \mathbb{R}^1$ are learnable parameters. $u_m \in \mathbb{R}^1$ is the score describing whether a candidate idiom is the correct answer.

u_a and u_m denote the score of one candidate idiom. We further define the $\{u_{ai}\}_{i=1}^n$ and $\{u_{mi}\}_{i=1}^n$ as the scores of all candidate idioms, where n denotes the number of candidate idioms. Then we add them up:

$$u_{si} = u_{ai} + u_{mi} \qquad (12)$$

and pass u_{si} through softmax function:

$$p_i = \frac{e^{u_{si}}}{\sum_{k=1}^n e^{u_{sk}}} \qquad (13)$$

p_i is the possibility for the i-th candidate idiom to be the correct answer. This is the end of inferring but not training.

3.4 Extra Loss

Because Chinese idioms are used in more unique and specific context than common words, we choose the answer from all Chinese idioms that appear in the whole cloze test dataset as an extra loss for training. Formally, we use $\boldsymbol{h}_c$ to predict the correct answer from the whole vocabulary of candidate Chinese idioms:

$$\boldsymbol{u}_c = \boldsymbol{W}_{cv}\boldsymbol{h}_c + \boldsymbol{b}_v \qquad (14)$$

6

where $\boldsymbol{W}_{cv} \in \mathbb{R}^{v \times b}$ and $\boldsymbol{b}_v \in \mathbb{R}^v$ are learnable parameters; v denotes the number of all candidate Chinese idioms which is much larger than n.

$$q = \mathrm{softmax}(\boldsymbol{u}_c) \tag{15}$$

$q \in \mathbb{R}^v$ are possibilities for all candidate idioms being the correct answer. In this way, the model can learn relationships between much more idioms every time. Due to the uniqueness and specificity of Chinese idioms, this will not cause limited noises but improve the performance significantly. Without Extra Loss, relationships between only given candidate idioms are considered every time.

When inferring, the max possibility of $\{p_i\}_{i=1}^n$ is the final result. For training, the cross entropy loss of $\{p_i\}_{i=1}^n$ is defined as l_p, and the cross entropy loss of q is defined as l_q. The final loss is:

$$l = l_p + \beta l_q \tag{16}$$

where β is a hyper-parameter to determine the weight of the loss l_q. Empirically, we suggest setting the value of β as 0.5. l is the final loss for training.

4 Experiment

4.1 Training Details

In this section, we will introduce the details and hyper-parameters for training our model.

Dataset ChID dataset (Zheng et al., 2019) is used in experiments. Table 1 shows a simple example of the dataset. Given a sentence with a blank and several candidate Chinese idioms, an examinee is required to choose a Chinese idioms which best matches the context surrounding the blank. The corpus of ChID contain news, novels, and essays. News and novels are treated as in-domain data, which contains a training set, a development set **Dev**, and a test set **Test**. Essays are reserved for out-of-domain test **Out**, which can evaluate the generalization ability. In this way, the model is trained on news and novels but evaluated on essays. **Ran** and **Sim** are two test sets which have the same sentences as **Test**. In **Ran**, candidate idioms are not similar to the golden answer. In **Sim**, candidate idioms are similar idioms to golden answer.

BPretrained Model Pretrained RoBERTa-base (Liu et al., 2019) for Chinese with 12 layers and word embeddings from (Song et al., 2018; Li et al., 2018; Qiu et al., 2018) are used.

Hyper-parameters n is 7 because there are seven candidate idioms for every blank in ChID dataset (Zheng et al., 2019). v is 3848 because ChID dataset (Zheng et al., 2019) contains 3848 candidate idioms in total. The hidden size of attention m is 100. β as 0.5.

Optimizer The optimizer is Adam (Kingma and Ba, 2014) for BERT with linear schedule and a warm-up ratio of 0.05. The learning rate for RoBERTa is 2e-5, and for other parameters is 1e-3.

Parameters number The number of parameters of our model for experiments is 322M. The learnable parameters are initialized by (He et al., 2015).

GPU & Environment The model is running on a GPU of NVIDIA GeForce RTX 2080 Ti. Due to the limited GPU RAM, we use gradient accumulation for training. The operating system is Ubuntu 18.04. We use PyTorch 1.4.0 (Paszke et al., 2019) and Transformers 2.4.1 (Wolf et al., 2019) to implement our model. We also use mixed precision training with NVIDIA Apex 0.1 (Micikevicius et al., 2017) to accelerate our model. It takes an average of 42 hours per epoch, and the model achieves the best result within 10 epochs.

Metrics The metric for evaluation is the accuracy, which is implemented by Scikit-learn (Pedregosa et al., 2011).

4.2 Comparison

The description of other models are as follows:

AR Attentive Reader (AR) (Hermann et al., 2015). AR uses an attention mechanism to read the sentence.

SAR Stanford Attentive Reader (SAR) (Chen et al., 2016). SAR is a improvement based on AR.

CR Chengyu Reader (CR) (Jiang et al., 2018). CR extracts the summary of definition and adopts a similar attention mechanism of AR.

EAR Enhanced Attentive Reader (EAR) (Fu and Zhang, 2019) EA Reader contains a method called Multi-Space Context Fusion and integrates the method with the attention mechanism of AR.

X-RoBERTa We design AR-RoBERTa, SAR-RoBERTa, CR-RoBERTa, and EAR-RoBERTa to make a fair comparison. The LSTMs of them are all replaced by RoBERTa-base which has 12 layers,

	Dev	Test	Ran	Sim	Out
Human	-	87.1	97.6	82.2	86.2
AR (Hermann et al., 2015)	72.7	72.4	82.0	66.2	62.9
SAR (Chen et al., 2016)	71.7	71.5	80.0	64.9	61.7
CR (Jiang et al., 2018)	74.1	73.5	82.8	68.5	65.2
EAR (Fu and Zhang, 2019)	74.6	74.5	84.4	67.9	65.5
AR-RoBERTa (Hermann et al., 2015; Liu et al., 2019)	77.1	77.1	89.0	68.9	70.9
SAR-RoBERTa (Chen et al., 2016; Liu et al., 2019)	76.3	76.7	88.5	68.0	69.8
CR-RoBERTa (Jiang et al., 2018; Liu et al., 2019)	78.0	78.3	89.9	70.0	71.7
EAR-RoBERTa (Fu and Zhang, 2019; Liu et al., 2019)	78.7	79.2	90.5	71.7	72.3
Our model	**83.0**	**83.1**	**92.3**	**76.1**	**77.6**

Table 4: Comparison of accuracies of different models on ChID dataset.

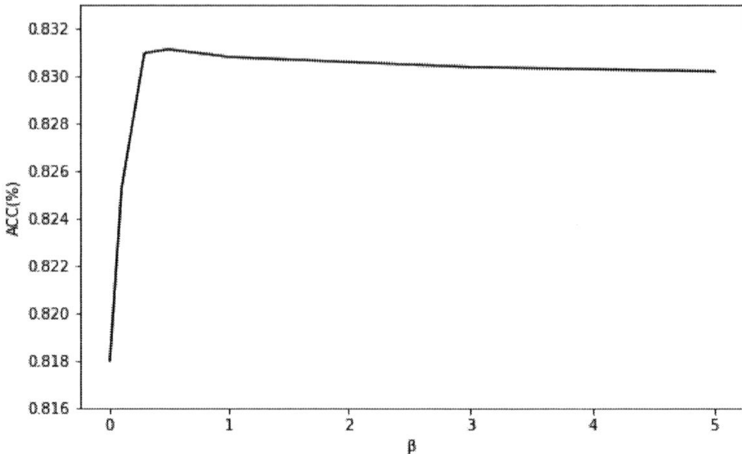

Figure 4: Performance of our model with different β on **Test**.

which is the same as our model. Both LSTM and RoBERTa provides contextual information.

Table 4 shows the accuracies of all methods. The result of human is given by (Zheng et al., 2019). Our model outperforms all other models in **Dev**, **Test**, **Ran**, **Sim**, and **Out**. Besides, our model has much better generalization ability. For example, comparing with EAR-RoBERTa, our model has a 3.9% improvement on **Test** but 5.3% on **Out**.

4.3 Extra Loss Studies

This section explores how β influence the accuracy of our model on **Test**. Figure 4 shows the results. When $\beta = 0$, the Extra Loss is not used, which shows the performance of our model that does not use Extra Loss. The accuracy increase very quickly when $\beta < 0.3$. The accuracy reaches the highest point when $\beta = 0.5$. The accuracy start decreasing slowly when $\beta > 1$. A larger β makes the extra loss

l_q too important and overshadow the normal loss l_p, which makes the model deviate from its purpose. Extra Loss gives a significant improvement and costs very few computing resources.

5 Conclusion

In this paper, we propose a model for the Chinese idiom cloze test. We introduce the definition and propose Attribute Attention to balance the importance of different representations of the Chinese idiom. We add Extra Loss calculated by choosing the answer from the whole vocabulary of Chinese idioms to improve the performance further, which costs very few computing resources. In experiments, our model outperforms state-of-the-art method.

References

Samuel W.K. Chan and Mickey W.C. Chong. 2008. An agent-based approach to Chinese word segmentation. In *Proceedings of the Sixth SIGHAN Workshop on Chinese Language Processing*.

Danqi Chen, Jason Bolton, and Christopher D Manning. 2016. A thorough examination of the cnn/daily mail reading comprehension task. *arXiv preprint arXiv:1606.02858*.

Jacob Devlin, Ming-Wei Chang, Kenton Lee, and Kristina Toutanova. 2019. BERT: Pre-training of deep bidirectional transformers for language understanding. In *Proceedings of the 2019 Conference of the North American Chapter of the Association for Computational Linguistics: Human Language Technologies, Volume 1 (Long and Short Papers)*, pages 4171–4186, Minneapolis, Minnesota. Association for Computational Linguistics.

Erik-Lân Do Dinh, Steffen Eger, and Iryna Gurevych. 2018a. Killing four birds with two stones: Multi-task learning for non-literal language detection. In *Proceedings of the 27th International Conference on Computational Linguistics*, pages 1558–1569, Santa Fe, New Mexico, USA. Association for Computational Linguistics.

Erik-Lân Do Dinh, Steffen Eger, and Iryna Gurevych. 2018b. One size fits all? a simple LSTM for non-literal token and construction-level classification. In *Proceedings of the Second Joint SIGHUM Workshop on Computational Linguistics for Cultural Heritage, Social Sciences, Humanities and Literature*, pages 70–80, Santa Fe, New Mexico. Association for Computational Linguistics.

A. Fathima Shirin and C. Raseek. 2018. Replacing idioms based on their figurative usage. In *2018 International Conference on Emerging Trends and Innovations in Engineering and Technological Research (ICETIETR)*, pages 1–6.

Afsaneh Fazly, Paul Cook, and Suzanne Stevenson. 2009. Unsupervised type and token identification of idiomatic expressions. *Computational Linguistics*, 35(1):61–103.

Michael Flor and Beata Beigman Klebanov. 2018. Catching idiomatic expressions in EFL essays. In *Proceedings of the Workshop on Figurative Language Processing*, pages 34–44, New Orleans, Louisiana. Association for Computational Linguistics.

Chengzhen Fu, Yuntao Li, and Yan Zhang. 2019. Atnet: Answering cloze-style questions via intra-attention and inter-attention. In *Advances in Knowledge Discovery and Data Mining*, pages 242–252, Cham. Springer International Publishing.

Chengzhen Fu and Yan Zhang. 2019. Ea reader: Enhance attentive reader for cloze-style question answering via multi-space context fusion. In *Proceedings of the AAAI Conference on Artificial Intelligence*, volume 33, pages 6375–6382.

Matt Gedigian, John Bryant, Srini Narayanan, and Branimir Ciric. 2006. Catching metaphors. In *Proceedings of the Third Workshop on Scalable Natural Language Understanding*, pages 41–48, New York City, New York. Association for Computational Linguistics.

Kaiming He, Xiangyu Zhang, Shaoqing Ren, and Jian Sun. 2015. Delving deep into rectifiers: Surpassing human-level performance on imagenet classification. In *The IEEE International Conference on Computer Vision (ICCV)*.

Karl Moritz Hermann, Tomas Kocisky, Edward Grefenstette, Lasse Espeholt, Will Kay, Mustafa Suleyman, and Phil Blunsom. 2015. Teaching machines to read and comprehend. In C. Cortes, N. D. Lawrence, D. D. Lee, M. Sugiyama, and R. Garnett, editors, *Advances in Neural Information Processing Systems 28*, pages 1693–1701. Curran Associates, Inc.

Zhiying Jiang, Boliang Zhang, Lifu Huang, and Heng Ji. 2018. Chengyu cloze test. In *Proceedings of the Thirteenth Workshop on Innovative Use of NLP for Building Educational Applications*, pages 154–158, New Orleans, Louisiana. Association for Computational Linguistics.

Graham Katz and Eugenie Giesbrecht. 2006. Automatic identification of non-compositional multi-word expressions using latent semantic analysis. In *Proceedings of the Workshop on Multiword Expressions: Identifying and Exploiting Underlying Properties*, pages 12–19, Sydney, Australia. Association for Computational Linguistics.

Diederik P Kingma and Jimmy Ba. 2014. Adam: A method for stochastic optimization. *arXiv preprint arXiv:1412.6980*.

Zhenzhong Lan, Mingda Chen, Sebastian Goodman, Kevin Gimpel, Piyush Sharma, and Radu Soricut. 2019. Albert: A lite bert for self-supervised learning of language representations. *arXiv preprint arXiv:1909.11942*.

Shen Li, Zhe Zhao, Renfen Hu, Wensi Li, Tao Liu, and Xiaoyong Du. 2018. Analogical reasoning on chinese morphological and semantic relations. In *Proceedings of the 56th Annual Meeting of the Association for Computational Linguistics (Volume 2: Short Papers)*, pages 138–143. Association for Computational Linguistics.

Changsheng Liu and Rebecca Hwa. 2018. Heuristically informed unsupervised idiom usage recognition. In *Proceedings of the 2018 Conference on Empirical Methods in Natural Language Processing*, pages 1723–1731, Brussels, Belgium. Association for Computational Linguistics.

Pengfei Liu, Kaiyu Qian, Xipeng Qiu, and Xuanjing Huang. 2017. Idiom-aware compositional distributed semantics. In *Proceedings of the 2017 Conference on Empirical Methods in Natural Language Processing*, pages 1204–1213, Copenhagen, Denmark. Association for Computational Linguistics.

Yinhan Liu, Myle Ott, Naman Goyal, Jingfei Du, Mandar Joshi, Danqi Chen, Omer Levy, Mike Lewis, Luke Zettlemoyer, and Veselin Stoyanov. 2019. Roberta: A robustly optimized bert pretraining approach. *arXiv preprint arXiv:1907.11692*.

Paulius Micikevicius, Sharan Narang, Jonah Alben, Gregory Diamos, Erich Elsen, David Garcia, Boris Ginsburg, Michael Houston, Oleksii Kuchaiev, Ganesh Venkatesh, et al. 2017. Mixed precision training. *arXiv preprint arXiv:1710.03740.*

Adam Paszke, Sam Gross, Francisco Massa, Adam Lerer, James Bradbury, Gregory Chanan, Trevor Killeen, Zeming Lin, Natalia Gimelshein, Luca Antiga, et al. 2019. Pytorch: An imperative style, high-performance deep learning library. In *Advances in Neural Information Processing Systems 32*, pages 8024–8035. Curran Associates, Inc.

F. Pedregosa, G. Varoquaux, A. Gramfort, V. Michel, B. Thirion, O. Grisel, M. Blondel, P. Prettenhofer, R. Weiss, V. Dubourg, J. Vanderplas, A. Passos, D. Cournapeau, M. Brucher, M. Perrot, and E. Duchesnay. 2011. Scikit-learn: Machine learning in Python. *Journal of Machine Learning Research*, 12:2825–2830.

Yuanyuan Qiu, Hongzheng Li, Shen Li, Yingdi Jiang, Renfen Hu, and Lijiao Yang. 2018. Revisiting correlations between intrinsic and extrinsic evaluations of word embeddings. In *Chinese Computational Linguistics and Natural Language Processing Based on Naturally Annotated Big Data*, pages 209–221. Springer.

Giancarlo Salton, Robert Ross, and John Kelleher. 2016. Idiom token classification using sentential distributed semantics. In *Proceedings of the 54th Annual Meeting of the Association for Computational Linguistics (Volume 1: Long Papers)*, pages 194–204, Berlin, Germany. Association for Computational Linguistics.

Victor Sanh, Lysandre Debut, Julien Chaumond, and Thomas Wolf. 2019. Distilbert, a distilled version of bert: Smaller, faster, cheaper and lighter. *arXiv preprint arXiv:1910.01108.*

Ekaterina Shutova, Lin Sun, and Anna Korhonen. 2010. Metaphor identification using verb and noun clustering. In *Proceedings of the 23rd International Conference on Computational Linguistics (Coling 2010)*, pages 1002–1010, Beijing, China. Coling 2010 Organizing Committee.

Yan Song, Shuming Shi, Jing Li, and Haisong Zhang. 2018. Directional skip-gram: Explicitly distinguishing left and right context for word embeddings. In *Proceedings of the 2018 Conference of the North American Chapter of the Association for Computational Linguistics: Human Language Technologies, Volume 2 (Short Papers)*, pages 175–180, New Orleans, Louisiana. Association for Computational Linguistics.

I. Spasic, L. Williams, and A. Buerki. 2017. Idiom—based features in sentiment analysis: Cutting the gordian knot. *IEEE Transactions on Affective Computing*, pages 1–1.

Weiwei Sun and Jia Xu. 2011. Enhancing Chinese word segmentation using unlabeled data. In *Proceedings of the 2011 Conference on Empirical Methods in Natural Language Processing*, pages 970–979, Edinburgh, Scotland, UK. Association for Computational Linguistics.

Chunqi Wang and Bo Xu. 2017. Convolutional neural network with word embeddings for Chinese word segmentation. In *Proceedings of the Eighth International Joint Conference on Natural Language Processing (Volume 1: Long Papers)*, pages 163–172, Taipei, Taiwan. Asian Federation of Natural Language Processing.

Liang Wang, Sujian Li, Wei Zhao, Kewei Shen, Meng Sun, Ruoyu Jia, and Jingming Liu. 2018. Multi-perspective context aggregation for semi-supervised cloze-style reading comprehension. In *Proceedings of the 27th International Conference on Computational Linguistics*, pages 857–867, Santa Fe, New Mexico, USA. Association for Computational Linguistics.

Thomas Wolf, Lysandre Debut, Victor Sanh, Julien Chaumond, Clement Delangue, Anthony Moi, Pierric Cistac, Tim Rault, R'emi Louf, Morgan Funtowicz, and Jamie Brew. 2019. Huggingface's transformers: State-of-the-art natural language processing. *ArXiv*, abs/1910.03771.

Ge Xu, Xinfan Meng, and Houfeng Wang. 2010. Build Chinese emotion lexicons using a graph-based algorithm and multiple resources. In *Proceedings of the 23rd International Conference on Computational Linguistics (Coling 2010)*, pages 1209–1217, Beijing, China. Coling 2010 Organizing Committee.

Zhuosheng Zhang, Yafang Huang, and Hai Zhao. 2018. Subword-augmented embedding for cloze reading comprehension. In *Proceedings of the 27th International Conference on Computational Linguistics*, pages 1802–1814, Santa Fe, New Mexico, USA. Association for Computational Linguistics.

Chujie Zheng, Minlie Huang, and Aixin Sun. 2019. ChID: A large-scale Chinese IDiom dataset for cloze test. In *Proceedings of the 57th Annual Meeting of the Association for Computational Linguistics*, pages 778–787, Florence, Italy. Association for Computational Linguistics.

Relation Extraction with Contextualized Relation Embedding (CRE)

Xiaoyu Chen[*]
Dept. of Computer Science
Stanford University
codchen03@gmail.com

Rohan Badlani[*]
Dept. of Computer Science
Stanford University
rohan.badlani@cs.stanford.edu

Abstract

Relation extraction (RE) is the task of identifying relation instance(s) between two entities given a corpus whereas Knowledge base (KB) modeling is the task of representing a knowledge base, in terms of relations between entities. This paper proposes an architecture for the relation extraction (RE) task that integrates semantic information with knowledge base (KB) modeling in a novel manner. Existing approaches for relation extraction either don't utilize knowledge base modelling or use separately trained KB models for the RE task. We present a model architecture that internalizes KB modeling in relation extraction. This model applies a novel approach to encode sentences into contextualized relation embeddings (CRE), which can then be used together with parameterized entity embeddings to score relation instances. The proposed CRE model achieves state of the art performance on datasets derived from The New York Times Annotated Corpus[1] and FreeBase[2]. The source code has been made available[3] to reproduce the results.

1 Introduction

Relation extraction (RE) is a sub-task under the broad category of information extraction (IE) that aims to identify relationship(s) between named entities based on textual information (corpus). The groundtruth relationship(s) between an entity pair can be either internal, if each sentence in the corpus is explicitly labeled, or external, in the form of relation instances in a standalone knowledge base (KB). Such knowledge bases, like Freebase

---

[*]equal contribution

[1]https://catalog.ldc.upenn.edu/LDC2008T19

[2]https://developers.google.com/freebase

[3]https://github.com/codchen/CRE

Bollacker et al. (2008), are collaboratively edited by human beings and thus offer high informational fidelity.

In this paper, we focus on the problem of predicting the collection of relations for a new entity pair based on the usage of that entity pair in its respective collection of sentences. To this end, we assume the general construction that given a dataset with a set of named entity pairs and each entity pair's respective collection of sentences as input along with entity pair's respective collection of relations as output, our goal is to train a model with the objective of predicting collection of *relevant* relation(s) for a new entity pair based on its contextual usage.

Distant supervision Mintz et al. (2009) is the most popular approach for this problem, that has achieved its success by leveraging knowledge base information for relation extraction tasks. However, this restricts the usage of semantic information present in knowledge bases, since the distant supervision work mainly incorporates the knowledge base information as labels instead of treating it as a graph and thereby losing the dense relationships between different entities. Knowledge base modelling is an independent area of research and there has been some recent work on utilizing knowledge base modeling and incorporating internal structural information from them to the relation extraction task. Bordes et al. (2013), Trouillon et al. (2016).

Weston et al. (2013) conducted the first research work that utilized knowledge bases as a structural graph by training a TransE (Bordes et al. (2013)) KB model alongside a traditional distant supervision extractor. However, this has been a simple combination of both ideas but despite its simplicity, the model was able to beat the then-state-of-the-art models in Relation Extraction tasks. The work by Han et al. (2018), on the other hand,

Proceedings of Deep Learning Inside Out (DeeLIO):
The First Workshop on Knowledge Extraction and Integration for Deep Learning Architectures, pages 11–19
Online, November 19, 2020. ©2020 Association for Computational Linguistics

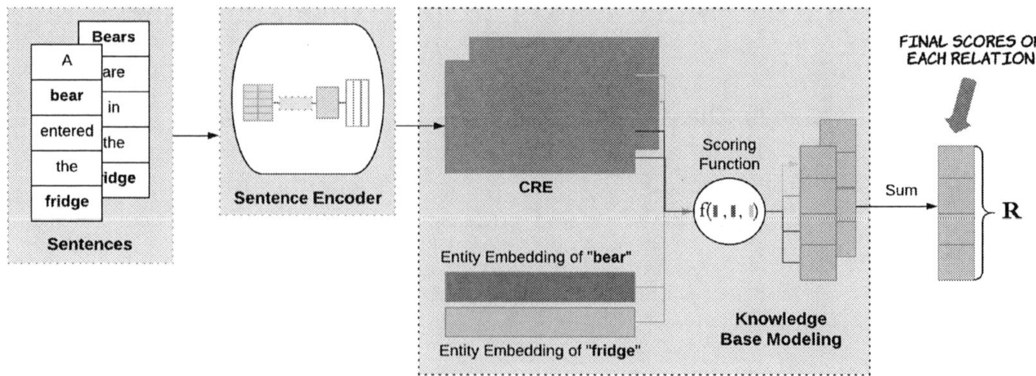

Figure 1: Contextualized Relation Embedding (CRE) Model Architecture

The details of "Sentence Encoder" can be found in figure 2.
The scoring function takes one CRE vector and two entity embedding vectors as inputs, and outputs a scalar score.

went a step further by sharing some model weights between the distant supervision extractor and the knowledge base model. However, although there is some shared architecture, but the objective function for the KB modelling and the distant supervision remain separate. Another notable work by Xu and Barbosa (2019) combines the two models through an additional objective function that guides the training but during prediction time there is no any shared architecture and hence knowledge base information is not really incorporated well for relation prediction.

The model presented in this paper differs from all previous work in that it is a single relation extraction model that internalizes knowledge base modeling. Instead of treating relation embeddings as parameters like in standalone knowledge embedding models (eg: TransE (Weston et al., 2013)), where such embeddings have no context of any textual information, our model expresses relation embeddings as context-aware latent states generated by encoding textual data. Such contextualized embeddings represent a natural link between the textual input and the knowledge base modeling objective, so that the end-to-end information transformation is completely internal to the model. The entity embeddings, on the other hand, are not contextualized and will still be trained as parameters of the same model, because they need to serve as bridges across different entity pairs and globalize the knowledge base modeling which is now based on contextualized relation embeddings localized to each entity pair. A significant innovation of this work is that each

sentence in which a pair of entities occurs, we represent each possible relation between them as a function of that entire sentence and score the relation for that entity pair and sentence using the representation of the relation.

2 Contextualized Relation Embedding

Let $\mathcal{R}$ stand for the set of all relations and $\mathcal{E}$ stand for set of all entities. Then, for the i-th entity pair, H_i and T_i stand for the subject and object respectively, both belonging to $\mathcal{E}$. $\mathcal{R}'_i \subset \mathcal{R}$ stand for the set of relations existing between the i-th entity pair. S_i stands for the collection of sentences that contain H_i as the subject and T_i as the object; S_i^{jk} stands for the k-th word of the j-th sentence in S_i, where each S_i^{jk} is delimited by spaces except for the subject and the object, whose phrasal integrities are preserved (e.g. if it is the subject/object of a sentence, *the United States* will be considered as a single "word").

We propose a novel neural network model (called CRE model) that implicitly combines knowledge base to detect relationships between entities, given a corpus of sentences containing those entities. The overall architecture of a CRE model is shown in figure 1, which consists of a sentence encoding step and a knowledge base modeling step. During the sentence encoding step, the model transforms each S_i^{jk} into E-dimensional embeddings. Specifically, we apply pretrained skip-gram embeddings Mikolov et al. (2013), treating all named entities as unknown, which results in a W-dimensional embedding for each word. We

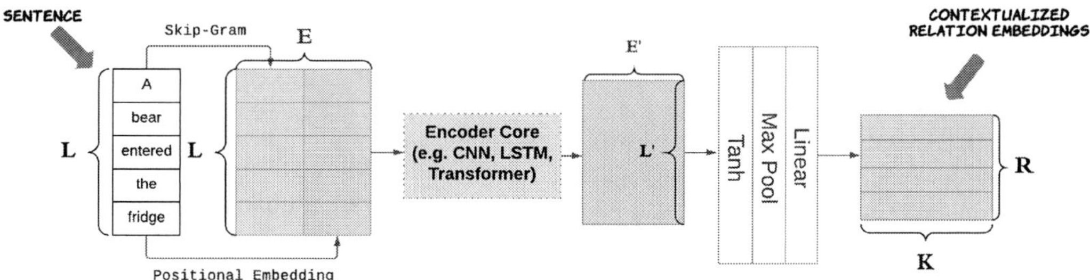

Figure 2: Single Sentence Encoding Process

apply a positional embedding based on Zeng et al. (2014), where each word's index in the positional "vocabulary" is defined as its relative distance to one of the named entities. Consider the sentence "A bear entered the fridge" and named entities "bear" and "fridge". The word "A" will have -1 as its positional embedding index with respect to "bear" and -4 with respect to "fridge", whereas "entered" will have $+1$ with respect to "bear" and -2 with respect to "fridge". For each word (including the two named entities), we represent it as its skip-gram word embedding of dimension W, concatenated with its positional embeddings (each of dimension P) with respect to the two named entities, to form a final embedding of dimension E, where $E = W + 2 * P$. The skip-gram embeddings are fixed during training, whereas the positional embeddings are learnt. This leads to a sentence embedding of $L * E$, where L is the maximum length of each sentence. We utilize the above mentioned sentence embeddings and learn an encoder that encodes each sentence into a $R * K$ embedding, which can be represented as $|\mathcal{R}|$ K-dimensional embeddings, each of which corresponds to a distinct relation in $\mathcal{R}$. Figure 2 illustrates the sentence encoding process for a single sentence.

It is worth noting that the sentence encoder is a generic framework where we can plug in any model architecture (both for positional encoding and sentence encoding). In our experiments, we found that neural network based encoders tend to result in better performance. We think this is due to their ability to extract both semantic and syntactic information. We denote sentence j's representation of r's relation for entity pair i as CRE_i^{jr}.

In order to provide the model more context, we explicitly apply a K-dimensional embedding for each part of the entity pair represented by H_i and T_i respectively. These entity embeddings

are learnt as parameters during training, similar to the positional embeddings above. We utilize the relation embeddings (contextualized relation embeddings) from the sentences and these entity embeddings to form relation triplet embeddings. Specifically, this will result in R triplets for each sentence, since we computed R relation embeddings for each sentence. This allows us to apply different knowledge based models and further enhances the generalization of our model. Depending on the choice of knowledge based model, we use the relation triplet embeddings to compute its score based on the scoring function of the respective knowledge base model. For example, if TransE Bordes et al. (2013) is chosen as the underlying knowledge base model with H_i and T_i as head and tail entity embeddings, then embeddings for relation r derived from sentence j will be scored as:

$$Score_i^{j,r} = 1 - tanh(||H_i + CRE_i^{jr} - T_i||);$$
$$where\ 0 \leq Score_i^{j,r} \leq 2$$
$$(1)$$

Since most knowledge base models are characterized by their scoring functions, it is straightforward to swap in any knowledge base model here for scoring purposes.

Finally, the model aggregates scores for the same relation across all sentences so that we can obtain a single score for each relation given an entity pair:

$$Score_i^r = \sum_j Score_i^{j,r} \qquad (2)$$

For experiments in this paper, we adopted summation as the aggregation function since we do not have prior knowledge about our dataset and thus want to take into account the "opinion" of all sentences equally, but it is by no means prescriptive. One can certainly use maximum, minimum or mean as the aggregation functions instead of sum in case the dataset is such that any single sentence's outcome can be regarded as reliable.

We train the model with a binary cross entropy loss, after normalizing relation scores and targets and we use an $L2$ regularization that helps prevent overfitting.

$$NS_i^r = \frac{Score_i^r}{\sum_{r'} Score_i^{r'}} \tag{3}$$

$$m_i^r = \frac{I[r \in \mathcal{R}_i']}{|\mathcal{R}_i'|} \tag{4}$$

$$L_i^r = -m_i^r * log(NS_i^r)) + (m_i^r - \frac{1}{|\mathcal{R}_i'|}) * log(1 - NS_i^r) \tag{5}$$

$$L_i = \sum_r L_{ir} + \lambda * \sum ||w||^2 \tag{6}$$

We use the normalized scores to predict the relations for the given entity pair. Note that normalization is still necessary for quantitative evaluation. We pool together scores for different entity pairs to form a precision-recall curve, so scores need to be comparable and normalization brings them to the same scale. The top-k prediction can formulated as:

$$Top_i^k = argmax_r^k(NS_i^r)$$
$$TopScore_i^k = NS_i^{Top_i^k} \tag{7}$$

3 Experiments

3.1 Data and Experimental Setup

For our experiments, we use the textual data from The New York Times (NYT) Annotated Corpus Riedel et al. (2010), and the knowledge base are derived from the most recent FreeBase Bollacker et al. (2008) dump. Note that entities in each NYT sentence are already annotated. The NYT and Freebase presents a more challenging task for relation extraction models than FreeBase and Wikipedia texts due to their heterogeneous nature, since FreeBase itself is largely derived from Wikipedia. We construct the dataset through the following procedure:

1. Filter out any relation instance from FreeBase dump if the mapping between the ID of either of its two entities and its corresponding English phrase is not available.

2. Find the top 500K entities based on the number of relation instances they participate in, and further filter out any relation instance if either of its two entities is not in the top 500K list.

3. Inner join the NYT dataset with the filtered Freebase by aligning NYT entity annotations and Freebase entity English phrases. In other words, no example in the NYT dataset that contains unseen entities in the filter Freebase is preserved, and vice versa.

4. Backfill an N/A relation for any entity pair present in the filtered NYT dataset that has no relation instance in the filtered Freebase.

After this procedure, we have a dataset that contains 465K sentences, 35K entities, 233K entity pairs, and 238 relations. As most entities in this world do not possess direct relations with other entities, the dataset is extremely unbalanced, where only 5K entity pairs out of the 233K have non-N/A relation. These 5K entity pairs contribute 20K sentences out of the 465K. Because of this imbalance, we performed train-test splits for positive pairs and negative pairs separately, so that test set gets around 1200 positive pairs and 57K negative pairs. Since this test set is still severely imbalanced and we don't want our model to be biased in favor an N/A prediction, we further randomly sample the negative pairs in the test set so that the number of sentences consisting of negative pairs is roughly the same as that of any positive relation. We did not perform similar filtering to the training set from the outset, but randomly applied such filtering at the beginning of each training epoch, in order to utilize all training data we have.

3.2 Evaluation Metrics

In order to quantitatively evaluate the performance of our model, we measure precision over various recall levels. Specifically, we examine precision-recall curves for top-1 predictions, top-3 predictions, and top-5 predictions. Top-1 predictions, which only includes the relation with the highest score among all relations for a given entity pair, are widely used in related

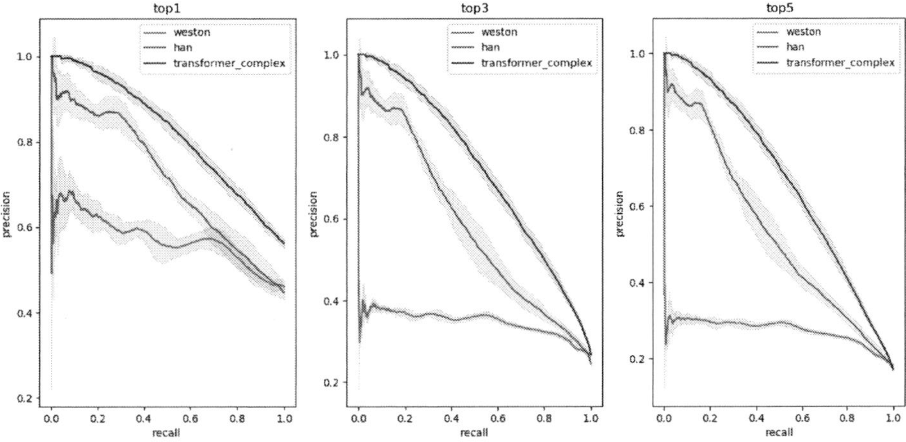

Figure 3: Weston et al. vs. Han et al. vs. CRE Model

literature, but we believe it alone does not provide a comprehensive view, since each entity pair can have multiple relations. Besides the precision-recall curve, we also measure the mean reciprocal rank (MRR) among top-3 predictions and top-5 predictions.

On the qualitative side, we examine the number of distinct top-1 relation predictions, in order to check if our model achieves high precision just by heavily favoring certain relations, given the unbalanced nature of our dataset.

3.3 Baseline Models

As discussed in Section 2, our proposed model provides a deep integration of knowledge bases in the relation prediction task. We select two baseline models to compare performance: one from Weston et al. (2013) as a representative of weak integration between knowledge bases and relation extraction, and the other from Han et al. (2018) to represent a semi-integrated setup. Both models have already been briefly described in the Introduction section. Since the state of art of these models is not publically available, we performed hyperparameter tuning for both models on our dataset, since they may not be exactly the same as the datasets used in their respective work.

3.4 Model Configurations

As shown in the model details section, there can be a myriad of options for various components of our proposed CRE model. In this evaluation, we will focus on the effect of different choices of sentence-to-CRE encoders as well as underlying knowledge

base models. Every other aspect will be kept fixed as described in the preceding section.

For sentence-to-CRE encoders, we will explore 3 options:

- A single 1D convolutional layer with hidden state dimension of 230 and window size of 3.

- A single LSTM layer with hidden state dimension of 230.

- A double-layered transformer encoder with hidden state dimension of 100 and 5-head attention Vaswani et al. (2017).

All these encoders are followed by a $tanh$ activation layer and a linear layer to project the low-dimensional hidden state onto $|\mathcal{R}|K$-dimensional space. 230 is selected as the hidden dimension for fair comparison purpose because it is the CNN hidden state dimension used in Han et al. (2018). The complexity of encoders evaluated here are limited by computational resources available for this work, so it is possible to find more sophisticated encoders that can achieve further improvements. For the transformer based encoder, an additional linear projection and tanh activation is applied at the front to reduce the number of parameters that need to be trained to a manageable level.

For knowledge base model, we explore 2 options:

- TransE with embedding dimension of 50.

- ComplEx Trouillon et al. (2016) with embedding dimension of 25 for the real part and 25 for the imaginary part.

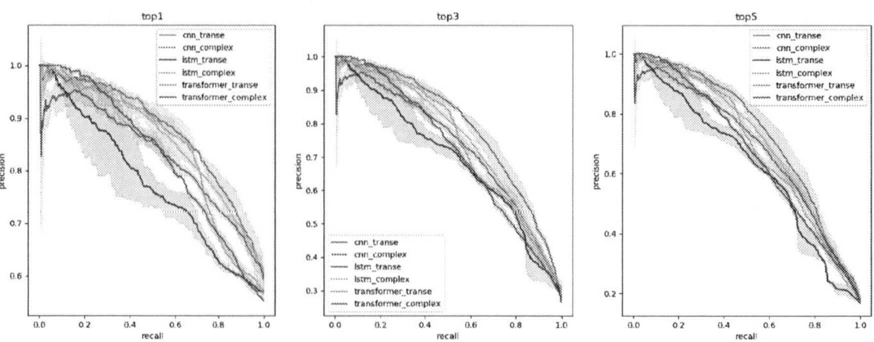

Figure 4: CRE Models with different configurations

Left: precision-recall curves of the most confident prediction for each entity pairs
Middle: precision-recall curves of the top 3 most confident predictions for each entity pairs
Right: precision-recall curves of the top 5 most confident predictions for each entity pairs

Model	MRR among Top-3	MRR among Top-5
Weston et al.	0.6010	0.6194
Han et al.	0.5786	0.6005
CRE(transformer+ComplEx)	**0.6413**	**0.6588**

Table 1: MRR comparison with baseline models

The dimensions chosen here are based on reports from each model's respective paper.

By combining these options, we will explore 6 different model configurations in total. We use Adam optimizer for training and consider the model to have converged when the loss on the current epoch is no less than the average loss of the last ten epochs. Each model is then used to make predictions on the same held-out test set.

In order to test for statistical significance, we divided the dataset into 3 different subsets randomly and recorded the results of each model on all three subsets.

3.5 Results

3.5.1 The best model configuration

We compare the performance of the CRE models across different configurations, which is illustrated in figure 4. From the results, we can see that the more sophisticated knowledge base model (ComplEx) outperforms the simpler alternative (TransE) at lower recall levels (less than 0.25), but under-performs at higher recall levels. Similarly, for different choices of sentence-to-CRE encoders, we observe that the more complex transformer encoder is almost perfect before recall rises above 0.25.

The most consistent configuration, from a quantitative perspective, is the combination of CNN and TransE. These results are reinforced by the MRR comparison among different CRE configurations, as shown in table 2. We can see that the model that achieved the best precision-recall result (CNN+TransE) also dominates in terms of MRR, whereas the worst results for both metrics are attributable to the LSTM+TransE configuration.

3.5.2 Comparison with baseline models

Figure 3 shows the precision-recall curve comparisons between baseline models and a CRE-based model with Transformer+ComplEx configuration. Each model's confidence interval was obtained via variance among precisions at the same recall level of 9 different runs: 3 runs for each of 3 different random subset of the training/testing dataset. The CRE model was able to outperform both baseline models.

Interestingly, Weston's approach achieved top-1 prediction accuracy comparable with what was reported in its original paper, but saw a particularly sharp drop in precision as the number of predictions examined increases. This contrast is unsurprising though, because Weston's approach only re-scores its most confident predictions, so models trained this way have no capability of making multiple

Model	MRR among Top-3	MRR among Top-5
CNN+TransE	**0.6925**	**0.7059**
CNN+ComplEx	0.6681	0.6805
LSTM+TransE	0.6234	0.6506
LSTM+ComplEx	0.6802	0.6938
transformer+TransE	0.6332	0.6549
transformer+ComplEx	0.6413	0.6588

Table 2: MRR comparison between different configurations of CRE

predictions for a single entity pair.

In addition, we observed the mean reciprocal rank for CRE model is significantly higher than baseline models, as shown in table 1, which corresponds to the improvement we saw in terms of precision-recall curve.

3.5.3 Qualitative evaluation

Table 3 shows most frequent relations and the number of times each model concludes one of them to be the most likely relation given an entity pair, as well as the ground truth. It can be observed that the CRE models tend to generate a less skewed distribution of these frequent relations compared to Han's, which is the better of the two baseline models in terms of quantitative performance.

4 Discussion

Our experiments from figure 3 clearly demonstrate that models utilizing contextualized relation embeddings that internalize both relation extractor modeling and knowledge base modeling tend to perform much better on relation extraction task than architectures like Weston et al. (2013) and Han et al. (2018) that join a relation extractor and a knowledge base model in some arbitrary way. We believe this is due to the fact that the "internal knowledge base models" within CRE models are context-aware. As a result, CRE models can take advantage of the contextual information contained in the corpus more effectively.

We demonstrate the generality and flexibility of the proposed CRE model that can work with different encoders and knowledge base models. Moreover, it can be observed from Table 3 that the CRE-models generate less skewed distribution of frequent relations compared to the baseline models, thus demonstrating that the CRE model provides robust predictions and works well even with imbalanced datasets.

It can be observed from Figure 4 that more

complex configurations for our model tend to achieve stellar results in the low recall arena but lose steam when recall levels are high. This may be explained by the insufficient training epochs due to resource constraints. As a result, these complex models did not get the chance to optimize for the less seen prediction targets. However, it can been seen from Table 3 that the transformer-based CRE model was able to correctly uncover some rare relations, like *programCreator*, which was missed by the CNN-based CRE model, despite it having better overall quantitative results. It is reasonable to expect that given a more balanced dataset with sufficient training time, the transformer-based CRE model may obtain a better quantitative result than its CNN counterpart.

Since contextual knowledge plays a big role in the performance of CRE models, it will be interesting to see how such models may perform over prediction on input texts that are heterogeneous to the New York Times. For example, an alternative input text source could be a collection of academic publications, which is of very different genre compared to the New York Times. If our hypothesis on why these models work well is correct, then we would expect to see some degradation in performance, though it should be no worse than context-free approaches. This can be overcome, of course, by utilizing pre-trained CRE models and finetuning on the new text body, so that the model can learn about the new context.

5 Conclusion and Future Work

In this paper, we introduced a novel contextualized relation embedding (CRE) model for relation extraction that incorporates knowledge base modeling in a comprehensive and efficient manner. We demonstrate both empirically and qualitatively that the CRE model is able to achieve state of the art results on relation extraction task on the New York times dataset with Freebase as a knowledge

Relation Name	Weston et al.	Han et al.	CRE+CNN	CRE+Transformer	Fact
location.contains	1085	1178	761	840	597
person.nationality	66	19	189	159	173
location.containedBy	198	205	435	346	316
people.placeOfBirth	7	0	16	17	91
people.placeOfDeath	1	0	0	22	47
usRepresentative.state	0	0	0	5	11
tvProgram.programCreator	0	0	0	1	2

Table 3: Top relation prediction counts by each model compared to truth

source. We demonstrate the flexibility of the model by using different encoders and knowledge based modeling schemes which are a testament to the modular nature of this model, which can easily be upgraded with alternative configurations with ease. Finally, we showcase that CRE model tend to generate a less skewed distributions of predicted relations and the model is robust to imbalances in the dataset.

Interesting directions of future work may include utilizing CRE pre trained models and evalauting if these models can be finetuned to work in low-resource situations when the testing set distribution is different than the training distribution. Another interesting direction may be utilizing pre-trained BERT-based Devlin et al. (2018) models as sentence encoders and fine-tune them for the relation extraction task, since such models are already trained on large amount of textual data and thus may hold contextual knowledge that might be useful for this task. This may also reveal some hidden connections between contextualized word embeddings and contextualized relation embeddings.

References

Kurt Bollacker, Colin Evans, Praveen Paritosh, Tim Sturge, and Jamie Taylor. 2008. Freebase: A collaboratively created graph database for structuring human knowledge. In *Proceedings of the 2008 ACM SIGMOD International Conference on Management of Data*, SIGMOD '08, page 1247–1250, New York, NY, USA. Association for Computing Machinery.

Antoine Bordes, Nicolas Usunier, Alberto Garcia-Duran, Jason Weston, and Oksana Yakhnenko. 2013. Translating embeddings for modeling multi-relational data. In *Advances in Neural Information Processing Systems 26*, pages 2787–2795. Curran Associates, Inc.

Jacob Devlin, Ming-Wei Chang, Kenton Lee, and Kristina Toutanova. 2018. Bert: Pre-training of deep bidirectional transformers for language understanding.

Xu Han, Zhiyuan Liu, and Maosong Sun. 2018. Neural knowledge acquisition via mutual attention between knowledge graph and text.

Tomas Mikolov, Ilya Sutskever, Kai Chen, Greg Corrado, and Jeffrey Dean. 2013. Distributed representations of words and phrases and their compositionality. *CoRR*, abs/1310.4546.

Mike Mintz, Steven Bills, Rion Snow, and Daniel Jurafsky. 2009. Distant supervision for relation extraction without labeled data. In *Proceedings of the Joint Conference of the 47th Annual Meeting of the ACL and the 4th International Joint Conference on Natural Language Processing of the AFNLP*, pages 1003–1011, Suntec, Singapore. Association for Computational Linguistics.

Sebastian Riedel, Limin Yao, and Andrew McCallum. 2010. Modeling relations and their mentions without labeled text. In *Machine Learning and Knowledge Discovery in Databases*, pages 148–163, Berlin, Heidelberg. Springer Berlin Heidelberg.

Théo Trouillon, Johannes Welbl, Sebastian Riedel, Éric Gaussier, and Guillaume Bouchard. 2016. Complex embeddings for simple link prediction. *CoRR*, abs/1606.06357.

Ashish Vaswani, Noam Shazeer, Niki Parmar, Jakob Uszkoreit, Llion Jones, Aidan N. Gomez, Lukasz Kaiser, and Illia Polosukhin. 2017. Attention is all you need. *CoRR*, abs/1706.03762.

Jason Weston, Antoine Bordes, Oksana Yakhnenko, and Nicolas Usunier. 2013. Connecting language and knowledge bases with embedding models for relation extraction. *CoRR*, abs/1307.7973.

Peng Xu and Denilson Barbosa. 2019. Connecting language and knowledge with heterogeneous representations for neural relation extraction. *CoRR*, abs/1903.10126.

Daojian Zeng, Kang Liu, Siwei Lai, Guangyou Zhou, and Jun Zhao. 2014. Relation classification via convolutional deep neural network. In *Proceedings of COLING 2014, the 25th International Conference on Computational Linguistics: Technical Papers*, pages 2335–2344, Dublin, Ireland. Dublin City University and Association for Computational Linguistics.

Generalization to Mitigate Synonym Substitution Attacks

Basemah Alshemali
College of Computer Science and
Engineering
Taibah University
Almadinah, KSA
College of Engineering and Applied Science
University of Colorado at Colorado Springs
Colorado Springs, USA
balshema@uccs.edu

Jugal Kalita
College of Engineering and Applied Science
University of Colorado at Colorado Springs
Colorado Springs, USA
jkalita@uccs.edu

Abstract

Studies have shown that deep neural networks
are vulnerable to adversarial examples – per-
turbed inputs that cause DNN-based models
to produce incorrect results. One robust adversarial attack in the NLP domain is the synonym substitution. In attacks of this variety, the adversary substitutes words with synonyms. Since synonym substitution perturbations aim to satisfy all lexical, grammatical,
and semantic constraints, they are difficult to
detect with automatic syntax check as well as
by humans. In this work, we propose the first
defensive method to mitigate synonym substitution perturbations that can improve the robustness of DNNs with both clean and adversarial data. We improve the generalization of
DNN-based classifiers by replacing the embeddings of the important words in the input samples with the average of their synonyms' embeddings. By doing so, we reduce model sensitivity to particular words in the input samples.
Our algorithm is generic enough to be applied
in any NLP domain and to any model trained
on any natural language.

1 Introduction

Deep Neural Networks (DNNs) have achieved re-
markable success in various machine learning tasks,
including computer vision (Krizhevsky et al., 2012;
He et al., 2019), speech recognition (Hinton et al.,
2012; Chen et al., 2019), and natural language processing (NLP) (Kim, 2014; Pirinen, 2019; Kambhatla et al., 2018). However, studies have found
that DNNs are vulnerable to adversarial examples –
artificially modified input samples that lead DNNs
to produce incorrect results, while not being de-
tectable by humans (Szegedy et al., 2014). These
vulnerabilities have been exposed in the domains
of computer vision (Goodfellow et al., 2015; Papernot et al., 2016; Carlini and Wagner, 2017), speech

(Alzantot et al., 2017; Carlini and Wagner, 2018),
and NLP (Ebrahimi et al., 2018; Jin et al., 2020).

Based on the adversary's level of perturbation,
three categories of adversarial attacks in NLP systems have been proposed: Character-level, token-
level, and sentence-level adversarial attacks (Alshemali and Kalita, 2020; Zhang et al., 2020). One robust existing token-level adversarial attack in NLP
is black-box synonym substitution (Alzantot et al.,
2018; Ren et al., 2019; Zhang et al., 2019; Jin et al.,
2020). In attacks of this variety, the adversary substitutes tokens with synonyms. Since synonym
substitution perturbations aim to satisfy all lexical,
grammatical, and semantic constraints, they are difficult to detect with automatic syntax check as well
as by humans.

In this work, we propose a defensive method to
mitigate synonym substitution perturbations. We
propose to improve the generalization of DNN-
based models by replacing the embeddings of the
important tokens in the input samples with the average of their synonyms' embeddings. By doing
so, we reduce model sensitivity to particular tokens
in the input samples. Experimenting on two popular datasets, for two types of text classification
tasks, demonstrates that the proposed defense is
not only capable of defending against these adversarial attacks, but is also capable of improving the
performance of DNN-based models when tested on
benign data. To our knowledge, our defense is the
first proposed method that can effectively (1) Improve the robustness of DNN-based models against
synonym substitution adversarial attacks and (2)
Improve the generalization of DNN-based models
with both clean and adversarial data.

2 Related Work

Alzantot et al. (2018) developed a black-box synonym substitution attack to generate adversarial

Proceedings of Deep Learning Inside Out (DeeLIO):
The First Workshop on Knowledge Extraction and Integration for Deep Learning Architectures, pages 20–28
Online, November 19, 2020. ©2020 Association for Computational Linguistics

samples for sentiment analysis. They first computed the nearest neighbors of a token based on the Euclidean distance in the embedding space. Then, they picked the token that maximizes the target label prediction when replacing the original token. Their adversarial examples successfully fooled their LSTM model's output with a 100% success rate, using the IMDB dataset (Maas et al., 2011).

Ren et al. (2019) proposed a black-box synonym substitution attack for text classification tasks. They employed word saliency to select the token to be replaced. For each token, they selected the synonym that causes the most significant change in the classification probability after replacement. They experimented with three datasets: IMDB, AG's News (Zhang et al., 2015), and Yahoo! Answers[1] using the word-level CNN of Kim (2014), the character-level CNN of Zhang et al. (2015), a Bi-directional LSTM, and an LSTM. Their results showed that, under their attack, the classification accuracies on the three datasets IMDB, AG's News, and Yahoo! Answers were reduced by an average of 81.05%, 33.62%, and 38.65% respectively.

Zhang et al. (2019) adopted the Metropolis-Hastings (M-H) sampling approach (Metropolis et al., 1953; Hastings, 1970) to generate black-box synonym substitution perturbations against text classification and textual entailment tasks. They used the M-H approach to replace targeted words with synonyms, followed by a language model to enforce the fluency of the sentence after replacing the words. Their attack successfully changed the output of their Bi-LSTM model and the Bi-DAF model (Seo et al., 2017) with 98.7% and 86.6% success rates, respectively, using the IMDB dataset, and the SNLI dataset (Bowman et al., 2015).

Jin et al. (2020) also proposed a black-box synonym substitution attack to evaluate text classification systems. They first identified important tokens for the target model, then gathered the top tokens whose cosine similarity with the selected tokens are greater than a threshold. They kept the candidates that altered the prediction of the target model. Using their attack, they evaluated the word-level CNN and a word-level LSTM, using the AG's News and IMDB datasets. Their results suggested that their attack reduced the accuracy of all target models by at least 64.2%.

---

[1] https://webscope.sandbox.yahoo.com/catalog.php?

3 Methodology

This paper proposes improving the generalization of DNN-based models by reducing a model's sensitivity to particular tokens in the input samples. This effectively mitigates black-box synonym substitution perturbations. We propose a method that combines word importance ranking, synonym extraction, word embedding averaging, and majority voting techniques to mitigate adversarial perturbations. Figure 1 illustrates the overall schema of the proposed approach. The proposed approach for mitigating adversarial text consists of four main steps:

- **Step 1:** Determine the N important tokens in the input sequence.

- **Step 2:** Build a synonym set for each important token.

- **Step 3:** Replace the embedding of each important token by the average of its synonyms' embeddings.

- **Step 4:** Perform a majority voting for the N replacements based on their predictions.

3.1 Scoring Function

Given a sequence of tokens, only some key tokens act as influential signals for the model's prediction. Therefore, we use a selection mechanism to choose the tokens that most significantly influence the final prediction results. We use the Replace-1 scoring function $R1S()$ of Gao et al. (2018) to score the importance of tokens in an input sequence according to the observed results from the targeted model.

By assuming the input sequence $x = x_1x_2...x_n$, where x_i is the token at the ith position, we measure the effect of the x_i token on the output of the targeted model (F). The scoring function $R1S()$ measures the effect of x_i on the model by replacing x_i with x_i'. More formally:

$$R1S(x_i) = F(x_1, x_2, ..., x_{i-1}, x_i, ..., x_n) - \\ F(x_1, x_2, ..., x_{i-1}, x_i', ..., x_n), \quad (1)$$

where x_i' is chosen to be out-of-vocabulary (OOV) and it is obtained by inserting, deleting, or substituting a letter in x_i for a random letter. $R1S()$ measures the importance of a token by calculating the effect of replacing it with an OOV token, while observing the model's prediction. The token's importance is thus calculated as the prediction change

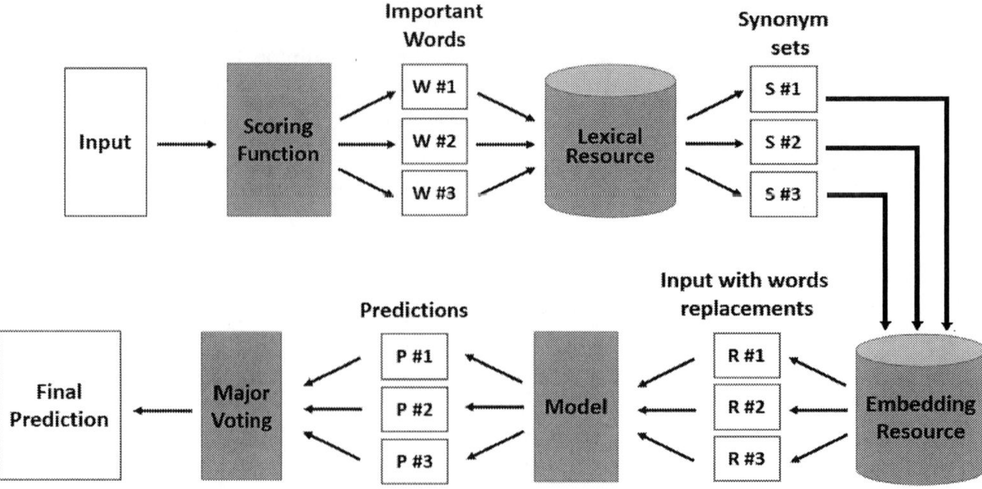

Figure 1: Schema of the proposed defensive method. The proposed defense involves the following steps: Step 1: Extract the important tokens in the input sample (here, we extract the three most important tokens). Step 2: Build a synonym set for each important token. Step 3: Replace the embedding of each important token by the average of its synonyms' embeddings. Step 4: Perform a majority voting for the replacements based on their predictions.

before and after replacing it with an OOV. By calculating the effect of replacing x_i with OOV, the importance of all tokens in the input sample can be measured and ranked. This step is employed to report the N most important tokens in an input sample. In our experiments, setting N to be 5 produces the best results.

3.2 Synonym Extraction

For a given token with a high importance score obtained in Step 1, we build a synonym set ($Synset$) for the selected token. Synonyms can be found in WordNet[2] (Miller, 1995), a large lexical resource for the English language. For each token, we use WordNet to build a synonym set that contains all possible synonyms of the token. More formally,

$$Synset(token) = \{syn_1, syn_2, ..., syn_m\},$$

(2)

where m is the quantity of the token's synonyms that exist in the lexical resource (WordNet). If a token does not have any synonyms in the lexical resource, the processing moves to the next important token. In this step, we use WordNet as a lexical resource, but the proposed defense can use any other lexical resource (e.g. Wiktionary[3]).

[2]https://wordnet.princeton.edu/
[3]https://www.wiktionary.org/

3.3 Embedding Averaging

In the previous steps, we determine the N important tokens in an input sample (Step 1), and then extract a synonym set for each one of the important tokens (Step 2). In the third step, for each important token, we replace its embedding by the average of its synonyms' embeddings. More formally,

$$E(token) = \frac{1}{m} \sum_{i=1}^{m} E(syn_i),$$

(3)

where $E()$ represents the word embeddings resource, and m is the count of synonyms in the synonym set of the token.

3.4 Majority Voting

In the previous step, for each important token, we replace the embedding of the token by the average of its synonyms' embeddings. In this step, the model makes a prediction after each replacement, and assigns each replacement a vote based on its prediction. The model's final prediction will be the prediction with the majority of the votes. An example of this step is illustrated in Figure 2. In this figure, the model made three predictions and the final classification is positive, based on the votes. The proposed approach with all steps is shown in Algorithm 1.

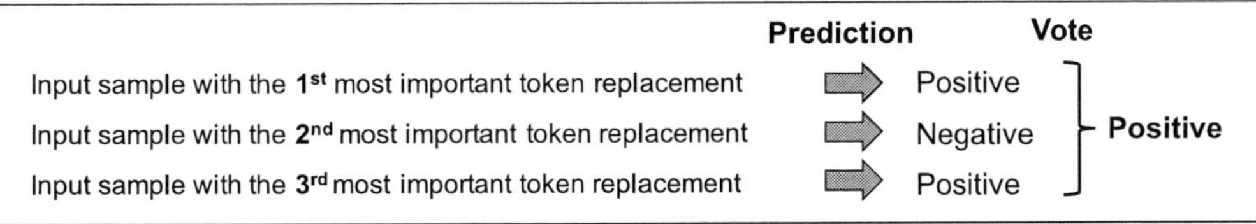

Figure 2: Step 4: The model makes a prediction after each replacement, and assigns each replacement a vote based on its prediction. The model's final prediction is the prediction with the majority of the votes.

Algorithm 1: The overall procedure of the proposed defensive method.

input : Input sample X, classifier $F()$, Replace-1 scoring function to extract important tokens in an input sample $R1S()$, lexical resource to extract synonyms $Synset()$, word embeddings resource to represent tokens $E()$, prediction set P, majority voting method $V()$.

output : $F(X)$

$R1S(X) = \{token_1, token_2, ..., token_n\}$

for $c \leftarrow 1$ **to** n **do**

    $Synset(token_c) = \{syn_1, syn_2, ..., syn_m\}$

    $E(token_c) = \frac{1}{m}\sum_{i=1}^{m} E(syn_i)$

    $S = X$

    $S \leftarrow E(token_c)$

    $P \leftarrow F(S)$

end

$F(X) = V(P)$

Return $F(X)$

In this paper, we proposed a simple and structure-free defensive strategy which can be successful in hardening DNNs against synonym substitution based adversarial attacks. As shown in Section 5, the proposed defense yielded great performance. The advantage of our approach is that it can use any embeddings and lexical resources. It does not require any additional data to train, or modify the architecture of the models. Our implementation is generic enough to be applied in any domain and to models trained on any natural language.

4 Experiments

We implemented the proposed defensive method using Python, Numpy, Tensorflow, Scikit-learn, and Pandas libraries.

4.1 Corpus

To study the efficiency of our defense, we used the Internet Movie Database (Maas et al., 2011). IMDB is a sentiment classification dataset which involves binary labels annotating the sentiment of sentences in movie reviews. IMDB consists of 25,000 training samples and 25,000 test samples, labeled as positive or negative. The average length of samples in IMDB is 262 words.

4.2 Targeted Classification Models

To evaluate our proposed approach, several experiments on the word-level CNN model of Kim (2014) and the Bi-directional LSTM model of Ren et al. (2019) were conducted. We replicated Kim's CNN architecture, which contains three convolutional layers, a max-pooling layer, and a fully-connected layer. The Bi-directional LSTM model involves a Bi-directional LSTM layer and a fully connected layer.

4.3 Adversarial Attacks

We evaluated our defensive method with two black-box synonym substitution attacks: The attack of Alzantot et al. (2018) and the attack of Ren et al. (2019), explained in Section 2.

4.4 Word Embeddings

We used the Global Vectors for Word Representation (GloVe) embedding space (Pennington et al., 2014) to generate word vectors of 300 dimensions.

4.5 Performance Evaluation

Classification accuracy is used as the metric to evaluate the performance of the proposed defensive model. Higher accuracy denotes a more effective approach.

5 Results

The CNN and Bi-LSTM models were trained on the IMDB training set, and achieved training accuracy scores similar to the original implementations.

Model	Model w/o defense	Model w/defense	Percent Increase
CNN	76.50	80.00	3.50
Bi-LSTM	73.44	78.90	5.46

Table 1: The accuracy of the classification models on the original benign data with and without our defensive method. No adversarial perturbations were used. "w/o defense" denotes using the model with no defense. "w/defense" denotes using the model with our defense. Percent Increase is the percent increase of the classification accuracy after using the defense.

Model	Attack	Model w/o defense	Model w/defense	Percent Increase
CNN	Alzantot et al.	35.00	74.20	39.20
CNN	Ren et al.	24.60	68.00	43.40
Bi-LSTM	Alzantot et al.	23.50	72.70	49.20
Bi-LSTM	Ren et al.	5.07	67.20	62.13

Table 2: The accuracy of the classifiers under adversarial attacks, with and without the defense applied. The accuracies of the models with the original data were 76.50% and 73.44% for the CNN and the Bi-LSTM, respectively.

Following the practices of previous studies that have explored adversarial examples (Alzantot et al., 2018; Ren et al., 2019; Zhang et al., 2019; Jin et al., 2020), and because the process of generating adversarial examples to evaluate the defense is time and resource-consuming, we randomly sampled 1280 examples from the IMDB testing set to evaluate the efficiency of the proposed defensive method. As shown in Section 3, for each sample, our defensive method first extracts the five important tokens. It then extracts their synonyms from the lexical resource. Overall, there were 2.15 synonyms per important token on average, as the majority of important tokens had 2 or 3 synonyms.

We first present how the defensive method behaves on benign data with no adversarial attacks. In Table 1, we report the accuracy of the targeted models on the original test samples, with and without the defense applied. Table 1 shows that the defense is capable of improving the performance of the models even when they are not under attack. The classification accuracy of the CNN increases by 3.50%, and that for the Bi-LSTM is also increased by 5.46%. This indicates that the defense is beneficial not only in adversarial situations, but also in secure situations with no adversarial attacks.

5.1 Effectiveness of the Defense

To evaluate the efficiency of our defense in adversarial situations, we used the adversarial attacks of Alzantot et al. (2018) and Ren et al. (2019) to perturb the 1280 benign samples and convert them to adversarial examples. A more effective defensive method should cause a smaller drop in model classification accuracy when said model is under attack. Table 2 shows the efficacy of various adversarial attacks and the defensive method.

Under the adversarial attacks of Alzantot et al. and Ren et al., the classification accuracy of the models dropped significantly. For the CNN, the accuracy degraded more than 41.50% and 51.90%, under the Alzantot et al. and Ren et al. attacks, respectively. Similarly, the accuracy of the Bi-LSTM model reduced more than 49.94% and 68.37%, under the same attacks. Our results suggest that (1) DNN-based models with higher original accuracy (with clean data) are more difficult to be attacked. For instance, as shown in Tables 1 and 2, the under-attack accuracy is higher for the CNN model compared with the Bi-LSTM model under all attacks. This agrees with the observation from previous research that, in general, models with higher original accuracy have higher under-attack accuracy (Jin et al., 2020). (2) The Bi-LSTM model is more vulnerable to the two attacks than the CNN model by a 12.45% accuracy difference on average. This supports the conclusion from previous research that, in the NLP domain, deep CNNs tend to be more robust than RNN models (Ren et al., 2019; Alshemali and Kalita, 2019). (3) While Alzantot et al. randomly selected the tokens to be replaced, Ren et al. employed the word saliency technique to determine the tokens to be replaced. This makes the attack of Ren et al. more effective than the attack of Alzantot et al. on both models by an average margin of 10.40% for the CNN and 18.43% for the Bi-LSTM.

After employing our defensive method, the ro-

Model	Attack	Model w/o defense	Model w/defense	Percent Increase
SVM	No-attack	88.28	92.35	4.06
SVM	Alzantot et al.	60.00	76.10	16.10
SVM	Ren et al.	55.00	74.15	19.15
XGBoost	No-attack	85.15	89.93	4.77
XGBoost	Alzantot et al.	49.61	70.00	20.39
XGBoost	Ren et al.	40.94	66.41	25.47

Table 3: The accuracy of the nonneural classification models under adversarial attacks, with and without the defense applied. Percent Increase is the percent increase of the classification accuracy with the defense applied.

bustness of the models significantly improved under all attacks. The effectiveness of the proposed defense is evaluated under the two attacks and the results are presented in Table 2. Our results show that the proposed defense effectively mitigated most of the adversarial examples generated by the two attacks. Under the Alzantot et al. attack, the defense increased the accuracies of the models by 39.20% and 49.20% for the CNN and Bi-LSTM, respectively. Under the Ren et al. attack, the accuracies of the models were improved by an average of 43.40% and 62.13% for the CNN and Bi-LSTM, respectively. Our results highlight that (1) Under the same attack, the proposed defense performs better with the Bi-LSTM model than with the CNN by an average difference of 14.36%; and (2) Under the same model, the proposed defense performs better in mitigating Ren et al.'s adversarial examples than in mitigating the adversarial examples generated by the attack of Alzantot et al., with an average difference of 8.56%. This is likely because Ren et al. used WordNet to obtain their synonyms, while Alzantot et al. considered the nearest neighbors of a token's embedding vector as its synonyms.

5.2 Nonneural Models

In this section, we evaluated the defense using two nonneural machine learning classification algorithms, that were selected due to their high performance on a variety of text classification tasks: (1) Support Vector Machine (SVM) (Cortes and Vapnik, 1995); and (2) Extreme Gradient Boosting (XGBoost) (Chen and Guestrin, 2016). We examined the performance of our defense with the SVM and XGBoost models, trained on the IMDB dataset, and using the GloVe embedding space.

To evaluate the defense with the SVM and XGBoost models, we used the adversarial attacks of Alzantot et al. (2018) and Ren et al. (2019) to perturb the same 1280 benign samples of IMDB re-

views (used in Section 5.1) and convert them to adversarial examples. Table 3 shows how the defense behaves with nonneural models on benign and adversarial data. Table 3 shows that the SVM model has more than 28.00% and 33.00% accuracy degradation under the Alzantot et al. and Ren et al. attacks, respectively. Similarly, the accuracy of the XGBoost model was reduced by 35.54% and 44.21%, under the same attacks, respectively.

By utilizing our defense, the robustness of the nonneural models improved under all attacks. Our results illustrate that the proposed defense is effectively able to mitigate most of the adversarial examples generated by the two attacks. Under the Alzantot et al. attack, the defense increased the accuracies of the models by 16.10% and 20.39% for SVM and XGBoost, respectively. Under the Ren et al. attack, the accuracies of the models were improved by 19.15% and 25.47% for SVM and XGBoost, respectively. Table 3 also shows that the defense improved the performance of the models with benign data. The classification accuracy of the SVM model increases by 4.06%, and that for the XGBoost is also increased by 4.77%.

5.3 News Categorization Task

In Sections 5.1 and 5.2, we evaluated the effectiveness of the discussed defense on the sentiment analysis task. Here, we evaluated it on the news categorization task, using the Bidirectional Encoder Representations from Transformers (BERT) embedding space and the BERT model (Devlin et al., 2019). This model was trained on the AG's News categorization dataset (Zhang et al., 2015). We used the 12-layer BERT model, also called the base-uncased version[4].

AG's News is a news categorization dataset which contains news articles categorized into four classes: World, Sports, Business and Sci/Tech.

---

[4]https://github.com/huggingface/transformers

Attack	Model w/o defense	Model w/defense	Percent Increase
No-attack	65.56	68.00	2.44
Alzantot et al.	35.00	58.60	23.60
Ren et al.	30.00	59.61	29.61

Table 4: The classification accuracy of the BERT model under adversarial attacks, with and without the defense applied. Percent Increase is the percent increase of the classification accuracy with the defense applied.

The total number of training samples is 120,000 and testing 7,600. The average number of words per sample is 278.6. We randomly selected 1280 samples from the AG's News testing set to evaluate the effectiveness of the proposed defensive method. We used the adversarial attacks of Alzantot et al. and Ren et al. to perturb the 1280 benign samples and convert them to adversarial examples. Table 4 shows the efficacy of the defensive method with various adversarial attacks.

Even for the powerful BERT, which has achieved great performance in various NLP tasks, adversarial attacks can still reduce its classification accuracy by about 30.56% with the attack of Alzantot et al. and by 35.56% with the attack of Ren et al.. These accuracy drops are unprecedented, however, employing our defense boosted the robustness of the BERT model under all attacks. Table 4 shows that, under the Alzantot et al. attack, the defense improved the accuracy of the model by 23.60%. Similarly, under the Ren et al. attack, the accuracy of the model was increased by 29.61%.

5.4 Statistical Analysis

While the defended classifiers had higher accuracy scores than the undefended classifiers across all tasks, adversarial attacks, and datasets, it is important to determine whether the difference in performance of the defended models is statistically significant. Many researchers recommend McNemar's test (McNemar, 1947) for comparing the performance of two classifiers (Salzberg, 1997; Dietterich, 1998; Japkowicz and Shah, 2011; Costa et al., 2018) as it has a lower probability of Type I error. McNemar's is a non-parametric pairwise test designed for comparing two populations, or in this case, the predictions from two different classifiers on the same test dataset. In this paper, McNemar's test was applied to compare the performance of the defended models with their undefended counterparts (studied in Sections 5.1, 5.2, and 5.3). Here, we wish to compare the performance of the defended CNN with the undefended CNN, the defended SVM with the undefended SVM, etc.

We performed McNemar's test to determine if there was a significant difference between the accuracy of the defended models and that of the undefended ones. We tested the null hypothesis, which states that there is no significant difference in the accuracy of the models studied, and the alternative hypothesis, which states that there is a difference in the accuracy of the models studied. Several comparisons were performed, and the significance threshold for each individual pairwise test was adjusted to 0.05. In all cases, the difference between the defended models and the undefended models (the p-value) was significant (< 0.05). Thus, we reject the null hypothesis which assumed there was no difference between the classifiers, in favor of the alternative. The results show that there was a statistically significant difference in the accuracy of all models, which indicates that the defended models had significantly better performance.

6   Conclusion

In this paper, we proposed a structure-free defensive method that is capable of improving the performance of DNN-based models with both clean and adversarial data. Our findings show that replacing the embeddings of the important words in the input samples with the average of their synonyms' embeddings can significantly improve the generalization of DNN-based models. Our results indicate that the proposed defense is not only capable of defending against adversarial attacks, but is also capable of improving the performance of DNN-based models when tested on benign data. On average, the proposed defense improved the classification accuracy of the CNN and Bi-LSTM models by 41.30% and 55.66%, respectively, when tested under adversarial attacks. Extended investigation shows that our defensive method can improve the robustness of nonneural models, achieving an average of 17.62% and 22.93% classification accuracy increase on the SVM and XGBoost models, respectively. The proposed defensive method has also shown an average of 26.60% classification accuracy improvement when tested with the infamous BERT model. In further work, we plan to generalize our approach to achieve robustness against other types of adversarial attacks in NLP. We also hope to evaluate the defense with a variety of NLP systems, such as textual entailment systems.

References

Basemah Alshemali and Jugal Kalita. 2019. Toward mitigating adversarial texts. *International Journal of Computer Applications*, 178(50):1–7.

Basemah Alshemali and Jugal Kalita. 2020. Improving the reliability of deep neural networks in NLP: A review. *Knowledge-Based Systems*, 191(105210):1–19.

Moustafa Alzantot, Bharathan Balaji, and Mani Srivastava. 2017. Did you hear that? adversarial examples against automatic speech recognition. In *Proceedings of the 31st Conference on Neural Information Processing Systems*.

Moustafa Alzantot, Yash Sharma, Ahmed Elgohary, Bo-Jhang Ho, Mani Srivastava, and Kai-Wei Chang. 2018. Generating natural language adversarial examples. In *Proceedings of the Conference on Empirical Methods in Natural Language Processing*, pages 2890–2896.

Samuel R Bowman, Gabor Angeli, Christopher Potts, and Christopher D Manning. 2015. A large annotated corpus for learning natural language inference. In *Proceedings of the Conference on Empirical Methods in Natural Language Processing*, pages 632–642.

Nicholas Carlini and David Wagner. 2017. Towards evaluating the robustness of neural networks. In *2017 IEEE Symposium on Security and Privacy (SP)*, pages 39–57. IEEE.

Nicholas Carlini and David Wagner. 2018. Audio adversarial examples: Targeted attacks on speech-to-text. In *2018 IEEE Security and Privacy Workshops (SPW)*, pages 1–7. IEEE.

Tianqi Chen and Carlos Guestrin. 2016. Xgboost: A scalable tree boosting system. In *International Conference on knowledge discovery and data mining*, pages 785–794. ACM.

Xie Chen, Xunying Liu, Yu Wang, Anton Ragni, Jeremy HM Wong, and Mark JF Gales. 2019. Exploiting future word contexts in neural network language models for speech recognition. *IEEE/ACM Transactions on Audio, Speech, and Language Processing*, 27(9):1444–1454.

Corinna Cortes and Vladimir Vapnik. 1995. Support-vector networks. *Machine Learning*, 20(3):273–297.

Joana Costa, Catarina Silva, Mario Antunes, and Bernardete Ribeiro. 2018. Adaptive learning models evaluation in Twitter's timelines. In *International Joint Conference on Neural Networks*, pages 1–8. IEEE.

Jacob Devlin, Ming-Wei Chang, Kenton Lee, and Kristina Toutanova. 2019. BERT: Pre-training of deep bidirectional transformers for language understanding. In *The Conference of the North American Chapter of the Association for Computational Linguistics: Human Language Technologies*, pages 4171–4186.

Thomas G Dietterich. 1998. Approximate statistical tests for comparing supervised classification learning algorithms. *Neural Computation*, 10(7):1895–1923.

Javid Ebrahimi, Anyi Rao, Daniel Lowd, and Dejing Dou. 2018. Hotflip: White-box adversarial examples for NLP. In *The Annual Meeting of the Association for Computational Linguistics*, pages 31–36.

Ji Gao, Jack Lanchantin, Mary Lou Soffa, and Yanjun Qi. 2018. Black-box generation of adversarial text sequences to evade deep learning classifiers. In *IEEE Security and Privacy Workshops*, pages 50–56.

Ian J Goodfellow, Jonathon Shlens, and Christian Szegedy. 2015. Explaining and harnessing adversarial examples. In *International Conference on Learning Representations*.

W Keith Hastings. 1970. Monte carlo sampling methods using markov chains and their applications. *Oxford University Press*.

Tong He, Zhi Zhang, Hang Zhang, Zhongyue Zhang, Junyuan Xie, and Mu Li. 2019. Bag of tricks for image classification with convolutional neural networks. In *The IEEE Conference on Computer Vision and Pattern Recognition*.

Geoffrey Hinton, Li Deng, Dong Yu, George E Dahl, Abdel-rahman Mohamed, Navdeep Jaitly, Andrew Senior, Vincent Vanhoucke, Patrick Nguyen, Tara N Sainath, et al. 2012. Deep neural networks for acoustic modeling in speech recognition: The shared views of four research groups. *IEEE Signal Processing Magazine*, 29(6):82–97.

Nathalie Japkowicz and Mohak Shah. 2011. *Evaluating Learning Algorithms: A Classification Perspective*. Cambridge University Press.

Di Jin, Zhijing Jin, Joey Tianyi Zhou, and Peter Szolovits. 2020. Is BERT really robust? a strong baseline for natural language attack on text classification and entailment. In *the Association for the Advancement of Artificial Intelligence*.

Nishant Kambhatla, Anahita Mansouri Bigvand, and Anoop Sarkar. 2018. Decipherment of substitution ciphers with neural language models. In *the Conference on Empirical Methods in Natural Language Processing*, pages 869–874.

Yoon Kim. 2014. Convolutional neural networks for sentence classification. In *Proceedings of the Conference on Empirical Methods in Natural Language Processing*, pages 1746–1751.

Alex Krizhevsky, Ilya Sutskever, and Geoffrey E Hinton. 2012. Imagenet classification with deep convolutional neural networks. In *Advances in Neural Information Processing Systems*, pages 1097–1105.

Andrew L Maas, Raymond E Daly, Peter T Pham, Dan Huang, Andrew Y Ng, and Christopher Potts. 2011. Learning word vectors for sentiment analysis. In *The Annual Meeting of the Association for Computational Linguistics: Human Language Technologies*, pages 142–150.

Quinn McNemar. 1947. Note on the sampling error of the difference between correlated proportions or percentages. *Psychometrika*, 12(2):153–157.

Nicholas Metropolis, Arianna W Rosenbluth, Marshall N Rosenbluth, Augusta H Teller, and Edward Teller. 1953. Equation of state calculations by fast computing machines. *The Journal of Chemical Physics*, 21(6):1087–1092.

George A Miller. 1995. WordNet: A lexical database for English. *Communications of the ACM*, 38(11):39–41.

Nicolas Papernot, Patrick McDaniel, Somesh Jha, Matt Fredrikson, Z Berkay Celik, and Ananthram Swami. 2016. The limitations of deep learning in adversarial settings. In *IEEE European Symposium, Security and Privacy*, pages 372–387.

Jeffrey Pennington, Richard Socher, and Christopher Manning. 2014. Glove: Global vectors for word representation. In *Proceedings of the Conference on Empirical Methods in Natural Language Processing*, pages 1532–1543.

Tommi A Pirinen. 2019. Neural and rule-based Finnish NLP models—expectations, experiments and experiences. In *the International Workshop on Computational Linguistics for Uralic Languages*, pages 104–114.

Shuhuai Ren, Yihe Deng, Kun He, and Wanxiang Che. 2019. Generating natural language adversarial examples through probability weighted word saliency. In *The Annual Meeting of the Association for Computational Linguistics*, pages 1085 –1097.

Steven L Salzberg. 1997. On comparing classifiers: Pitfalls to avoid and a recommended approach. *Data Mining and Knowledge Discovery*, 1(3):317–328.

Minjoon Seo, Aniruddha Kembhavi, Ali Farhadi, and Hannaneh Hajishirzi. 2017. Bidirectional attention flow for machine comprehension. In *International Conference on Learning Representations*.

Christian Szegedy, Wojciech Zaremba, Ilya Sutskever, Joan Bruna, Dumitru Erhan, Ian Goodfellow, and Rob Fergus. 2014. Intriguing properties of neural networks. In *International Conference on Learning Representations*.

Huangzhao Zhang, Hao Zhou, Ning Miao, and Lei Li. 2019. Generating fluent adversarial examples for natural languages. In *Proceedings of the 57th Annual Meeting of the Association for Computational Linguistics*, pages 5564–5569.

Wei Emma Zhang, Quan Z Sheng, Ahoud Alhazmi, and Chenliang Li. 2020. Adversarial attacks on deep-learning models in natural language processing: A survey. *ACM Transactions on Intelligent Systems and Technology (TIST)*, 11(3):1–41.

Xiang Zhang, Junbo Zhao, and Yann LeCun. 2015. Character-level convolutional networks for text classification. In *Advances in Neural Information Processing Systems*, pages 649–657.

GenAug: Data Augmentation for Finetuning Text Generators

Steven Y. Feng[*,1] **Varun Gangal**[*,1] **Dongyeop Kang**,[2] **Teruko Mitamura**,[1] **Eduard Hovy**[1]
[1]Carnegie Mellon University
{syfeng,vgangal,teruko,hovy}@cs.cmu.edu
[2]University of California, Berkeley
dongyeopk@berkeley.edu

Abstract

In this paper, we investigate data augmentation for text generation, which we call *GenAug*. Text generation and language modeling are important tasks within natural language processing, and are especially challenging for low-data regimes. We propose and evaluate various augmentation methods, including some that incorporate external knowledge, for finetuning GPT-2 on a subset of Yelp Reviews. We also examine the relationship between the amount of augmentation and the quality of the generated text. We utilize several metrics that evaluate important aspects of the generated text including its diversity and fluency. Our experiments demonstrate that insertion of character-level synthetic noise and keyword replacement with hypernyms are effective augmentation methods, and that the quality of generations improves to a peak at approximately three times the amount of original data.

Method	Text
Original Review	got sick from the food . overpriced and the only decent thing was the bread pudding . wouldn't go back even if i was paid a million dollars to do so .
Synthetic Noise (10%)	got **seick** from the **fotod** . **overhpriced** and the only decent **ting** was the bread pudding . wouldn't go back even if i was paid a million dollars to do so .
Synonym Replacement (3 keywords)	got sick from the food . overpriced and the only decent thing was the **scratch pud** . wouldn't go back even if i was paid a **one thousand thousand** dollars to do so .
Hyponym Replacement (3 keywords)	got sick from the food . overpriced and the only decent thing was the **crescent roll corn pudding** . wouldn't go back even if i was paid a million **kiribati dollar** to do so .
Hypernym Replacement (3 keywords)	got sick from the food . overpriced and the only decent thing was the **baked goods dish** . wouldn't go back even if i was paid a **large integer** dollars to do so .
Random Insertion (10%)	got sick from the food **nauseous** . overpriced and the only decent thing was the bread pudding . wouldn't go back even if i was paid a million dollars **boodle** to do so .
Semantic Text Exchange (60% MRT)	got sick from the **coffee** . overpriced and the **food was good** . wouldn't **come back** if i was **in a long hand washing machine** .

Table 1: Example of a Yelp review and its variations using our augmentation methods. Changes are bolded.

1 Introduction

Text generation is an important but difficult task within natural language processing (NLP). A major goal is for dialogue agents to generate human-like text. The development of strong pretrained text generators like GPT-2 (Radford et al., 2019) has made it easier to perform generation for new domains or task specifications. These models are typically finetuned on downstream tasks such as classification; however, the first stage of their training is language modeling. Effective language models are important not only for generation but many NLP tasks.

In-domain examples are needed for finetuning. Otherwise, the generated text, though fluent English, will not faithfully imbibe domain properties such as the vocabulary preferred, domain shifts in word meaning, and domain distribution over properties such as sentiment. The learned language model will also poorly replicate the domain. However, many domains are low-data. These models do not have enough data to learn domain-specific aspects of the text, especially without sacrificing aspects such as its fluency and diversity.

One approach is with text data augmentation. There is constantly an increasing demand for large amounts of text data. Compared to fields such as computer vision, augmentation techniques for NLP are limited. Collecting and cleaning data manually requires time and effort. Also, certain domains do not have sufficient data available to begin with.

Prior work in text augmentation has focused on classification tasks, and there has been limited investigation for generation. A possible explanation is that generation is more complicated; rather than predicting the correct label, the text itself must be produced and should satisfy properties typical of human text such as being fluent, logical, and di-

---

* Equal contribution by the two authors.

Code: https://github.com/styfeng/GenAug

Proceedings of Deep Learning Inside Out (DeeLIO):
The First Workshop on Knowledge Extraction and Integration for Deep Learning Architectures, pages 29–42
Online, November 19, 2020. ©2020 Association for Computational Linguistics

verse. Evaluation of the text is also more difficult.

In this work, we focus on data augmentation for text generation. We call this *GenAug*, and to the best of our knowledge, are the first to investigate it. We explore various augmentation methods such as semantic text exchange (STE) (Feng et al., 2019) and replacing keywords within examples from a small subset of the Yelp Reviews dataset (Yelp). See Table 1 for examples.[1] We also assess the impact of augmentation amount: from 1.5x to 4x the original amount of training data.

We evaluate the quality of generated text by GPT-2 after finetuning on our augmented data compared to the original data only. We illustrate that several augmentation methods improve the quality of the generations. We also show that the quality follows a trend with the augmentation amount: it increases until a peak and decreases thereafter. Overall, our major contributions can be summarized as follows:

- We propose *GenAug*, which is data augmentation specifically for text generation.
- We introduce and evaluate various augmentation methods for GenAug including inserting synthetic noise and integrating external knowledge through lexical databases for keyword replacement. We demonstrate that synthetic noise and replacement with hypernyms improve the quality of generations.[2]
- We investigate the effects of the augmentation amount and discover that performance improves until approximately three times the original training data, where all aspects of the generated text are noticeably improved upon.[2]
- We propose and use a mix of new and existing metrics for evaluating aspects of the text including its diversity, fluency, semantic content preservation, and sentiment consistency.[3]

2 Methodology

2.1 Model: GPT-2

We use OpenAI's GPT-2 (Radford et al., 2019), specifically its default pretrained model with 117M parameters. GPT-2 is a large transformer-based language model trained to predict the next word given previous words in a text. It is trained on *WebText* - a variety of internet data from sources such as Reddit, and has been shown to generate fluent text given different input prompts.

We choose this model as it is reasonably sized, frequently used as a pretrained text generator, and would thus benefit significantly from our experiments and analysis. We use HuggingFace's implementation of GPT-2 (Wolf et al., 2019).

2.2 Dataset: Yelp Reviews (YR)

The Yelp Reviews (YR) dataset contains user reviews on businesses. We choose YR as it differs substantially in domain from the *"WebText"* data used to train GPT-2, which consisted mainly of newswire and discussion forum threads. Unlike other review corpora such as SST-2 (Socher et al., 2013), YR contains long reviews with many sentences, making generation non-trivial.

We randomly select a small subset of YR for our experiments: a training split of 50K, validation split of 15K, and test split of 2K. This is approximately 1% of YR, replicating a low-data regime. We call this *Yelp-LR* or *YLR* (LR stands for low-resource). We include a proportion of reviews of each star rating equal to the proportions within YR to replicate the distribution of sentiment in YR.[4]

Finetuning GPT-2 on YLR represents the gold or baseline model. For each augmentation experiment, we combine YLR with our augmented data and finetune GPT-2 on this combination while using the same 15K validation and 2K test splits.

2.3 Text Augmentation Methods (AM)

We explore various augmentation methods (AM) to produce different versions of our training reviews[5] (see Table 1 for examples), and analyze their effects on GPT-2's generations. We split each review in half; a prompt and a continuation portion. We finetune GPT-2 on the entire reviews, but different AM are applied to either the prompt portion or entire review. We feed the prompt portion of test reviews as input to generate continuations.

2.3.1 Random Insertion, Deletion, & Swap

We experiment with random insertion, deletion, and swap (the *"Random Trio"*) on our entire reviews. Wei and Zou (2019) used these along with synonym replacement for text classification, and we investigate their performance for generation.

For each training example, we randomly swap the positions of two words, insert a random syn-

---

[1]See Appendix §A for more augmentation examples.
[2]See Section §4 for results and analysis.
[3]See Section §2.5 for evaluation metrics.

[4]See Section §3.3 for preprocessing details for this dataset.
[5]We also tried syntactic paraphrasing using SCPNs (Wieting and Gimpel, 2017) but found the paraphrase quality poor and hard to control for meaning preservation and fluency.

onym of a word that is not a stopword[6] into a random location, and remove a word, with $\alpha = 5\%$ and 10% (5% and 10% of the words are changed). Hence, we produce six total variations per example.

2.3.2 Semantic Text Exchange (STE)

We investigate Semantic Text Exchange (STE) as introduced in Feng et al. (2019) on the entire reviews. STE adjusts text to fit the semantic context of a word/phrase called the replacement entity (RE). We use Feng et al. (2019)'s SMERTI-Transformer by training on a subset of YLR.[7] It inserts the RE into the text by replacing another entity, masks words similar to the replaced entity, and fills in these masks using a masked language model.

SMERTI is designed for shorter text due to the limited ability of the model to learn longer temporal dependencies.[8] We break each review into windows, and perform STE on each. Our augmentations are the concatenation of the semantically adjusted windows. For each window, a random RE is chosen. The candidates REs are 150 of the 200 most frequent nouns in SMERTI's training set.[9] We use masking rate thresholds (MRT) of 20%, 40%, and 60% , which represent the maximum proportion of the text that can be masked and replaced.

2.3.3 Synthetic Noise

We add character-level synthetic noise to the prompt portion of reviews. For every word, at every character, we perform a character insertion, deletion, or swapping of two side-by-side characters. The insertions are lowercase letters.

The three events have an equal chance of occurring at every character equal to one-third the overall level of noise. We ignore the first and last character of every word to more closely imitate natural noise and typos (Belinkov and Bisk, 2017). We produce 5%, 10%, and 15% noise variations per review. The noised prompt is combined with the original continuation to form the augmentations.

2.3.4 Keyword Replacement

We experiment with replacing keywords within entire reviews. We use RAKE (Rose et al., 2010) for keyword extraction. Candidate replacements are extracted from the lexical database WordNet (Miller, 1995). We replace up to three keywords for each review, resulting in a maximum of three

augmentations for each review. Unlike STE, our goal is not to adjust the text's overall semantics.

The keywords replaced are ordered by their RAKE score (e.g. the probability of being a keyword) and replaced with words with the same overall part-of-speech (POS). We use the Stanford POS Tagger (Toutanova et al., 2003). Previous replacements are kept intact as further ones occur. There are three replacement methods:

1. **Synonyms Replacement (WN-Syns)** replaces each chosen keyword with a randomly chosen synonym of the same POS, preserving the text's semantics as much as possible.
2. **Hyponyms Replacement (WN-Hypos)** replaces each chosen keyword with a randomly chosen hyponym of the same POS that has more specific meaning. Words can have multiple hyponyms which differ semantically.
3. **Hypernyms Replacement (WN-Hypers)** replaces each chosen keyword with the closest (lowest) hypernym of the same POS that carries more broad and high-level meaning.

2.4 Text Augmentation Amounts

We also assess the impact of the amount of augmentation on the generated text. Specifically, **1.5x**, **2x**, **3x**, and **4x** the original amount of data (e.g. 4x refers to each example having three augmentations). We use a combination of synthetic noise, STE, and keyword replacement, each augmenting $\frac{1}{3}$ the YLR training examples (WN-Syns, Hypos, and Hypers each augment $\frac{1}{9}$).

2.5 Evaluation Metrics

We evaluate generated continuations using various metrics assessing major aspects of the text including its diversity, fluency, semantic content preservation, and sentiment consistency. Arguably the two most important are text fluency and diversity.[10]

2.5.1 Diversity

We pick a broad range of diversity measures for both intra- and inter-continuation diversity.[11]

1. SELF-BLEU (SBLEU) (ZHU ET AL., 2018), for a sample population S, measures the mean similarity of each sample to other samples. It is expressed as $E_{s \sim S}[BLEU(s, S - \{s\})]$,

---

[6]We use the stopwords list from Onix.

[7]See Section §3.2 for SMERTI training details.

[8]Feng et al. (2019) perform STE on text ≤ 20 words long.

[9]See Appendix §B for sliding window algorithm details.

[10]We do not use BLEU (Papineni et al., 2002) as we only have a single ground-truth continuation per review.

[11]We evaluate diversity on the generated continuations only (not concatenated with their corresponding prompts).

where $BLEU(h, R)$ is the BLEU-4 score of a hypothesis h measured against a set of references R. We measure the average SBLEU of every batch of 100 continuations per test prompt.[12] Lower SBLEU values represent higher inter-continuation diversity.

2. UNIQUE TRIGRAMS (UTR) (Tevet and Berant, 2020; Li et al., 2016) measures the ratio of unique to total trigrams in a population of generations. Higher UTR represents greater diversity. Since UTR is defined at the population level, it can assess the extent of cross-continuation repetition.

3. TYPE-TOKEN RATIO (TTR) is the ratio of unique to total tokens in a piece of text, and serves as a measure of intra-continuation diversity. The higher the TTR, the more varied the vocabulary in a continuation.

4. RARE-WORDS (RWORDS) (See et al., 2019) is defined by the following:

$$E_{s \sim S}[\sum_{w \in s} - \log \frac{n_{train}(w)}{N_{train}}]$$

where $n_{train}(w)$ and N_{train} are the corpus frequency of word w and the total corpus word count, respectively. Our corpus here is the 50K YLR training split. Lower values indicate usage of more rare words (less frequent in the corpus) and higher diversity.

2.5.2 Fluency

Fluency, also known as naturalness or readability, is a measure of how fluent text is. The higher the fluency, the more it imitates grammatically and logically correct human text.[13]

1. PERPLEXITY (PPL) is defined as:

$$PPL(S) = exp(-\frac{1}{|S|} ln(p_M(S)))$$

where S is a piece of text and $p_M(S)$ is the probability assigned to S by the language model. We finetune GPT-2 on a two-million review subset of YR (with a 500K additional validation split) and use this finetuned model for PPL evaluation. Outputs less likely to be seen in YR will typically have higher PPL.

2. SLOR (syntactic log-odds ratio) (Kann et al., 2018) is our main fluency metric. It modifies PPL by normalizing for individual tokens (e.g. "Zimbabwe" is less frequent than "France" but just as fluent), and serves as a better measure. Higher SLOR represents higher fluency. The equation for SLOR is as follows:

$$SLOR(S) = \frac{1}{|S|}(ln(p_M(S)) - ln(\prod_{t \in S} p(t)))$$

where $|S|$ is the length of S (in tokens), $p_M(S)$ is the probability of S under language model M, and $p(t)$ are the unconditional probabilities of individual tokens (or unigrams) t in S. We use the same finetuned GPT-2 model on YR as for PPL mentioned above for SLOR. We use the proportional frequencies of unigrams in the two-million reviews as the unconditional unigram probabilities. Specifically, for tokens t: $p(t) = \frac{f(t)}{z+1}$, where $f(t)$ is the frequency of token t and $z = \sum_t f(t)$.

3. SPELLCHECK: For synthetic noise, we measure two spelling related metrics:

   (a) SPELLWORDS: average number of misspelled words per continuation.

   (b) SPELLCHARS: average number of character level mistakes per continuation.

These approximately measure how *noisy* the generations are, which can misleadingly improve diversity metrics. We use Sym-Spell (Garbe, 2019), which uses a Symmetric Delete Algorithm to quickly compute edit distances to a predefined dictionary. We set *verbosity* to *top*, a prefix length of ten, and consider a maximum edit distance of five.

2.5.3 Semantic Content Preservation (SCP)

SCP assesses how closely each generated continuation (hypothesis) matches in semantic content to the ground truth distribution of continuations (reference). Since the latter is unavailable in this case, we use the prompt itself as a proxy for reference.[14]

We use what we call the Prompt-Continuation BertScore (BPRO). BPRO computes average BertScore (Zhang et al., 2019a) between each continuation and the prompt. BertScore computes per-token BERT representations for both hypothesis and reference and aligns each hypothesis token to a reference token. We prefer BertScore over symbolic measures (e.g BLEU) since it does not rely on exact string matching alone and allows soft matches between different parts of the input pair.

---

[12]This is because we generate 100 continuations per test example. See Section §3.4 for more.

[13]We evaluate perplexity and SLOR on the concatenations of the generated continuations with their corresponding prompts, and Spellcheck on the generated continuations only.

[14]Datasets with multiple continuations per prompt are rare, and one continuation would be insufficient in most cases.

2.5.4 Sentiment Consistency

We finetune a BERT (Devlin et al., 2019) sentiment regressor on YLR by converting review stars into values between 0 and 1, inclusive, with higher values representing more positive sentiment.[15] We run the regressor on the ground-truth test reviews and the concatenation of our generated continuations with their corresponding prompts. We measure:

1. SENTSTD: average standard deviation of sentiment scores among each batch of 100 continuations (each concatenated with the input prompt) for a given test example. We do this for all 2000 test examples (100 prompt + continuation concatenations each) and take the average of the standard deviation values for each. A lower value indicates more consistent (lower spread) of sentiment, on average, among the continuations for each prompt.

2. SENTDIFF: average difference in sentiment score between each batch of 100 continuations (each concatenated with the single input prompt) and the corresponding ground-truth review in its entirety (essentially, the input prompt concatenated with the ground-truth continuation). We run this for all 2000 test examples (100 prompt + continuation concatenations each) and take the average of the differences. A lower value indicates sentiment of the continuations that, on average, more closely aligns with the ground-truth reviews.

3 Experiments

3.1 GPT-2 Finetuning

We finetune GPT-2 with a batch size of two. We try three different learning rates on YLR: 5e-4, 5e-5, and 5e-6, and find 5e-5 results in the lowest validation perplexity and use it for all experiments. We ensure the same hyperparameters and settings are used for each experiment. Final models correspond to epochs with the lowest validation perplexity.[16]

3.2 SMERTI-Transformer Training

We take a 25K subset of YLR's training split and a 7.5K subset of YLR's validation split. These serve as SMERTI's training and validation splits, respectively. This replicates the low-data regime, ensures SMERTI does not see additional data, and ensures SMERTI only learns from a portion of the data to prevent overfitting and repetition.

Each chosen example is split into chunks (or windows) of up to 30 tokens each,[17] resulting in 144.6K total training and 43.2K total validation examples for SMERTI. We mask 20%, 40%, and 60% of the words in $\frac{1}{3}$ of the examples each. We train SMERTI on this data and find the best performance after 9 epochs with a validation loss of 1.63. We use scaled dot-product attention and the same hyperparameters as Feng et al. (2019).[18]

3.3 Data Processing

For Yelp preprocessing, we filter out reviews that are blank, non-English, or contain URLs. For remaining ones, we remove repeated punctuations and uncommon symbols. For postprocessing, we noticed that many GPT-2 generations included trailing exclamation marks. We stripped these if more than four occurred in a row. Resulting blank continuations (very small portion of the total) were represented with a *<blank>* token and ignored during evaluation of most metrics.

3.4 Experimental Setup

For the separate method experiments, we choose one augmentation for each training example, for a total of 2x the amount of original data. Since each method has multiple variations per training example, we randomly select one of these for each.

For the augmentation amount experiments, we ensure that larger amounts are supersets of smaller amounts - e.g. 3x contains all of the augmentation examples within 2x, and so forth.

We generate 100 continuations per test example by feeding in the prompt portions (first 50% of words). We use the default end-of-text token, a nucleus sampling budget (Holtzman et al., 2019) of 0.9, and a length limit of 500 for the generations.

For all experiments, we run two sets of random seeds, where each set $\{rs_1, rs_2\}$ consists of rs_1: a seed for data preparation and selection, and rs_2: a seed for GPT-2 finetuning and generation. Our final evaluation results are the average results.

4 Results and Analysis

4.1 Evaluation Results

Tables 2 and 3 contain average evaluation results for the variations and amounts, respectively. See Appendix §F for significance p-values and Ap-

---

[15] See Appendix §C for regressor finetuning details.

[16] See Appendix §D for details of the finetuned models.

[17] See Appendix §B for sliding window algorithm details.

[18] See Appendix §E for further SMERTI training details.

pendix §G for PPL results.[19] Figures 1 to 4 contain graphs of the variation results, and Figures 5 to 8 contain graphs of the amount results. The horizontal line(s) on the graphs refer to the no-augmentation (gold and 1x) setting with Yelp-LR. Table 4 contains generation examples.[20]

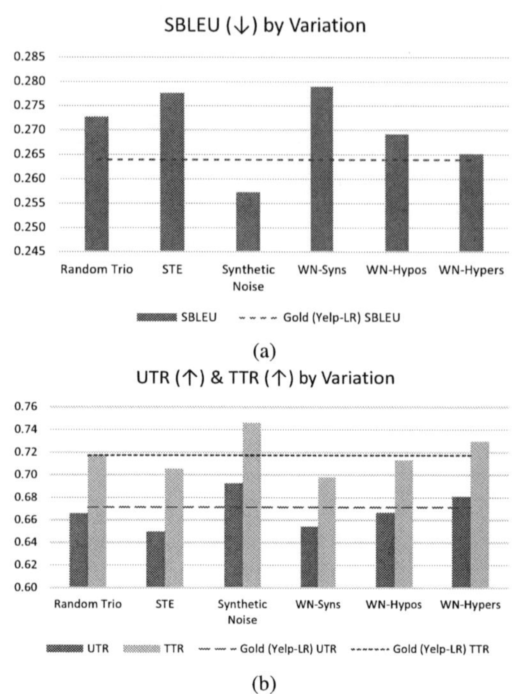

(a)

(b)

Figure 1: Graphs of a) average SBLEU and b) average UTR and TTR results by variation.

---

[19]Statistical significances are from paired two-tailed t-tests between the Yelp-LR and particular variation and amount results using an α of 0.05.

[20]See Appendix §H for more example generations.

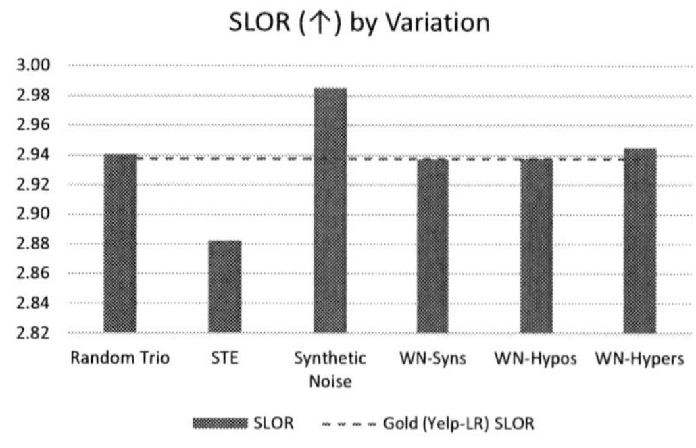

Figure 2: Graph of average SLOR results by variation.

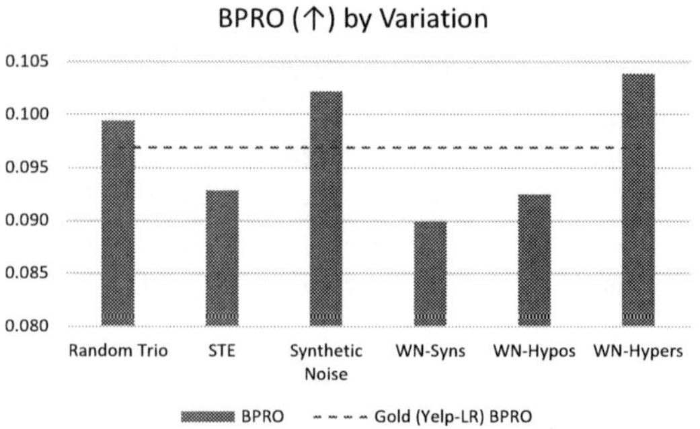

Figure 3: Graph of average BPRO results by variation.

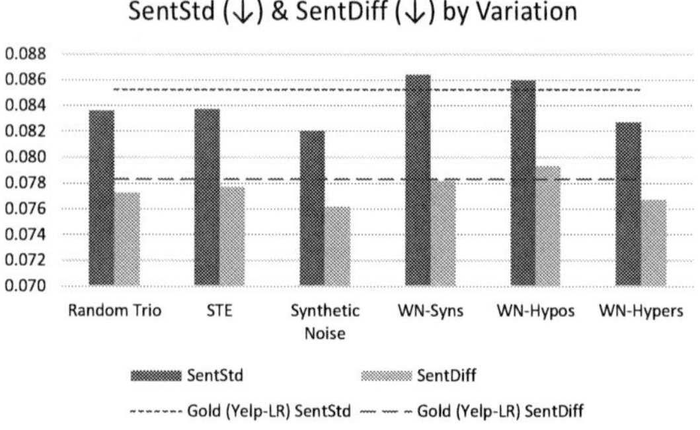

Figure 4: Graph of avg. sentiment results by variation.

4.2 Performance by Augmentation Method

We analyze the performance of each augmentation method using Table 2 and Figures 1 to 4.

4.2.1 Synthetic Noise and WN-Hypers

Synthetic Noise beats gold considerably on every metric. WN-Hypers does as well (other than SBLEU), but to a lesser extent on most metrics. Both clearly improve upon the gold setting.

To ensure Synthetic Noise's diversity improvements are not due to increased misspellings, we measure SpellWords and SpellChars. As seen in Table 5, Synthetic Noise actually decreases the average number of misspellings. This is likely because we only insert noise into the prompt portion of the training reviews, and GPT-2 is learning to be more robust to noise when finetuned on this data. This may also lead to increased generation quality.

WN-Hypers may improve performance as it slightly semantically adjusts the text. It does not keep semantics the same (unlike the goal of WN-Syns) but also does not drift too far since we choose the closest hypernyms. Each one carries more high-level meaning, which may contribute to increasing text diversity and fluency. We hence show that the

Variations	Gold (Yelp-LR)	Random Trio	STE	Synthetic Noise	WN-Syns	WN-Hypos	WN-Hypers
SBLEU ($\downarrow$)	0.2639	0.2727	0.2776	**0.2572**	0.2789	0.2691	0.2651
UTR ($\uparrow$)	0.6716	0.6660	0.6495	**0.6925**	0.6540	0.6669	**0.6808**
TTR ($\uparrow$)	0.7173	**0.7176***	0.7056	**0.7461**	0.6978	0.7129	**0.7296**
RWords ($\downarrow$)	-6.0637	**-6.0718**	-6.0508	**-6.1105**	**-6.0801**	**-6.0895**	**-6.0841**
SLOR ($\uparrow$)	2.9377	**2.9404***	2.8822	**2.9851**	2.9368*	2.9373*	**2.9447**
BPRO ($\uparrow$)	0.0969	**0.0994**	0.0928	**0.1022**	0.0899	0.0925	**0.1038**
SentStd ($\downarrow$)	0.0852	**0.0836**	**0.0837**	**0.0821**	0.0864	0.0859*	**0.0827**
SentDiff ($\downarrow$)	0.0783	**0.0773**	**0.0777***	**0.0762**	**0.0782***	0.0793	**0.0768**

Table 2: Average results by variation. Bold values indicate results better than Gold (Yelp-LR). Arrows beside each metric indicate whether lower or higher is better. * indicates insignificant values (using an α of 0.05).

Amounts	1x	1.5x	2x	3x	4x
SBLEU ($\downarrow$)	0.2639	0.2724	0.2669	**0.2607**	**0.2583**
UTR ($\uparrow$)	0.6716	0.6632	0.6678	**0.6837**	0.6707*
TTR ($\uparrow$)	0.7173	0.7115	**0.7257**	**0.7535**	**0.7420**
RWords ($\downarrow$)	-6.0637	**-6.0732**	**-6.0874**	**-6.1023**	**-6.0938**
SLOR ($\uparrow$)	2.9377	**2.9435**	**2.9666**	**3.0001**	2.9258
BPRO ($\uparrow$)	0.0969	**0.0971***	**0.1005**	**0.1067**	**0.0995**
SentStd ($\downarrow$)	0.0852	**0.0840**	**0.0839**	**0.0784**	**0.0810**
SentDiff ($\downarrow$)	0.0783	**0.0777***	**0.0775**	**0.0752**	**0.0771**

Table 3: Average results by amount. Bold values indicate results better than 1x (Yelp-LR). Arrows beside each metric indicate whether lower or higher is better. * indicates insignificant values (using an α of 0.05).

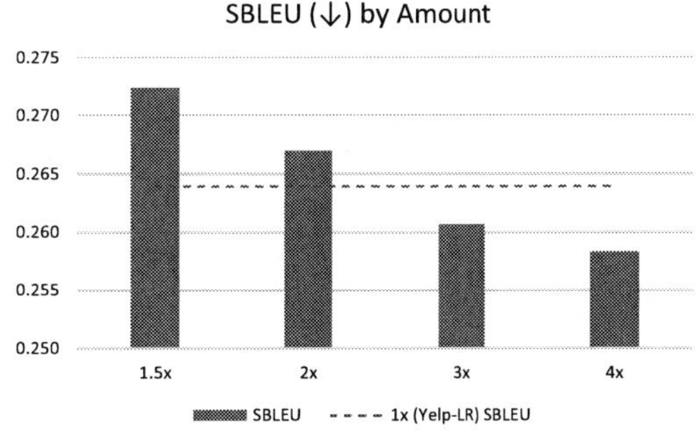

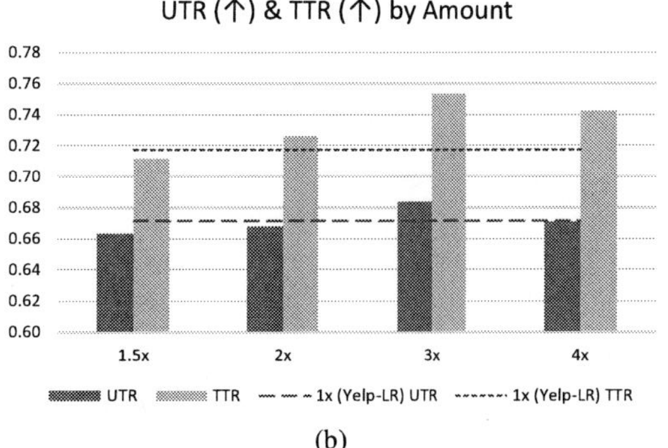

Figure 5: Graphs of a) average SBLEU and b) average UTR and TTR results by amount.

integration of external knowledge for GenAug can improve performance.

Unlike WN-Hypos, where replacements can be esoteric and rare, WN-Hypers' are typically more common words with higher chance of being seen by GPT-2 while training and appearing naturally at test-time. An example is replacing *dog* with *animal* (WN-Hypers) vs. *corgi* (WN-Hypos). Further, except quantified statements (e.g. *"All dogs bark"*), most WN-Hypers examples retain *faithfulness*[21] (Maynez et al., 2020) to the original, e.g. *"3 dogs walked home"* entails *"3 animals walked home"*.

4.2.2 STE and WN-Syns

STE and WN-Syns perform noticeably worse than gold. STE decreases fluency, diversity, and BPRO, albeit the sentiment-related metrics improve. WN-Syns decreases diversity and BPRO.

A possible explanation for STE is that SMERTI works best for shorter text.[22] Our sliding window is also problematic as text between windows may have semantic inconsistencies. For example, in Table 1, the chosen REs are *coffee* and *hand*; *hand*

results in *washing machine*, making the last part semantically inconsistent with the first part about *coffee*. This likely results in reduced fluency and BPRO. Reduced fluency is also not unexpected as Feng et al. (2019) showed STE reduces SLOR.

A possible explanation for WN-Syns is that synonyms keep the semantic content almost exactly the same, unlike the other augmentation techniques which vary the semantics of the text more. Hence, GPT-2 may be overfitting to the augmented data.

4.2.3 WN-Hypos and Random Trio

Lastly, WN-Hypos and Random Trio also do not perform very well. WN-Hypos performs worse

---

[21] Sentence Y being *Faithful* to Sentence X implies Y does not *hallucinate* or state information not already implied by X.

[22] See Section §2.3.2 for an explanation.

Method	Text
Prompt	i got my hair and make up done here for my wedding on 12 29 13 . everything was amazing . hannah styled my hair and the results were pure perfection . i
Original	wish my hair could look like that everyday . i only have positive things to say about this place and would definitely recommend this place . i loved everything about this place !
Gold (Yelp-LR)	went home feeling amazing. you get a full set that changes throughout the year. thanks so much again hannah! you did an awesome job for me and my mom.
Synthetic Noise	am forever thankful for hannah and her store. she's been so nice and accommodating to my needs. she explained my wants and what i could do and she never backed off. i will definitely be back to her store. this is a terrific place for professional hair and make up
WN-Hypers	am so happy i came here and will absolutely continue coming here to get my perfect cut. i left well satisfied. i love this place! thanks yelpers and thank you hannah and make up artist anthony! you've earned my trust
2x	highly recommend this salon. they even have some coupons on their site. i also got my eyebrows and lip waxing here. very affordable too! i'll be back for sure
3x	couldn't believe how beautifully my hair turned out. my stylist was very quick and made sure to check on my hair every step of the way. the environment is a bit loud, but the receptionists and staff make up for it with a great quality of service and product. the price is right for the quality of the work. you'll definitely want to check this place out. i can't wait to return
4x	have to say i will definitely return to this salon. it's very romantic and upscale, all of the staff is very friendly and welcoming. i would definitely recommend this place to anyone who wants a beautiful hairdresser

Table 4: Examples of generated continuations from GPT-2 finetuned on select augmentation methods & amounts. *Prompt* is the first half of the original Yelp review fed in as input, and *Original* is the ground-truth continuation.

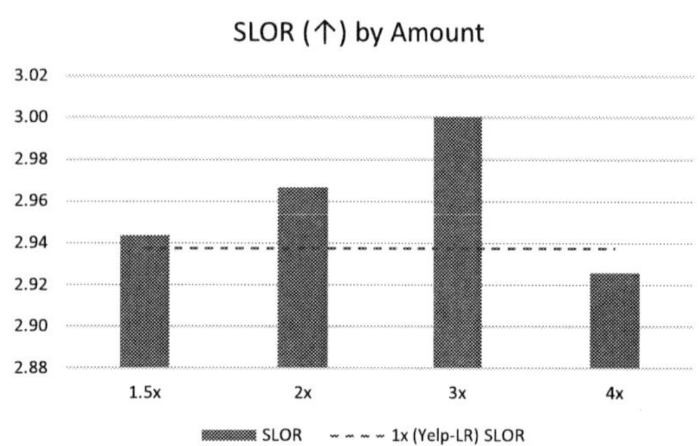

Figure 6: Graph of average SLOR results by amount.

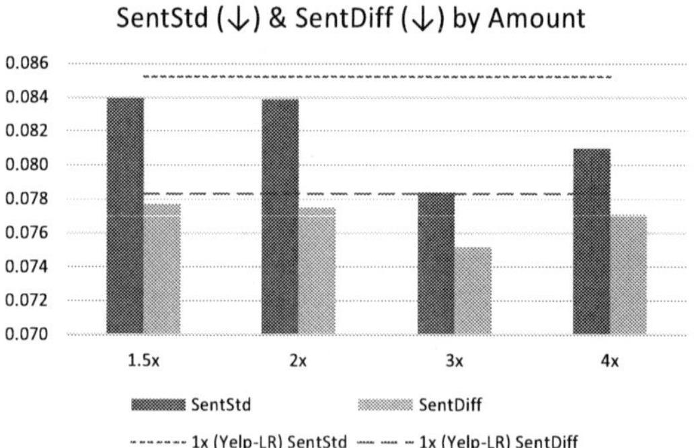

Figure 8: Graph of avg. sentiment results by amount.

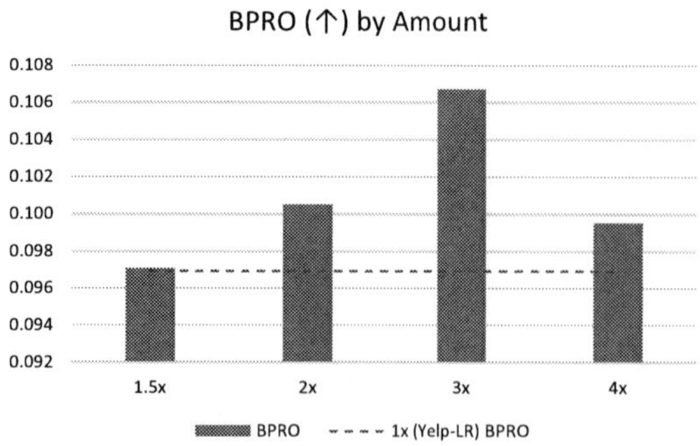

Figure 7: Graph of average BPRO results by amount.

Spellcheck	Gold (Yelp-LR)	Synthetic Noise
SpellWords (↓)	3.0024	**2.6274**
SpellChars (↓)	4.5804	**3.9190**

Table 5: Average Spellcheck results.

than gold on almost all metrics, but to a lesser extent. For Random Trio, overall diversity is decreased, but BPRO and sentiment-related metrics improve. A couple of Random Trio's metric improvements are minor and statistically insignificant.

This is likely due to Random Trio's techniques involving almost complete randomness (at the word-level), resulting in high variations in the metric results, leading to statistical insignificance and poor generations. Its random techniques appear much less suitable for GenAug than data augmentation for classification (Wei and Zou, 2019).

For WN-Hypos, we observe that some hyponyms diverge more from the parent than others (e.g. *food → beverage* vs. *food → micronutrient*), which can cause large drifts in meaning. Similar to Random Trio, this word-level *random-*

ness is likely leading to poor generations. Further, many hyponyms are esoteric words that GPT-2 has likely rarely (or never) seen (e.g *dragon→wyvern*), further decreasing performance. See the example in Table 1 (notice the word *kiribati*). Hence, we show that incorporation of external knowledge for GenAug can also decrease performance.

4.2.4 Overall Performance

Overall, Synthetic Noise and WN-Hypernyms are the best performing methods for GenAug on YLR (see Table 4 for example generations), and the others perform noticeably worse and are hence not recommended in their current state.

4.3 Performance by Augmentation Amount

Table 3 and Figures 5 to 8 show that quality of the generated text improves from 1.5x to 3x data augmentation, and decreases from 3x to 4x (except for SBLEU). 3x beats gold considerably on every metric, while 2x and 4x beat gold noticeably on most metrics as well (see Table 4 for example continuations). 1.5x performs noticeably worse than gold on text diversity.

Quality of the text really improves from 2x and onward, reaching a peak at 3x, and dropping afterward (especially in SLOR). For GenAug on YLR, 3x augmentation appears optimal, and more can reduce performance. This could be attributed to overfitting since many augmentation methods modify the original text to a limited degree. Augmentation at high amounts would thus have a similar (but lesser) effect to training on repeated examples.

5 Related Work

There has been work using GPT-2 as a component in the data augmentation process for training classifiers (Kumar et al., 2020; Papanikolaou and Pierleoni, 2020). We investigate augmentation for *finetuning GPT-2 itself*, and in fact deal with a precondition for the former - without a language model conforming to the domain, generated text would be further from the domain distribution.

There is also work on data augmentation for training NLP classifiers such as Wei and Zou (2019), Lu et al. (2006), and Kobayashi (2018). We adopt some techniques from Wei and Zou (2019) for our experiments, but in general, augmentation techniques for classification do not necessarily work well for generation. The distribution learned in the latter case, $P(x_c|x), x_c \in |V|^*$, is more complex than the former, $P(y|x), y \in Y \subset N$, due to a higher dimensional output variable (where Y is the label set, x_c denotes continuation, and $|V|$ refers to the vocabulary).

Generation of adversarial examples (AVEs) to evaluate robustness of NLP tasks is another area being investigated. Jia and Liang (2017) construct AVEs for span-based QA by adding sentences with distractor spans to passages. Zhang et al. (2019b) use word swapping to craft AVEs for paraphrase detection. Unlike these works, we are not concerned with test-time invariance or test-time model behavior on augmented examples, as long as these augmented examples improve training.

Kang et al. (2018) and Glockner et al. (2018) use WordNet relations to construct AVEs for textual entailment. However, to the best of our knowledge, we are the first ones to explore such methods using WordNet and lexical databases for text data augmentation for generative models.

6 Conclusion and Future Work

We introduced and investigated *GenAug*: data augmentation for text generation, specifically finetuning text generators, through various augmentation methods. We finetuned GPT-2 on a subset of the Yelp Reviews dataset, and demonstrated that insertion of character-level synthetic noise and keyword replacement with hypernyms are effective augmentation methods. We also showed that the quality of generated text improves to a peak at approximately three times the amount of original training data.

Potential future directions include exploring augmentation based on a) linguistic principles like compositionality (Andreas, 2020) and b) using more complex lexical resources - e.g. Framenet (Baker et al., 1998). One can also investigate further augmentation techniques using word replacement such as exploring the *contextual augmentation* method used in Kobayashi (2018). Further, methods of improving semantic text exchange (STE) on longer texts can be investigated, which would make it more effective for data augmentation. Lastly, there is potential in exploring data augmentation for other domains such as dialogue and related tasks such as style transfer (Kang et al., 2019), and investigating interesting aspects of it such as dialogue personalization (Li et al., 2020).

Acknowledgments

We thank the three anonymous reviewers for their comments and feedback.

References

Jacob Andreas. 2020. Good-enough compositional data augmentation. In *Proceedings of the 58th Annual Meeting of the Association for Computational Linguistics*, pages 7556–7566, Online. Association for Computational Linguistics.

Collin F Baker, Charles J Fillmore, and John B Lowe. 1998. The berkeley framenet project. In *36th Annual Meeting of the Association for Computational Linguistics and 17th International Conference on Computational Linguistics, Volume 1*, pages 86–90.

Yonatan Belinkov and Yonatan Bisk. 2017. Synthetic and natural noise both break neural machine translation. *arXiv preprint arXiv:1711.02173*.

Jacob Devlin, Ming-Wei Chang, Kenton Lee, and Kristina Toutanova. 2019. BERT: Pre-training of deep bidirectional transformers for language understanding. In *Proceedings of the 2019 Conference of the North American Chapter of the Association for Computational Linguistics: Human Language Technologies, Volume 1 (Long and Short Papers)*, pages 4171–4186, Minneapolis, Minnesota. Association for Computational Linguistics.

Steven Y. Feng, Aaron W. Li, and Jesse Hoey. 2019. Keep calm and switch on! preserving sentiment and fluency in semantic text exchange. In *Proceedings of the 2019 Conference on Empirical Methods in Natural Language Processing and the 9th International Joint Conference on Natural Language Processing (EMNLP-IJCNLP)*, pages 2701–2711, Hong Kong, China. Association for Computational Linguistics.

Wolf Garbe. 2019. Symspell. https://github.com/wolfgarbe/SymSpell.

Max Glockner, Vered Shwartz, and Yoav Goldberg. 2018. Breaking NLI systems with Sentences that Require Simple Lexical Inferences. In *Proceedings of the 56th Annual Meeting of the Association for Computational Linguistics (Volume 2: Short Papers)*, volume 2, pages 650–655.

Ari Holtzman, Jan Buys, Li Du, Maxwell Forbes, and Yejin Choi. 2019. The curious case of neural text degeneration. *arXiv preprint arXiv:1904.09751*.

Robin Jia and Percy Liang. 2017. Adversarial examples for evaluating reading comprehension systems. In *Proceedings of the 2017 Conference on Empirical Methods in Natural Language Processing*, pages 2021–2031, Copenhagen, Denmark. Association for Computational Linguistics.

Dongyeop Kang, Varun Gangal, and Eduard Hovy. 2019. (male, bachelor) and (female, Ph.D) have different connotations: Parallelly annotated stylistic language dataset with multiple personas. In *Proceedings of the 2019 Conference on Empirical Methods in Natural Language Processing and the 9th International Joint Conference on Natural Language Processing (EMNLP-IJCNLP)*, pages 1696–1706, Hong Kong, China. Association for Computational Linguistics.

Dongyeop Kang, Tushar Khot, Ashish Sabharwal, and Eduard Hovy. 2018. Adventure: Adversarial Training for Textual Entailment with knowledge-guided examples. In *Proceedings of the 56th Annual Meeting of the Association for Computational Linguistics (Volume 1: Long Papers)*, volume 1, pages 2418–2428.

Katharina Kann, Sascha Rothe, and Katja Filippova. 2018. Sentence-level fluency evaluation: References help, but can be spared! In *Proceedings of the 22nd Conference on Computational Natural Language Learning*, pages 313–323, Brussels, Belgium. Association for Computational Linguistics.

Diederik P. Kingma and Jimmy Ba. 2015. Adam: A method for stochastic optimization. In *3rd International Conference on Learning Representations, ICLR 2015, San Diego, CA, USA, May 7-9, 2015, Conference Track Proceedings*.

Sosuke Kobayashi. 2018. Contextual augmentation: Data augmentation by words with paradigmatic relations. In *Proceedings of the 2018 Conference of the North American Chapter of the Association for Computational Linguistics: Human Language Technologies, Volume 2 (Short Papers)*, pages 452–457, New Orleans, Louisiana. Association for Computational Linguistics.

Varun Kumar, Ashutosh Choudhary, and Eunah Cho. 2020. Data augmentation using pre-trained transformer models. *arXiv preprint arXiv:2003.02245*.

Aaron W Li, Veronica Jiang, Steven Y. Feng, Julia Sprague, Wei Zhou, and Jesse Hoey. 2020. Aloha: Artificial learning of human attributes for dialogue agents. In *Proceedings of Thirty-Fourth AAAI Conference on Artificial Intelligence (AAAI-20)*, pages 8155–8163.

Jiwei Li, Michel Galley, Chris Brockett, Jianfeng Gao, and Bill Dolan. 2016. A diversity-promoting objective function for neural conversation models. In *Proceedings of the 2016 Conference of the North American Chapter of the Association for Computational Linguistics: Human Language Technologies*, pages 110–119, San Diego, California. Association for Computational Linguistics.

Xinghua Lu, Bin Zheng, Atulya Velivelli, and Chengxiang Zhai. 2006. Enhancing text categorization with semantic-enriched representation and training data augmentation. *Journal of the American Medical Informatics Association : JAMIA*, 13:526–35.

Joshua Maynez, Shashi Narayan, Bernd Bohnet, and Ryan McDonald. 2020. On faithfulness and factuality in abstractive summarization. *arXiv preprint arXiv:2005.00661*.

George A Miller. 1995. Wordnet: a lexical database for english. *Communications of the ACM*, 38(11):39–41.

Onix. Onix text retrieval toolkit stopword list 1. http://www.lextek.com/manuals/onix/stopwords1.html.

Yannis Papanikolaou and Andrea Pierleoni. 2020. Dare: Data augmented relation extraction with gpt-2. *arXiv preprint arXiv:2004.13845*.

Kishore Papineni, Salim Roukos, Todd Ward, and Wei-Jing Zhu. 2002. Bleu: a method for automatic evaluation of machine translation. In *Proceedings of the 40th annual meeting on association for computational linguistics*, pages 311–318. Association for Computational Linguistics.

Alec Radford, Jeffrey Wu, Rewon Child, David Luan, Dario Amodei, and Ilya Sutskever. 2019. Language models are unsupervised multitask learners. *OpenAI Blog*, 1(8):9.

Stuart Rose, Dave Engel, Nick Cramer, and Wendy Cowley. 2010. Automatic keyword extraction from individual documents. *Text mining: applications and theory*, 1:1–20.

Abigail See, Aneesh Pappu, Rohun Saxena, Akhila Yerukola, and Christopher D. Manning. 2019. Do massively pretrained language models make better storytellers? In *Proceedings of the 23rd Conference on Computational Natural Language Learning (CoNLL)*, pages 843–861, Hong Kong, China. Association for Computational Linguistics.

Richard Socher, Alex Perelygin, Jean Wu, Jason Chuang, Christopher D Manning, Andrew Y Ng, and Christopher Potts. 2013. Recursive deep models for semantic compositionality over a sentiment treebank. In *Proceedings of the 2013 conference on empirical methods in natural language processing*, pages 1631–1642.

Guy Tevet and Jonathan Berant. 2020. Evaluating the evaluation of diversity in natural language generation. *arXiv preprint arXiv:2004.02990*.

Kristina Toutanova, Dan Klein, Christopher D. Manning, and Yoram Singer. 2003. Feature-rich part-of-speech tagging with a cyclic dependency network. In *Proceedings of the 2003 Conference of the North American Chapter of the Association for Computational Linguistics on Human Language Technology - Volume 1*, NAACL '03, page 173–180, USA. Association for Computational Linguistics.

Ashish Vaswani, Noam Shazeer, Niki Parmar, Jakob Uszkoreit, Llion Jones, Aidan N Gomez, Łukasz Kaiser, and Illia Polosukhin. 2017. Attention is all you need. In *Advances in Neural Information Processing Systems*, pages 5998–6008.

Jason Wei and Kai Zou. 2019. EDA: Easy data augmentation techniques for boosting performance on text classification tasks. In *Proceedings of the 2019 Conference on Empirical Methods in Natural Language Processing and the 9th International Joint Conference on Natural Language Processing (EMNLP-IJCNLP)*, pages 6382–6388, Hong Kong, China. Association for Computational Linguistics.

John Wieting and Kevin Gimpel. 2017. Revisiting recurrent networks for paraphrastic sentence embeddings. In *Proceedings of the 55th Annual Meeting of the Association for Computational Linguistics (Volume 1: Long Papers)*, pages 2078–2088, Vancouver, Canada. Association for Computational Linguistics.

Thomas Wolf, Lysandre Debut, Victor Sanh, Julien Chaumond, Clement Delangue, Anthony Moi, Pierric Cistac, Tim Rault, R'emi Louf, Morgan Funtowicz, and Jamie Brew. 2019. Huggingface's transformers: State-of-the-art natural language processing. *ArXiv*, abs/1910.03771.

Yelp. Yelp open dataset. https://www.yelp.com/dataset.

Tianyi Zhang, Varsha Kishore, Felix Wu, Kilian Q Weinberger, and Yoav Artzi. 2019a. Bertscore: Evaluating text generation with bert. *arXiv preprint arXiv:1904.09675*.

Yuan Zhang, Jason Baldridge, and Luheng He. 2019b. Paws: Paraphrase adversaries from word scrambling. In *Proceedings of the 2019 Conference of the North American Chapter of the Association for Computational Linguistics: Human Language Technologies, Volume 1 (Long and Short Papers)*, pages 1298–1308.

Yaoming Zhu, Sidi Lu, Lei Zheng, Jiaxian Guo, Weinan Zhang, Jun Wang, and Yong Yu. 2018. Texygen: A benchmarking platform for text generation models. In *The 41st International ACM SIGIR Conference on Research; Development in Information Retrieval*, SIGIR '18, page 1097–1100, New York, NY, USA. Association for Computing Machinery.

Appendices

A   Augmentation Variation Examples

See Tables 6 and 7 for further examples of Yelp review variations using our augmentation methods.

B   SMERTI Sliding Window Algorithm

We use 30-word windows, consisting of 10 words of context (the last 10 words of the previous window) and 20 new words.[23] In the context portion of each window, we cannot insert the RE nor mask or replace any words. In the new 20-word portion of each window, we can insert the new RE and mask and replace other words. This ensures when SMERTI performs STE on each window, it is able to utilize some context from the previous window but is unable to modify and blemish the STE already performed on the previous window.

C   Sentiment Regressor Finetuning

The BERT sentiment regressor is finetuned on the same Yelp-LR 50K training and 15K validation splits. The final classifer we use is after three epochs of finetuning. Details as follows:

- Star rating conversion: 1 star = 0, 2 star = 0.25, 3 star = 0.5, 4 star = 0.75, 5 star = 1
- Finetuning details:
    - max_seq_length: 128
    - per_gpu_eval_batch_size: 32
    - per_gpu_train_batch_size: 32
    - learning_rate: 2e-5

D   Finetuned Model Details

Note: BE below stands for "best epoch", and VPPL for "validation perplexity".

- Two-million review subset of Yelp (for PPL and SLOR eval): BE = 4, VPPL = 9.1588
- Seed set 1 finetuned models:
    - gpt2_gold: BE = 3, VPPL = 11.7309
    - gpt2_noise: BE = 3, VPPL = 12.0408
    - gpt2_STE: BE = 3, VPPL = 12.1892
    - gpt2_syns: BE = 2, VPPL = 11.9844
    - gpt2_hypos: BE = 2, VPPL = 11.9638
    - gpt2_hypers: BE = 2, VPPL = 12.0131
    - gpt2_random: BE = 2, VPPL = 11.9297
    - gpt2_1.5x: BE = 3, VPPL = 11.8958
    - gpt2_2x: BE = 3, VPPL = 11.9113

- gpt2_3x: BE = 2, VPPL = 12.2064
- gpt2_4x: BE = 1, VPPL = 12.3574
- Seed set 2 finetuned models:
    - gpt2_gold: BE = 3, VPPL = 11.7387
    - gpt2_noise: BE = 2, VPPL = 12.0230
    - gpt2_STE: BE = 3, VPPL = 12.1711
    - gpt2_syns: BE = 2, VPPL = 11.9282
    - gpt2_hypos: BE = 2, VPPL = 11.9583
    - gpt2_hypers: BE = 2, VPPL = 11.9957
    - gpt2_random: BE = 2, VPPL = 11.9558
    - gpt2_1.5x: BE = 3, VPPL = 11.8943
    - gpt2_2x: BE = 2, VPPL = 12.0209
    - gpt2_3x: BE = 2, VPPL = 12.1710
    - gpt2_4x: BE = 1, VPPL = 12.3288

E   SMERTI-Transformer Training

Similar to Feng et al. (2019), we use scaled dot-product attention and the same hyperparameters as Vaswani et al. (2017). We use the Adam optimizer (Kingma and Ba, 2015) with $\beta_1 = 0.9, \beta_2 = 0.98$, and $\epsilon = 10^{-9}$. We increase the learning rate (LR) linearly for the first $warmup\_steps$ training steps, and then decrease the LR proportionally to the inverse square root of the step number. We set $factor = 1$, $warmup\_steps = 2000$, and use a batch size of 4096.

F   Statistical Significance p-values

See Tables 8 and 10 for p-values of results by variation and amount, respectively. These are the results from paired two-tailed t-tests against Yelp-LR (Gold and 1x) results. We test statistical significance of all metrics other than RWords and PPL, and use an alpha of 0.05.

G   Perplexity (PPL) Results

See Tables 9 and 11 for average PPL results by variation and amount, respectively. Synthetic Noise, 2x, and 3x beat gold (Yelp-LR), similar to SLOR. However, WN-Hypers has higher PPL than gold (unlike SLOR). This is likely due to WN-Hypers having outputs that contain rarer tokens, thus increasing PPL. We note again that SLOR normalizes for this and is a better measure of fluency overall.

H   Generated Continuation Examples

See Tables 12 and 13 for further examples of generated continuations from the various experiments.

---

[23]The first window is 20 words long and has no context. If a review is at most 25 words long, we perform STE on the entire review (without the sliding window algorithm).

Method	Text
Original Review	fantastic selection of wines and always served at the proper temperature . the ambiance is stellar dark and cool like a wine cellar and the bands that i have seen there have been very good . check out their jazz band on monday night .
Synthetic Noise (15%)	fantastic **selectoin** of wines and always **sevred** at the **prouper temperaure** . the **ambfiaynce** is **sftellar dak** and cool like a wine cellar and the bands that i have seen there have been very good . check out their jazz band on monday night .
Synonym Replacement (3 keywords)	**wondrous option** of wines and always served at the **right** temperature . the ambiance is stellar dark and cool like a wine cellar and the bands that i have seen there have been very good . check out their jazz band on monday night .
Hyponym Replacement (3 keywords)	fantastic **write-in** of wines and always served at the proper **melting point** . the ambiance is stellar **gloom** and cool like a wine cellar and the bands that i have seen there have been very good . check out their jazz band on monday night .
Hypernym Replacement (3 keywords)	fantastic **action** of wines and always served at the proper **fundamental quantity** . the ambiance is stellar **illumination** and cool like a wine cellar and the bands that i have seen there have been very good . check out their jazz band on monday night .
Random Swap (10%)	fantastic selection of **cool** and always served at the proper temperature . the ambiance **i** stellar dark and **wines** like a wine cellar and **out** bands that **have** have seen there **is** been very good . check **the** their jazz band on monday night .
Semantic Text Exchange (60% MRT)	fantastic selection of wines and always served at the **same meat** . the **food is always fresh** and **the service is always friendly** and i have **to say** there have been very good . **they are out of the deal .**

Table 6: Example of a Yelp review and its variations using our augmentation methods. Changes are bolded.

Method	Text
Original Review	the girls working were so nice . they set up a table for us and gave honest , helpful opinions about the food . adorable store too ! great experience overall . we loved the breakfast sandwich .
Synthetic Noise (5%)	the girls working **wre** so **nwice** . they set up a table for us **ad** gave honest , **hlpful** opinions about the food . adorable store too ! great experience overall . we loved the breakfast sandwich .
Synonym Replacement (3 keywords)	the girls working were so nice . they set up a table for us and gave honest , helpful **view** about the food . **lovely storage** too ! great experience overall . we loved the breakfast sandwich .
Hyponym Replacement (3 keywords)	the girls working were so nice . they set up a table for us and gave honest , helpful **conclusion** about the food . adorable **beauty parlor** too ! great **familiarization** overall . we loved the breakfast sandwich .
Hypernym Replacement (3 keywords)	the girls working were so nice . they set up a table for us and gave honest , helpful **belief** about the food . adorable **mercantile establishment** too ! great **education** overall . we loved the breakfast sandwich .
Random Deletion (10%)	the girls working were so nice . they set up a table for us and gave honest , helpful opinions about food . adorable too ! experience overall . we the breakfast sandwich .
Semantic Text Exchange (60% MRT)	the **guys** working were **very** nice . they set up a **set** for us and gave **us a good time , very fun and fun and fun and fun fun with the ingredients** . adorable store too ! great experience overall . **we will definitely return .**

Table 7: Example of a Yelp review and its variations using our augmentation methods. Changes are bolded (except for Random Deletion where words were removed).

Variations	Random Trio	STE	Synthetic Noise	WN-Syns	WN-Hypos	WN-Hypers
SBLEU	4.288E-104	1.863E-164	5.521E-51	4.324E-283	1.164E-33	0.0018
UTR	4.566E-37	6.497E-261	0.0000	1.698E-288	5.311E-23	5.630E-102
TTR	0.6104*	2.390E-92	0.0000	2.358E-288	2.589E-16	2.149E-135
SLOR	0.1346*	2.694E-108	7.820E-117	0.6114*	0.8618*	0.0001
BPRO	1.071E-15	7.136E-31	2.828E-39	7.113E-94	3.217E-42	1.866E-100
SentStd	3.393E-05	0.0001	8.833E-14	0.0029	0.0570*	1.267E-11
SentDiff	0.0017	0.0709*	1.932E-08	0.7293*	0.0010	9.370E-08
SpellWords	N/A	N/A	0.0000	N/A	N/A	N/A
SpellChars	N/A	N/A	0.0000	N/A	N/A	N/A

Table 8: p-values of results by variation. Note: * indicates insignificant values (using an alpha of 0.05).

Variations	Gold (Yelp-LR)	Random Trio	STE	Synthetic Noise	WN-Syns	WN-Hypos	WN-Hypers
Perplexity ($\downarrow$)	71.9447	72.5887	76.6056	**71.1775**	73.2042	73.6881	77.7176

Table 9: Average perplexity results by variation. Note: bold values are better (lower) than gold (Yelp-LR).

Amounts	1.5x	2x	3x	4x
SBLEU	1.457E-98	1.001E-13	3.879E-12	1.112E-27
UTR	6.668E-71	4.738E-14	1.082E-84	0.2463*
TTR	7.868E-32	5.653E-65	0.0000	1.432E-295
SLOR	0.0020	3.404E-46	4.057E-151	7.017E-06
BPRO	0.6436*	1.571E-28	9.270E-121	7.356E-11
SentStd	0.0012	0.0004	3.190E-64	1.137E-23
SentDiff	0.0632*	0.0105	2.567E-18	0.0030

Table 10: p-values of results by amount. Note: * indicates insignificant values (using an alpha of 0.05).

Amounts	1x (Yelp-LR)	1.5x	2x	3x	4x
Perplexity ($\downarrow$)	71.9447	74.5190	**69.8858**	**67.2170**	74.9576

Table 11: Average perplexity results by amount. Note: bold values are better (lower) than 1x (Yelp-LR).

Method	Text
Prompt	the veal piccata was exquisite and my husband thoroughly enjoyed lobster ravioli . shared the house salad and it was fresh and
Original	plenty for two . thank you for our complimentary desert , it was the perfect finish . staff was awesome as always .
Gold (Yelp-LR)	excellent! also the baked dates were good, made to order. our server was attentive and friendly. i'm sure it will be back soon
Synthetic Noise	delicious. lobster ravioli was also excellent, crispy and savory. our waiter was attentive and had a funny attitude. the potatoes we ordered were absolutely fabulous. everything on the plate was perfection and very well presented. we will be back for sure.
WN-Hypers	tasty. portion size was perfect and meal was exactly how we were looking for. prices were a tad high for the amount of food but the quality was top notch. we will be back.
2x	tasty and decadent! also enjoyed the stuffed crab cakes, they were incredibly fresh and absolutely the perfect combination of creamy, flaky goodness! highly recommend this amazing restaurant! if you are looking for some unique and wonderful, fantastic meals, then come here and you will not be disappointed! great way to end an otherwise boring evening.
3x	the dressing was yummy. the only suggestion i would make is the price of the ravioli is a bit high. but, if you are looking for something light and hearty, this is the place to go. you could pay about $ 20 or so for a meal for two people
4x	delicious. excellent wine selection and the atmosphere was fine and classy. only downside was the parking. otherwise, a great place to hang out and eat with your family and friends.

Table 12: Examples of generated continuations from GPT-2 finetuned on select augmentation methods & amounts. *Prompt* is the first half of the original Yelp review fed in as input, and *Original* is the ground-truth continuation.

Method	Text
Prompt	good to very good gym . some of the machines need to be moved out to make room for newer
Original	more useful equip . need another smith machine def and poss another flat bench . and please add some hammer strength
Gold (Yelp-LR)	machines. good food selection. good staff, reasonable prices, and a quiet atmosphere. gym was clean and well kept, and the associate helped me check out the yoga area to help me decide on a new class i would take. i would highly recommend
Synthetic Noise	equipment. it's also very bright and well maintained. the gym is in a really convenient location. i would highly recommend if you like to workout at a good price.
WN-Hypers	machines. the men's room is a good size. i liked that there's a separate swimming pool area to cool off and dip in the pool. i would visit again for sure.
2x	machines and the trainers there was also quite impressive but the ac didn't work so i stopped going.
3x	machines. staff is pretty awesome. clean facility with lots of cardio equipment. after some recent renovations, it's nice to have a nice place to do work. pricing is very reasonable.
4x	equipment. the equipment is expected and the fitness staff was friendly and knowledgeable. it's a nice facility. i would recommend.

Table 13: Examples of generated continuations from GPT-2 finetuned on select augmentation methods & amounts. *Prompt* is the first half of the original Yelp review fed in as input, and *Original* is the ground-truth continuation.

Common Sense or World Knowledge? Investigating Adapter-Based Knowledge Injection into Pretrained Transformers

Anne Lauscher♣ Olga Majewska♠ Leonardo F. R. Ribeiro◇
Iryna Gurevych◇ Nikolai Rozanov♠ Goran Glavaš♣
♣Data and Web Science Group, University of Mannheim, Germany
♠Wluper, London, United Kingdom
◇Ubiquitous Knowledge Processing (UKP) Lab, TU Darmstadt, Germany
{anne,goran}@informatik.uni-mannheim.de
{olga,nikolai}@wluper.com
www.ukp.tu-darmstadt.de

Abstract

Following the major success of neural language models (LMs) such as BERT or GPT-2 on a variety of language understanding tasks, recent work focused on injecting (structured) knowledge from external resources into these models. While on the one hand, joint pretraining (i.e., training from scratch, adding objectives based on external knowledge to the primary LM objective) may be prohibitively computationally expensive, post-hoc fine-tuning on external knowledge, on the other hand, may lead to the catastrophic forgetting of distributional knowledge. In this work, we investigate models for complementing the distributional knowledge of BERT with conceptual knowledge from ConceptNet and its corresponding Open Mind Common Sense (OMCS) corpus, respectively, using *adapter training*. While overall results on the GLUE benchmark paint an inconclusive picture, a deeper analysis reveals that our adapter-based models substantially outperform BERT (up to 15-20 performance points) on inference tasks that require the type of conceptual knowledge explicitly present in ConceptNet and OMCS. We also open source all our experiments and relevant code under: https://github.com/wluper/retrograph.

1 Introduction

Self-supervised neural models like ELMo (Peters et al., 2018), BERT (Devlin et al., 2019; Liu et al., 2019b), GPT (Radford et al., 2018, 2019), or XL-Net (Yang et al., 2019) have rendered language modeling a very suitable pretraining task for learning language representations that are useful for a wide range of language understanding tasks (Wang et al., 2018, 2019). Although shown versatile w.r.t. the types of knowledge (Rogers et al., 2020) they encode, much like their predecessors – static word embedding models (Mikolov et al., 2013; Pennington et al., 2014) – neural LMs still only "consume" the distributional information from large corpora. Yet, a number of structured knowledge sources exist – knowledge bases (KBs) (Suchanek et al., 2007; Auer et al., 2007) and lexico-semantic networks (Miller, 1995; Liu and Singh, 2004; Navigli and Ponzetto, 2010) – encoding many types of knowledge that are underrepresented in text corpora.

Starting from this observation, most recent efforts focused on injecting factual (Zhang et al., 2019; Liu et al., 2019a; Peters et al., 2019) and linguistic knowledge (Lauscher et al., 2019; Peters et al., 2019) into pretrained LMs and demonstrated the usefulness of such knowledge in language understanding tasks (Wang et al., 2018, 2019). *Joint pretraining models*, on the one hand, augment distributional LM objectives with additional objectives based on external resources (Yu and Dredze, 2014; Nguyen et al., 2016; Lauscher et al., 2019) and train the extended model from scratch. For models like BERT, this implies computationally expensive retraining from scratch of the encoding transformer network. *Post-hoc fine-tuning* models (Zhang et al., 2019; Liu et al., 2019a; Peters et al., 2019), on the other hand, use the objectives based on external resources to fine-tune the encoder's parameters, pretrained via distributional LM objectives. If the amount of fine-tuning data is substantial, however, this approach may lead to catastrophic forgetting of distributional knowledge obtained in pretraining (Goodfellow et al., 2014; Kirkpatrick et al., 2017).

In this work, similar to the concurrent work of Wang et al. (2020), we turn to the recently proposed *adapter-based fine-tuning* paradigm (Rebuffi et al., 2018; Houlsby et al., 2019), which remedies the shortcomings of both joint pretraining and standard post-hoc fine-tuning. Adapter-based training injects additional parameters into the encoder and only tunes their values: original transformer parameters are kept fixed. Be-

Proceedings of Deep Learning Inside Out (DeeLIO):
The First Workshop on Knowledge Extraction and Integration for Deep Learning Architectures, pages 43–49
Online, November 19, 2020. ©2020 Association for Computational Linguistics

cause of this, adapter training preserves the distributional information obtained in LM pretraining, without the need for any distributional (re-)training. While (Wang et al., 2020) inject factual knowledge from Wikidata (Vrandečić and Krötzsch, 2014) into BERT, in this work, we investigate two resources that are commonly assumed to contain *general-purpose* and *common sense* knowledge:[1] Concept-Net (Liu and Singh, 2004; Speer et al., 2017) and the Open Mind Common Sense (OMCS) corpus (Singh et al., 2002), from which the ConceptNet graph was (semi-)automatically extracted. For our first model, dubbed CN-ADAPT, we first create a synthetic corpus by randomly traversing the ConceptNet graph and then learn adapter parameters with masked language modelling (MLM) training (Devlin et al., 2019) on that synthetic corpus. For our second model, named OM-ADAPT, we learn the adapter parameters via MLM training directly on the OMCS corpus.

We evaluate both models on the GLUE benchmark, where we observe limited improvements over BERT on a subset of GLUE tasks. However, a more detailed inspection reveals large improvements over the base BERT model (up to 20 Matthews correlation points) on language inference (NLI) subsets labeled as requiring World Knowledge or knowledge about Named Entities. Investigating further, we relate this result to the fact that ConceptNet and OMCS contain much more of what in downstream is considered to be factual world knowledge than what is judged as common sense knowledge. Our findings pinpoint the need for more detailed analyses of compatibility between (1) the types of knowledge contained by external resources; and (2) the types of knowledge that benefit concrete downstream tasks; within the emerging body of work on injecting knowledge into pretrained transformers.

2 Knowledge Injection Models

In this work, we are primarily set to investigate if injecting specific types of knowledge (given in the external resource) benefits downstream inference that clearly requires those exact types of knowledge. Because of this, we use the arguably most straightforward mechanisms for injecting the ConceptNet and OMCS information into BERT, and leave the exploration of potentially more effective knowledge injection objectives for future work. We

---

inject the external information into adapter parameters of the adapter-augmented BERT (Houlsby et al., 2019) via BERT's natural objective – masked language modelling (MLM). OMCS, already a corpus in natural language, is directly subjectable to MLM training – we filtered out non-English sentences. To subject ConceptNet to MLM training, we need to transform it into a synthetic corpus.

Unwrapping ConceptNet. Following established previous work (Perozzi et al., 2014; Ristoski and Paulheim, 2016), we induce a synthetic corpus from ConceptNet by randomly traversing its graph. We convert relation strings into NL phrases (e.g., `synonyms` to *is a synonym of*) and duplicate the object node of a triple, using it as the subject for the next sentence. For example, from the path "*alcoholism* $\xrightarrow{causes}$ *stigma* $\xrightarrow{hasContext}$ *christianity* $\xrightarrow{partOf}$ *religion*" we create the text "*alcoholism causes stigma. stigma is used in the context of christianity. christianity is part of religion.*". We set the walk lengths to 30 relations and sample the starting and neighboring nodes from uniform distributions. In total, we performed 2,268,485 walks, resulting with the corpus of 34,560,307 synthetic sentences.

Adapter-Based Training. We follow Houlsby et al. (2019) and adopt the adapter-based architecture for which they report solid performance across the board. We inject *bottleneck adapters* into BERT's transformer layers. In each transformer layer, we insert two bottleneck adapters: one after the multi-head attention sub-layer and another after the feed-forward sub-layer. Let $\mathbf{X} \in \mathbb{R}^{T \times H}$ be the sequence of contextualized vectors (of size H) for the input of T tokens in some transformer layer, input to a bottleneck adapter. The bottleneck adapter, consisting of two feed-forward layers and a residual connection, yields the following output:

$$Adapter(\mathbf{X}) = \mathbf{X} + f\left(\mathbf{X}\mathbf{W}_d + \mathbf{b}_d\right)\mathbf{W}_u + \mathbf{b}_u$$

where $\mathbf{W}_d$ (with bias $\mathbf{b}_d$) and $\mathbf{W}_u$ (with bias $\mathbf{b}_u$) are adapter's parameters, that is, the weights of the linear down-projection and up-projection sub-layers and f is the non-linear activation function. Matrix $\mathbf{W}_d \in \mathbb{R}^{H \times m}$ compresses vectors in $\mathbf{X}$ to the *adapter size* $m < H$, and the matrix $\mathbf{W}_u \in \mathbb{R}^{m \times H}$ projects the activated down-projections back to transformer's hidden size H. The ratio H/m determines how many times fewer parameters we optimize with adapter-based training compared to standard fine-tuning of all transformer's parameters.

3 Evaluation

We first briefly describe the downstream tasks and training details, and then proceed with the discussion of results obtained with our adapter models.

3.1 Experimental Setup.

Downstream Tasks. We evaluate BERT and our two adapter-based models, CN-ADAPT and OM-ADAPT, with injected knowledge from ConceptNet and OMCS, respectively, on the tasks from the GLUE benchmark (Wang et al., 2018):

CoLA (Warstadt et al., 2018): Binary sentence classification, predicting grammatical acceptability of sentences from linguistic publications;

SST-2 (Socher et al., 2013): Binary sentence classification, predicting binary sentiment (positive or negative) for movie review sentences;

MRPC (Dolan and Brockett, 2005): Binary sentence-pair classification, recognizing sentences which are are mutual paraphrases;

STS-B (Cer et al., 2017): Sentence-pair regression task, predicting the degree of semantic similarity for a given pair of sentences;

QQP (Chen et al., 2018): Binary classification task, recognizing question paraphrases;

MNLI (Williams et al., 2018): Ternary natural language inference (NLI) classification of sentence pairs. Two test sets are given: a matched version (MNLI-m) in which the test domains match the domains from training data, and a mismatched version (MNLI-mm) with different test domains;

QNLI: A binary classification version of the Stanford Q&A dataset (Rajpurkar et al., 2016);

RTE (Bentivogli et al., 2009): Another NLI dataset, ternary entailment classification for sentence pairs;

Diag (Wang et al., 2018): A manually curated NLI dataset, with examples labeled with specific types of knowledge needed for entailment decisions.

Training Details. We inject our adapters into a BERT Base model (12 transformer layers with 12 attention heads each; $H = 768$) pretrained on lowercased corpora. Following (Houlsby et al., 2019), we set the size of all adapters to $m = 64$ and use GELU (Hendrycks and Gimpel, 2016) as the

adapter activation f. We train the adapter parameters with the Adam algorithm (Kingma and Ba, 2015) (initial learning rate set to $1e^{-4}$, with 10000 warm-up steps and the weight decay factor of 0.01). In downstream fine-tuning, we train in batches of size 16 and limit the input sequences to $T = 128$ wordpiece tokens. For each task, we find the optimal hyperparameter configuration from the following grid: learning rate $l \in \{2 \cdot 10^{-5}, 3 \cdot 10^{-5}\}$, epochs in $n \in \{3, 4\}$.

3.2 Results and Analysis

GLUE Results. Table 1 reveals the performance of CN-ADAPT and OM-ADAPT in comparison with BERT Base on GLUE evaluation tasks. We show the results for two snapshots of OM-ADAPT, after 25K and 100K update steps, and for two snapshots of CN-ADAPT, after 50K and 100K steps of adapter training. Overall, none of our adapter-based models with injected external knowledge from ConceptNet or OMCS yields significant improvements over BERT Base on GLUE. However, we observe substantial improvements (of around 3 points) on RTE and on the Diagnostics NLI dataset (Diag), which encompasses inference instances that require a specific type of knowledge.

Since our adapter models draw specifically on the conceptual knowledge encoded in ConceptNet and OMCS, we expect the positive impact of injected external knowledge – assuming effective injection – to be most observable on test instances that target the same types of conceptual knowledge. To investigate this further, we measure the model performance across different categories of the Diagnostic NLI dataset. This allows us to tease apart inference instances which truly test the efficacy of our knowledge injection methods. We show the results obtained on different categories of the Diagnostic NLI dataset in Table 2. The improvements of our adapter-based models over BERT Base on these phenomenon-specific subsections of the Diagnostics NLI dataset are generally much more pronounced: e.g., OM-ADAPT (25K) yields a 7% improvement on inference that requires factual or common sense knowledge (KNO), whereas CN-ADAPT (100K) yields a 6% boost for inference that depends on lexico-semantic knowledge (LS). These results suggest that (1) ConceptNet and OMCS do contain the specific types of knowledge required for these inference categories and that (2) we managed to inject that knowledge into BERT by training

Model	CoLA MCC	SST-2 Acc	MRPC F1	STS-B Spear	QQP F1	MNLI-m Acc	MNLI-mm Acc	QNLI Acc	RTE Acc	Diag MCC	Avg –
BERT Base	52.1	93.5	**88.9**	85.8	71.2	**84.6**	83.4	90.5	66.4	34.2	75.1
OM-Adapt (25K)	49.5	93.5	88.8	85.1	71.4	84.4	83.5	**90.9**	67.5	35.7	75.0
OM-Adapt (100K)	**53.5**	93.4	87.9	**85.9**	71.1	84.2	**83.7**	90.6	68.2	34.8	75.3
CN-Adapt (50K)	49.8	**93.9**	**88.9**	85.8	**71.6**	84.2	83.3	90.6	**69.7**	37.0	**75.5**
CN-Adapt (100K)	48.8	92.8	87.1	85.7	71.5	83.9	83.2	90.8	64.1	**37.8**	74.6

Table 1: Results on test portions of GLUE benchmark tasks. Numbers in brackets next to adapter-based models (25K, 50K, 100K) indicate the number of update steps of adapter training on the synthetic ConceptNet corpus (for CN-Adapt) or on the original OMCS corpus (for OM-Adapt). **Bold**: the best score in each column.

Model	LS	KNO	LOG	PAS	All
BERT Base	38.5	20.2	26.7	39.6	34.2
OM-Adapt (25K)	39.1	**27.1**	26.1	39.5	35.7
OM-Adapt (100K)	37.5	21.2	27.4	41.0	34.8
CN-Adapt (50K)	40.2	24.3	30.1	**42.7**	37.0
CN-Adapt (100K)	**44.2**	25.2	**30.4**	41.9	37.8

Table 2: Breakdown of Diagnostics NLI performance (Matthews correlation), according to information type needed for inference (coarse-grained categories): Lexical Semantics (LS), Knowledge (KNO), Logic (LOG), and Predicate Argument Structure (PAS).

Model	CS	World	NE
BERT Base	**29.0**	10.3	15.1
OM-Adapt (25K)	28.5	25.3	31.4
OM-Adapt (100K)	24.5	17.3	22.3
CN-Adapt (50K)	25.6	21.1	26.0
CN-Adapt (100K)	24.4	**25.6**	**36.5**

Table 3: Results (Matthews correlation) on Common Sense (CS), World Knowledge (World), and Named Entities (NE) categories of the Diagnostic NLI dataset.

adapters on these resources.

Fine-Grained Knowledge Type Analysis. In our final analysis, we "zoom in" our models' performances on three fine-grained categories of the Diagnostics NLI dataset – inference instances that require Common Sense Knowledge (CS), World Knowledge (World), and knowledge about Named Entities (NE), respectively. The results for these fine-grained categories are given in Table 3. These results show an interesting pattern: our adapter-based knowledge-injection models massively outperform BERT Base (up to 15 and 21 MCC points, respectively) for NLI instances labeled as requiring World Knowledge or knowledge about Named Entities. In contrast, we see drops in performance on instances labeled as requiring common sense

knowledge. This initially came as a surprise, given the common belief that OMCS and ConcepNet contain the so-called *common sense* knowledge. Manual scrutiny of the diagnostic test instances from both CS and World categories uncovers a noticeable mismatch between the kind of information that is considered common sense in KBs like ConceptNet and what is considered common sense knowledge in the downstream. In fact, the majority of information present in ConceptNet and OMCS falls under the World Knowledge definition of the Diagnostic NLI dataset, including factual geographic information (`stockholm [partOf] sweden`), domain knowledge (`roadster [isA] car`) and specialized terminology (`indigenous [synonymOf] aboriginal`).

In contrast, many of the CS inference instances require complex, high-level reasoning, understanding metaphorical and idiomatic meaning, and making far-reaching connections. We display NLI Diagnostics examples from the World Knowledge and Common Sense categories in Table 4. In such cases, explicit conceptual links often do not suffice for a correct inference and much of the required knowledge is not explicitly encoded in the external resources. Consider, e.g., the following CS NLI instance: [`premise`: *My jokes fully reveal my character* ; `hypothesis`: *If everyone believed my jokes, they'd know exactly who I was* ; `entailment`]. While ConceptNet and OMCS may associate *character* with *personality* or *personality* with *identity*, the knowledge that the phrase *who I was* may refer to *identity* is beyond the explicit knowledge present in these resources. This sheds light on the results in Table 3: when the knowledge required to tackle the inference problem at hand is available in the external resource, our adapter-based knowledge-injected models significantly outperform the baseline transformer; otherwise, the benefits of knowledge injection are neg-

Knowledge	Premise	Hypothesis	ConceptNet?
World	*The sides came to an agreement after their meeting in **Stockholm**.*	*The sides came to an agreement after their meeting in **Sweden**.*	`stockholm [partOf] sweden`
	*Musk decided to offer up his personal Tesla **roadster**.*	*Musk decided to offer up his personal **car**.*	`roadster [isA] car`
	*The Sydney area has been inhabited by **indigenous** Australians for at least 30,000 years.*	*The Sydney area has been inhabited by **Aboriginal** people for at least 30,000 years.*	`indigenous [synonymOf] aboriginal`
Common Sense	*My jokes fully reveal my character.*	*If everyone believed my jokes, they'd know exactly who I was.*	
	The systems thus produced are incremental: dialogues are processed word-by-word, shown previously to be essential in supporting natural, spontaneous dialogue.	*The systems thus produced support the capability to interrupt an interlocutor mid-sentence.*	
	He deceitfully proclaimed: "This is all I ever really wanted."	*He was satisfied.*	

Table 4: Premise-hypothesis examples from the diagnostic NLI dataset tagged for commonsense and world knowledge, and relevant ConceptNet relations, where available.

ligible or non-existent. The promising results on *world knowledge* and *named entities* portions of the Diagnostics dataset suggest that our methods does successfully inject external information into the pretrained transformer and that the presence of the required knowledge for the task in the external resources is an obvious prerequisite.

4 Conclusion

We presented two simple strategies for injecting external knowledge from ConceptNet and OMCS corpus, respectively, into BERT via bottleneck adapters. Additional adapter parameters store the external knowledge and allow for the preservation of the rich distributional knowledge acquired in BERT's pretraining in the original transformer parameters. We demonstrated the effectiveness of these models in language understanding settings that require precisely the type of knowledge that one finds in ConceptNet and OMCS, in which our adapter-based models outperform BERT by up to 20 performance points. Our findings stress the importance of having detailed analyses that compare (a) the types of knowledge found in external resources being injected against (b) the types of knowledge that a concrete downstream reasoning tasks requires. We hope this work motivates further research effort in the direction of fine-grained knowledge typing, both of explicit knowledge in external resources and the implicit knowledge stored in pretrained transformers.

Acknowledgments

Anne Lauscher and Goran Glavaš are supported by the Eliteprogramm of the Baden-Württemberg Stiftung (AGREE grant). Leonardo F. R. Ribeiro has been supported by the German Research Foundation as part of the Research Training Group AIPHES under the grant No. GRK 1994/1. This work has been supported by the German Research Foundation within the project "Open Argument Mining" (GU 798/25-1), associated with the Priority Program "Robust Argumentation Machines (RATIO)" (SPP-1999). The work of Olga Majewska was conducted under the research lab of Wluper Ltd. (UK/ 10195181).

References

Sören Auer, Christian Bizer, Georgi Kobilarov, Jens Lehmann, Richard Cyganiak, and Zachary Ives. 2007. Dbpedia: A nucleus for a web of open data. In *The semantic web*, pages 722–735. Springer.

Luisa Bentivogli, Peter Clark, Ido Dagan, and Danilo Giampiccolo. 2009. The fifth pascal recognizing textual entailment challenge. In *TAC*.

Daniel Cer, Mona Diab, Eneko Agirre, Iñigo Lopez-Gazpio, and Lucia Specia. 2017. SemEval-2017 task 1: Semantic textual similarity multilingual and crosslingual focused evaluation. In *Proceedings of the 11th International Workshop on Semantic Evaluation (SemEval-2017)*, pages 1–14, Vancouver, Canada. Association for Computational Linguistics.

Zihan Chen, Hongbo Zhang, Xiaoji Zhang, and Leqi Zhao. 2018. Quora question pairs.

Jacob Devlin, Ming-Wei Chang, Kenton Lee, and Kristina Toutanova. 2019. Bert: Pre-training of deep bidirectional transformers for language understanding. In *Proceedings of the 2019 Conference of the North American Chapter of the Association for Computational Linguistics: Human Language Technologies, Volume 1 (Long and Short Papers)*, pages 4171–4186.

William B Dolan and Chris Brockett. 2005. Automatically constructing a corpus of sentential paraphrases. In *Proceedings of the Third International Workshop on Paraphrasing (IWP2005)*.

Ian J Goodfellow, Mehdi Mirza, Aaron Courville Da Xiao, and Yoshua Bengio. 2014. An empirical investigation of catastrophic forgeting in gradient-based neural networks. In *In Proceedings of International Conference on Learning Representations (ICLR*. Citeseer.

Dan Hendrycks and Kevin Gimpel. 2016. Gaussian error linear units (gelus).

Neil Houlsby, Andrei Giurgiu, Stanislaw Jastrzebski, Bruna Morrone, Quentin De Laroussilhe, Andrea Gesmundo, Mona Attariyan, and Sylvain Gelly. 2019. Parameter-efficient transfer learning for nlp. In *International Conference on Machine Learning*, pages 2790–2799.

Diederik P Kingma and Jimmy Ba. 2015. Adam: A method for stochastic optimization. In *Proceedings of ICLR*.

James Kirkpatrick, Razvan Pascanu, Neil Rabinowitz, Joel Veness, Guillaume Desjardins, Andrei A Rusu, Kieran Milan, John Quan, Tiago Ramalho, Agnieszka Grabska-Barwinska, et al. 2017. Overcoming catastrophic forgetting in neural networks. *Proceedings of the national academy of sciences*, 114(13):3521–3526.

Anne Lauscher, Ivan Vulić, Edoardo Maria Ponti, Anna Korhonen, and Goran Glavaš. 2019. Informing unsupervised pretraining with external linguistic knowledge. *arXiv preprint arXiv:1909.02339*.

Hugo Liu and Push Singh. 2004. Conceptnet—a practical commonsense reasoning tool-kit. *BT technology journal*, 22(4):211–226.

Weijie Liu, Peng Zhou, Zhe Zhao, Zhiruo Wang, Qi Ju, Haotang Deng, and Ping Wang. 2019a. K-bert: Enabling language representation with knowledge graph. *arXiv preprint arXiv:1909.07606*.

Yinhan Liu, Myle Ott, Naman Goyal, Jingfei Du, Mandar Joshi, Danqi Chen, Omer Levy, Mike Lewis, Luke Zettlemoyer, and Veselin Stoyanov. 2019b. RoBERTa: A robustly optimized bert pretraining approach. *arXiv preprint arXiv:1907.11692*.

Tomas Mikolov, Ilya Sutskever, Kai Chen, Greg S Corrado, and Jeff Dean. 2013. Distributed representations of words and phrases and their compositionality. In *Advances in neural information processing systems*, pages 3111–3119.

George A Miller. 1995. Wordnet: a lexical database for english. *Communications of the ACM*, 38(11):39–41.

Roberto Navigli and Simone Paolo Ponzetto. 2010. Babelnet: Building a very large multilingual semantic network. In *Proceedings of the 48th annual meeting of the association for computational linguistics*, pages 216–225. Association for Computational Linguistics.

Kim Anh Nguyen, Sabine Schulte im Walde, and Ngoc Thang Vu. 2016. Integrating distributional lexical contrast into word embeddings for antonym-synonym distinction. In *Proceedings of ACL*, pages 454–459.

Jeffrey Pennington, Richard Socher, and Christopher Manning. 2014. Glove: Global vectors for word representation. In *Proceedings of the 2014 conference on empirical methods in natural language processing (EMNLP)*, pages 1532–1543.

Bryan Perozzi, Rami Al-Rfou, and Steven Skiena. 2014. Deepwalk: Online learning of social representations. In *Proceedings of the 20th ACM SIGKDD International Conference on Knowledge Discovery and Data Mining*, KDD '14, page 701–710, New York, NY, USA. Association for Computing Machinery.

Matthew E Peters, Mark Neumann, Mohit Iyyer, Matt Gardner, Christopher Clark, Kenton Lee, and Luke Zettlemoyer. 2018. Deep contextualized word representations. In *Proceedings of NAACL-HLT*, pages 2227–2237.

Matthew E. Peters, Mark Neumann, Robert Logan, Roy Schwartz, Vidur Joshi, Sameer Singh, and Noah A. Smith. 2019. Knowledge enhanced contextual word representations. In *Proceedings of the 2019 Conference on Empirical Methods in Natural Language Processing and the 9th International Joint Conference on Natural Language Processing (EMNLP-IJCNLP)*, pages 43–54.

Alec Radford, Karthik Narasimhan, Tim Salimans, and Ilya Sutskever. 2018. Improving language understanding by generative pre-training. *OpenAI Technical Report*.

Alec Radford, Jeffrey Wu, Rewon Child, David Luan, Dario Amodei, and Ilya Sutskever. 2019. Language models are unsupervised multitask learners. *OpenAI Blog*, 1(8).

Pranav Rajpurkar, Jian Zhang, Konstantin Lopyrev, and Percy Liang. 2016. SQuAD: 100,000+ questions for machine comprehension of text. In *Proceedings of the 2016 Conference on Empirical Methods in Natural Language Processing*, pages 2383–2392, Austin, Texas. Association for Computational Linguistics.

Sylvestre-Alvise Rebuffi, Hakan Bilen, and Andrea Vedaldi. 2018. Efficient parametrization of multi-domain deep neural networks. In *CVPR*.

Petar Ristoski and Heiko Paulheim. 2016. Rdf2vec: Rdf graph embeddings for data mining. In *International Semantic Web Conference*, pages 498–514. Springer.

Anna Rogers, Olga Kovaleva, and Anna Rumshisky. 2020. A primer in bertology: What we know about how bert works. *arXiv preprint arXiv:2002.12327*.

Push Singh, Thomas Lin, Erik T Mueller, Grace Lim, Travell Perkins, and Wan Li Zhu. 2002. Open mind common sense: Knowledge acquisition from the general public. In *OTM Confederated International Conferences" On the Move to Meaningful Internet Systems"*, pages 1223–1237. Springer.

Richard Socher, Alex Perelygin, Jean Wu, Jason Chuang, Christopher D Manning, Andrew Ng, and Christopher Potts. 2013. Recursive deep models for semantic compositionality over a sentiment treebank. In *Proceedings of the 2013 conference on empirical methods in natural language processing*, pages 1631–1642.

Robert Speer, Joshua Chin, and Catherine Havasi. 2017. Conceptnet 5.5: An open multilingual graph of general knowledge. In *Thirty-First AAAI Conference on Artificial Intelligence*.

Fabian M Suchanek, Gjergji Kasneci, and Gerhard Weikum. 2007. Yago: a core of semantic knowledge. In *Proceedings of the 16th international conference on World Wide Web*, pages 697–706. ACM.

Denny Vrandečić and Markus Krötzsch. 2014. Wikidata: a free collaborative knowledgebase. *Communications of the ACM*, 57(10):78–85.

Alex Wang, Yada Pruksachatkun, Nikita Nangia, Amanpreet Singh, Julian Michael, Felix Hill, Omer Levy, and Samuel Bowman. 2019. Superglue: A stickier benchmark for general-purpose language understanding systems. In *Advances in Neural Information Processing Systems*, pages 3261–3275.

Alex Wang, Amanpreet Singh, Julian Michael, Felix Hill, Omer Levy, and Samuel Bowman. 2018. GLUE: A multi-task benchmark and analysis platform for natural language understanding. In *Proceedings of the Blacbox NLP Workshop*, pages 353–355.

Ruize Wang, Duyu Tang, Nan Duan, Zhongyu Wei, Xuanjing Huang, Cuihong Cao, Daxin Jiang, Ming Zhou, et al. 2020. K-adapter: Infusing knowledge into pre-trained models with adapters. *arXiv preprint arXiv:2002.01808*.

Alex Warstadt, Amanpreet Singh, and Samuel R Bowman. 2018. Neural network acceptability judgments. *arXiv preprint arXiv:1805.12471*.

Adina Williams, Nikita Nangia, and Samuel Bowman. 2018. A broad-coverage challenge corpus for sentence understanding through inference. In *Proceedings of the 2018 Conference of the North American Chapter of the Association for Computational Linguistics: Human Language Technologies, Volume 1 (Long Papers)*, pages 1112–1122.

Zhilin Yang, Zihang Dai, Yiming Yang, Jaime Carbonell, Ruslan Salakhutdinov, and Quoc V Le. 2019. Xlnet: Generalized autoregressive pretraining for language understanding. *arXiv preprint arXiv:1906.08237*.

Mo Yu and Mark Dredze. 2014. Improving lexical embeddings with semantic knowledge. In *Proceedings of ACL*, pages 545–550.

Zhengyan Zhang, Xu Han, Zhiyuan Liu, Xin Jiang, Maosong Sun, and Qun Liu. 2019. ERNIE: Enhanced language representation with informative entities. In *Proceedings of the 57th Annual Meeting of the Association for Computational Linguistics*, pages 1441–1451.

Entity Attribute Relation Extraction with Attribute-Aware Embeddings

Dan Iter[*]
Stanford University
daniter@stanford.edu

Xiao Yu
Google
yux@google.com

Fangtao Li
Google
lifangtao@google.com

Abstract

Entity-attribute relations are a fundamental component for building large-scale knowledge bases, which are widely employed in modern search engines. However, most such knowledge bases are manually curated, covering only a small fraction of all attributes, even for common entities. To improve the precision of model-based entity-attribute extraction, we propose attribute-aware embeddings, which embeds entities and attributes in the same space by the similarity of their attributes. Our model, EANET, learns these embeddings by representing entities as a weighted sum of their attributes and concatenates these embeddings to mention level features. EANET achieves up to 91% classification accuracy, outperforming strong baselines and achieves 83% precision on manually labeled high confidence extractions, outperforming Biperpedia (Gupta et al., 2014), a previous state-of-the-art for large scale entity-attribute extraction.

1 Introduction

Modern search engines often attempt to provide structured search results that reveal more facets of the search query than explicitly requested. These results rely on knowledge bases that contain tuples of the form (*entity, attribute, value*). However, the number of known entities and attributes in these knowledge bases is limited and there is a long tail of both entities and attributes that is too large to be manually curated. The goal of automatic entity-attribute extraction is to replace manual knowledge acquisition which is expensive and biased towards popular entities (Bollacker et al., 2008; Dong et al., 2014). Previous studies have proposed model-based approaches that use various NLP features, distant supervision and traditional machine learning methods for entity-attribute extraction but

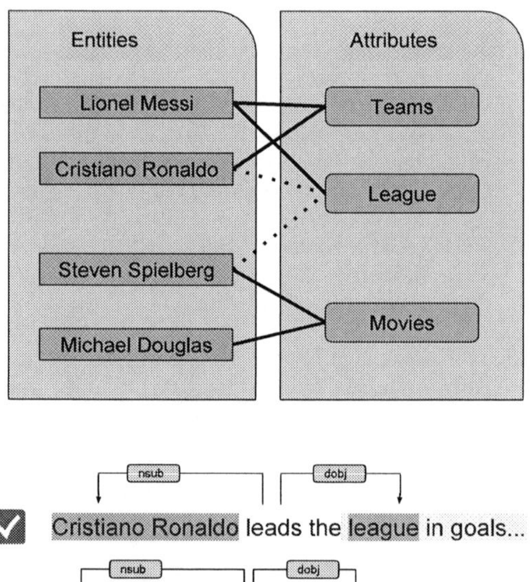

Figure 1: The top figure shows an example of known attributes (solid lines) and candidate attributes (dotted lines). Below are support sentences for the candidate entity-attribute pairs. The attributes of related entities can be used to improve entity representation and entity-attribute classification accuracy.

their precision has not been high enough to replace manually curated knowledge bases (Auer et al., 2007; Carlson et al., 2010; Gupta et al., 2014).

The key insight of this paper is that entities that share many attributes are often similar. This is an extension of the distributional hypothesis, (Harris, 1954; Weeds and Weir, 2003), which states that words with similar semantic meanings tend to appear in similar contexts, and builds on work that use referential attributes to estimate semantic relatedness (Gupta et al., 2015; Freitas et al., 2013). For the attribute-aware embeddings, we argue that a good representation for an entity can be

---

[*] Work done during an internship at Google.

Proceedings of Deep Learning Inside Out (DeeLIO):
The First Workshop on Knowledge Extraction and Integration for Deep Learning Architectures, pages 50–55
Online, November 19, 2020. ©2020 Association for Computational Linguistics

inferred from its most common attributes, which we may have access to from an external source of knowledge. In Figure 1, we want to classify two candidate relations given the other known relations. If the model has previously seen a link between *Teams* and *League* but not *Movies* and *League*, we can correctly predict that *Ronaldo* should have the *League* attribute and *Speilberg* should not, despite the surface form in the sentences being similar. We generalize this intuition by learning embeddings for each entity based on the most common attributes for that entity.

We propose EANET, a neural model that combines a path-embedding model from dependency parse trees, with **attribute-aware embeddings** which we describe in this paper. The proposed model captures both the dependency path for a given sentence between potential entity and attribute candidates, as well as a distributional representation for both entities and attributes based on an attribute distributional assumption. Our model learns general representations for specific entities with few mentions by learning embeddings based on attributes for those entities observed in the distant supervision.

2 Methods

2.1 Task Definition

The objective of this work is to determine, for a given term-pair (e, a), if a is an attribute of the entity e. In order to classify entity-attribute term pairs, we have access to a multiset of sentences $\mathcal{S}^{(e,a)}$ where the terms co-occur. These sentences only capture local information about how the entity and attribute terms relate at the sentence level. Our model also has access to global information from the set of known entity-attribute pairs from the training data. For each term-pair, (e, a), we are given a set of known true entity-attribute pairs $\mathcal{K}^e$ and $\mathcal{K}^a$, where $\mathcal{K}^e$ is a set where the entity is always e and $\mathcal{K}^a$ is a set where the attribute is always a. We learn a binary classifier on the input of entity-attribute pairs, their support sentences, and their known neighbors.

2.2 Path Embedding Model

Our baseline model is inspired by a hypernym classification model proposed by Shwartz et al. (2016), also using a pair of terms with a set of support sentences where the terms co-occur.

Sentences are represented with their shortest dependency path between two candidates, as proposed in (Fundel et al., 2006). The bottom of Figure 1 shows an example of the shortest path between an entity and attribute for one sentence. We converts each sentence from a string to a list of terms, where the first and last term is either the entity or the attribute. Each term in the dependency path is represented by the lemma of the term, the part-of-speech tag, the dependency label, the direction of the dependency path to the parent (left, right or root). Each of these features is embedded and concatenated to produce a sequence of vectors that represents the dependency path. The concatenation is the edge representation $\vec{v}_{edge} = [\vec{v}_{lemma}, \vec{v}_{pos}, \vec{v}_{dep}, \vec{v}_{dir}]$

The sequence of terms in each path is input into an LSTM to produce a single vector representation for the sentence, $\vec{v}_s$. This is repeated for each sentence producing one vector per sentence. The sentences are aggregated with a weighted mean of the sentence representations to form a representation of the multiset of sentences, $\vec{v}_{sents(e,a)}$.

2.3 Distributional Representation

As proposed by Shwartz et al. (2016), adding the word embedding or distributive representation for the candidate strings can improve the performance of the model. The embeddings of the two candidate terms in the entity-attribute pair are concatenated to each side of the aggregated sentences vector described in the previous section. The embeddings for e and a are simply $\vec{v}_e$ and $\vec{v}_a$. Thus the full representation of a entity-attribute pair is: $\vec{v}_{(e,a)} = [\vec{v}_e, \vec{v}_{sents(e,a)}, \vec{v}_a]$

2.4 Attribute-Aware Embeddings

We propose to use an attribute-aware representation in the classification model to leverage "similarity" between terms. In the entity-attribute relation setting, a strong signal of what entities are similar is how their attributes overlap. Therefore, we create an **attribute-aware embedding** for each entity and attribute that captures term similarity by shared attributes, rather than relying on *word embeddings*, which are learned from terms being in similar contexts. This helps to generalize to new unseen data for which we may know some related entities and attributes. Figure 2 illustrates the model and shows how the representations are combined in the classifier.

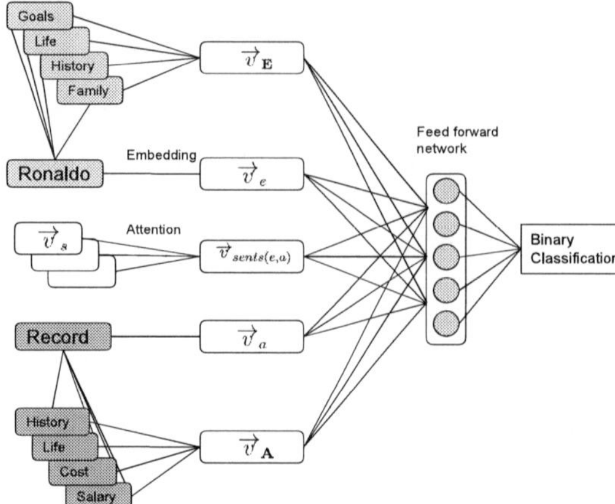

Figure 2: Model for binary classification of a pair of entity attribute candidates. For each entity and attribute, related attributes are aggregated into attribute-aware embeddings that are concatenated to the sentence and distributional representations.

2.5 Learning Attribute-Aware Embeddings

Entities are modeled as a weighted sum of their attributes. Similarly, attributes can be represented by the entities that they describe, which would create a symmetry in the model. However, empirically we found that attributes provide more signal so we use attributes to represent other attributes. Given an attribute, we can find all entities in the training data that have that attribute. We then find all the attributes for each entity. We take the ranked set of attributes by count (of entities) to associate with the attribute.

We initialize attribute embeddings with Glove (Pennington et al., 2014) word embeddings. For an entity, we take all the known attributes from $\mathcal{K}^e$. The representation of each entity is the weighted sum of the known attributes, with learned attention weights. The weights are shared between entities and attributes.

We concatenate these vectors to the full representation for the entity-attribute term-pair: $\vec{v}_{(e,a)} = [\vec{v}_{\mathbf{E}}, \vec{v}_e, \vec{v}_{sents(e,a)}, \vec{v}_a, \vec{v}_{\mathbf{A}}]$

In Figure 2 the 5 concatenated vectors are shown vertically in the middle and are input into a feed forward neural network, followed by a sigmoid layer and a logistic loss.

3 Dataset Creation

3.1 Dataset

We sample sentences from a subset of online news articles and label them with our distant supervision knowledge base (Mintz et al., 2009) using a query streams as the source of supervision, as in (Paşca et al., 2007). We sample 12.6 million entity-attribute pairs from a knowledge base, finding 6 million unique entities and 788 thousand unique attributes. Each sentence that contains an entity-attribute pair from our knowledge base is used as the support set for that pair. All pairs with less than 30 support sentences are discarded leaving 351 thousand distantly labeled positive examples and 14 million negatively labeled examples. Negative examples are sentences that contain a known entity and a known attribute but the entity is not annotated with this attribute in our knowledge base. We split the positive examples into roughly 75% train, 20% test and 5% validation. Negative examples are randomly sampled so we sample equivalent amounts for test and validation but use about 14 million negative examples during training, weighing the two classes accordingly.

3.2 Annotations and Labels

True entity-attribute relations are sampled from our knowledge base. Negative examples of entity-attribute pairs are combinations of entities and attributes that appear together in sentence but are not in our knowledge base. We augment the negative examples with randomly sampled noun phrases (including modifiers) from sentences in our corpus. We also flip the order of true entity-attribute pairs and use them as negative examples because the relation is not symmetric. Support sentences for each pair are found by exact match of both terms.

Known attributes ($\mathcal{K}^e$) for each entity and known entities ($\mathcal{K}^a$) for each attribute are the top 20 most common attributes for that entity or attribute in the training data by the count of support sentences. If there are no known attributes for an entity, as is the case for our test data in the entity-split setting, we use the top 20 known attributes by co-occurrence with the entity in the support sentences.

4 Experiments

We evaluate our model on two basic metrics. (1) The ability of the model to fit the data and generalize to a held-out test set which is measured

	Entity Split	Random Split
Path	0.784	0.821
Dist.	0.772	0.882
Attr-Aware	**0.825**	0.905
EANET	0.824	**0.913**

Table 1: Accuracy of two baselines and two models with attribute-aware embeddings (in bold) for entity split and random split test datasets.

(Common)	Precision	F1
Biperpedia	0.547	0.707
EANET	0.837	0.911

Table 2: Precision and F1 for EANET and Biperpedia on 1000 extracted entity-attribute pairs each that were manually labeled.

by accuracy on the test set. (2) The ability of the model to extract high quality entity-attribute pairs which we evaluate with manual evaluation on a small set of extracted pairs.

4.1 Entity Attribute Classification

We compare two variations of our model to two strong baseline models that are also based on word and path embedding neural network models.

The baselines are the **Path** and **Dist.** (ie. distributional) models described in Section 2.2 and Section 2.3 respectively. The **Attr-Aware** model (ie. attribute-aware), uses both the path embeddings and our attribute-aware embeddings but does not include the word embeddings of the terms.

We evaluate two regimes; entity split and random split. Entity split separates test and train by entity so there is no overlap in entities. The random split naively splits the set of all entity-attribute pairs. In the random split, every entity-attribute pair is unique so for every candidate pair in the test set, the model has never seen any sentences where the entity and attribute appeared together during training. For example, from Fig 1, the training data may contain (Ronaldo, Teams) and (Spielberg, Movies) and the test data will have (Ronaldo, League) and (Spielberg, League). In this setting, we have some learned representation of the entity and the attribute separately but have not observed them together in the training data. The sentences used for the mention level representations are also split between training and test sets.

Table 1 shows the results for the two settings and the accuracy for each of the two baselines and the two proposed models described above. Models that use our proposed attribute-aware embeddings outperform the baselines in every setting. EANET achieves the highest accuracy on the random test split at 91.3%.

4.2 Entity Attribute Extraction

We present results for two evaluations with human labels; (1) we compare extracted entity-attribute pairs to those extracted by the previous state-of-the-art Biperpedia (Gupta et al., 2014) and (2) we report precision over a small set of longtail entity-attribute pairs that did not appear in our distant supervision.

Biperpedia: First we sample 20 entities from the most common entities in the test data. We sample the entities such that each entity belongs to a different knowledge graph class to fairly compare against Biperpedia which extracts attributes at the class level rather than the entity level. For each entity, we randomly sample 50 attributes extracted by EANET. We use the same entities for Biperpedia and sample 50 attributes each from those extracted by Biperpedia. 1000 high-confidence examples are extracted using each model and they are manually labeled.

Since Biperpedia extracts attributes at the class level (eg. *Country* instead of *USA*), the attributes are sampled from the class of the entity. The comparison is not fair because many errors come from the mapping from entity to class (eg. *Countries* have *Prime Ministers* but the *US* does not). Nevertheless, this is a good evaluation for how relevant attributes from Biperpedia are for a given queried entity.

From a total of 1000 manually labeled entity-attribute pairs from each model, EANET achieves 83.7% precision while Biperpedia achieves only 54.7% precision. Table 2 shows precision and F1 scores for EANET and Biperpedia for the 1000 entity-attribute pairs extracted for each model conditioned on the same 20 entities. The improvement in EANET comes from both more fine-grained typing, using entity level attributes rather than class level, and from higher precision classifications.

(Longtail)	Precision	F1
EANET	0.623	0.768

Table 3: Precision and F1 for EANET on 1000 extracted longtail entity-attribute pairs that were manually labeled. Neither the entities nor the attributes in these pairs appeared at all in our distant supervision.

Longtail: A goal of EANET is extracting longtail entity-attribute pairs that would likely be missed by human created knowledge bases. We manually labeled the top 1000 entity-attribute pairs by frequency where **neither** entity nor attribute appear in the distant supervision. EANET achieves 62.3% precision on 1000 manually labeled entity-attribute pairs. We expected the precision to be worse because the "known" attributes used for the attribute-aware embeddings are much noisier when neither the entity nor the attribute has been seen in any positive training data.

4.3 Error Analysis

For more insight into the performance of our model, we analyze the type of errors that our model makes and discuss possible trade-offs and possible future improvements.

Error Types. From manually annotating a small set of examples, we find that there are 6 general types of errors:

- x of y—a common pattern for entity-attribute pairs such as "the height of a person" but also often occurs with non-entity attribute pairs such as "a lot of people",

- IsA relationships,

- extracting the value rather than the attributes—extracting the name of a drug rather than the term "medication",

- incorrect entity extraction—extracting "medication" as an attribute for "heart" instead of "heart disease",

- general attribute—some terms such as "number" and "direction" are often attributed to rarer entities because they seem generic and similar to other common attributes and

- other miscellaneous errors.

In the comparison to Biperpedia we analyze the type of errors our model makes with common extractions. In this setting, most entities are frequent

High Confidence		
Label	Entity	Attribute
True	Britain	invasions
True	homeless	medical care
False	prostate cancer	Metformin
False	petroleum	migration
Longtail		
Label	Entity	Attribute
True	medical students	rotations
True	endophthalmitis	injections
False	SXSW	festival
False	third party	operating systems

Table 4: A few positive and negative examples from common and longtail extractions.

in the dataset. The most common errors are x of y, value extraction and incorrect entities. In all cases, it seems that generally high co-occurrence between terms is often a contributor to false positives and these are the most common cases of non-entity-attribute co-occurrence in the training data.

In the longtail evaluation, both the entities and attributes are relatively rare and do not occur in any of our training data. In this case, we see many IsA relationships and general attributes. The former could likely be remedied by using supervision of IsA relationships to generate negative training data. The latter is an overgeneralization by the model.

Some examples of correct and incorrect extractions are shown in Table 4.

5 Conclusion

We present EANET, a neural model for entity-attribute relation extraction from text. We describe a mechanism for learning attribute-aware embeddings for entities and attributes in our training data that capture similarities between entities by embedding the similarities between their known attributes. We show that our model outperforms the previous approaches for entity-attribute relation extraction and that it can be used to learn representations for longtail entities.

References

Sören Auer, Christian Bizer, Georgi Kobilarov, Jens Lehmann, Richard Cyganiak, and Zachary Ives. 2007. Dbpedia: A nucleus for a web of open data. In *The semantic web*, pages 722–735. Springer.

Kurt Bollacker, Colin Evans, Praveen Paritosh, Tim Sturge, and Jamie Taylor. 2008. Freebase: a collaboratively created graph database for structuring human knowledge. In *Proceedings of the 2008 ACM SIGMOD international conference on Management of data*, pages 1247–1250. AcM.

Andrew Carlson, Justin Betteridge, Bryan Kisiel, Burr Settles, Estevam R Hruschka, and Tom M Mitchell. 2010. Toward an architecture for never-ending language learning. In *Twenty-Fourth AAAI Conference on Artificial Intelligence*.

Xin Dong, Evgeniy Gabrilovich, Geremy Heitz, Wilko Horn, Ni Lao, Kevin Murphy, Thomas Strohmann, Shaohua Sun, and Wei Zhang. 2014. Knowledge vault: A web-scale approach to probabilistic knowledge fusion. In *Proceedings of the 20th ACM SIGKDD international conference on Knowledge discovery and data mining*, pages 601–610. ACM.

André Freitas, João Gabriel Oliveira, Seán O'riain, João CP Da Silva, and Edward Curry. 2013. Querying linked data graphs using semantic relatedness: A vocabulary independent approach. *Data & Knowledge Engineering*, 88:126–141.

Katrin Fundel, Robert Küffner, and Ralf Zimmer. 2006. Relex—relation extraction using dependency parse trees. *Bioinformatics*, 23(3):365–371.

Abhijeet Gupta, Gemma Boleda, Marco Baroni, and Sebastian Padó. 2015. Distributional vectors encode referential attributes. In *Proceedings of the 2015 Conference on Empirical Methods in Natural Language Processing*, pages 12–21, Lisbon, Portugal. Association for Computational Linguistics.

Rahul Gupta, Alon Halevy, Xuezhi Wang, Steven Euijong Whang, and Fei Wu. 2014. Biperpedia: An ontology for search applications. *Proceedings of the VLDB Endowment*, 7(7):505–516.

Zellig S. Harris. 1954. Distributional structure. *Word*, 10:146–162. Reprinted in J. Fodor and J. Katz, *The Structure of Language*, Prentice Hall, 1964 and in Z. S. Harris, *Papers in Structural and Transformational Linguistics*, Reidel, 1970, 775–794.

Mike Mintz, Steven Bills, Rion Snow, and Dan Jurafsky. 2009. Distant supervision for relation extraction without labeled data. In *Proceedings of the Joint Conference of the 47th Annual Meeting of the ACL and the 4th International Joint Conference on Natural Language Processing of the AFNLP: Volume 2-Volume 2*, pages 1003–1011. Association for Computational Linguistics.

Marius Paşca, Benjamin Van Durme, and Nikesh Garera. 2007. The role of documents vs. queries in extracting class attributes from text. In *Proceedings of the sixteenth ACM conference on Conference on information and knowledge management*, pages 485–494. ACM.

Jeffrey Pennington, Richard Socher, and Christopher Manning. 2014. Glove: Global vectors for word representation. In *Proceedings of the 2014 conference on empirical methods in natural language processing (EMNLP)*, pages 1532–1543.

Vered Shwartz, Yoav Goldberg, and Ido Dagan. 2016. Improving hypernymy detection with an integrated path-based and distributional method. In *Proceedings of the 54th Annual Meeting of the Association for Computational Linguistics (Volume 1: Long Papers)*, pages 2389–2398, Berlin, Germany. Association for Computational Linguistics.

Julie Weeds and David Weir. 2003. A general framework for distributional similarity. In *Proceedings of the 2003 conference on Empirical methods in natural language processing*.

Enhancing Question Answering by Injecting Ontological Knowledge through Regularization

Travis R. Goodwin and **Dina Demner-Fushman**
U.S. National Library of Medicine
National Institutes of Health
{firstname.lastname}@nih.gov

Abstract

Deep neural networks have demonstrated high performance on many natural language processing (NLP) tasks that can be answered directly from text, and have struggled to solve NLP tasks requiring external (e.g., world) knowledge. In this paper, we present OSCR (Ontology-based Semantic Composition Regularization), a method for injecting task-agnostic knowledge from an Ontology or knowledge graph into a neural network during pre-training. We evaluated the performance of BERT pre-trained on Wikipedia with and without OSCR by measuring the performance when fine-tuning on two question answering tasks involving world knowledge and causal reasoning and one requiring domain (healthcare) knowledge and obtained 33.3 %, 18.6 %, and 4 % improved accuracy compared to pre-training BERT without OSCR.

1 The Problem

"The detective flashed his badge to the police officer." The nearly effortless ease at which we, as humans, can understand this simple statement belies the depth of semantic knowledge needed for its understanding: What is a detective? What is a police officer? What is a badge? What does it mean to *flash* a badge? Why would the detective need to flash his badge to the police officer? Understanding this sentence requires knowing the answer to all these questions and relies on the reader's knowledge about this world: a detective investigates crime, police officers restrict access to the crime scene, and a badge can be a symbol of authority.

As shown in Figure 1, suppose we were interested in determining whether, upon showing the policeman his badge, it is more plausible that the detective would be let into the crime scene or that the police officer would confiscate the detective's badge? To answer this question, we would need

> **Premise:** The detective flashed his badge to the police officer.
>
> **Question:** What is the most likely *effect*?
>
> **A:** The police officer confiscated the detective's badge.
>
> **B:** The police officer let the detective enter the crime scene.

Figure 1: Example of a question requiring common-sense and causal reasoning (Roemmele et al., 2011) with entities highlighted.

to leverage our accumulated expectations about the world: although both scenarios are certainly possible, our accumulated expectations about the world suggest it would be very extraordinary for the police officer to confiscate the detective's badge rather than allow him to enter the crime scene.

Evidence of Grice's Maxim of Quantity (Grice, 1975), this shared knowledge of the world is rarely explicitly stated in text. Fortunately, some of this knowledge can be extracted from Ontologies and knowledge bases. For example ConceptNet (Speer et al., 2017) indicates that a *detective* is a TYPEOF *police officer*, and is CAPABLEOF *finding evidence*; that *evidence* can be LOCATEDAT a *crime scene*; and that a *badge* is a TYPEOF *authority symbol*.

While neural networks have been shown to obtain state-of-the-art performance on many types of question answering and reasoning tasks from raw data (Devlin et al., 2018; Rajpurkar et al., 2016; Manning, 2015), there has been less investigation into how to inject ontological knowledge into deep learning models, with most prior attempts embedding ontological information outside of the network itself (Wang et al., 2017).

In this paper, we present a pre-training regular-

Proceedings of Deep Learning Inside Out (DeeLIO):
The First Workshop on Knowledge Extraction and Integration for Deep Learning Architectures, pages 56–63
Online, November 19, 2020. ©2020 Association for Computational Linguistics

ization technique we call OSCR (Ontology-based Semantic Composition Regularization), which is capable of injecting world knowledge and ontological relationships into a deep neural network. We show that incorporating OSCR into BERT's pre-training injects sufficient world knowledge to improve fine-tuned performance in three question answering datasets. The main contributions of this work are:

1. OSCR, a regularization method for injecting ontological information and semantic composition into deep learning models;
2. Empirical evidence showing the impact of OSCR on two tasks requiring world knowledge, causal reasoning, and discourse understanding even with as few as 500 training example, as well as a task requiring medical domain knowledge; and
3. Experimental results showing that the same technique used to infer background knowledge about the world can also capture domain-specific knowledge in the case of medical question answering; and
4. An open-source implementation of OSCR and BERT supporting mixed-precision training, non-TPU model distribution, and enhanced numerical stability.

2   Background and Related Work

The idea of training a model on a related problem before training on the problem of interest has been shown to be effective for many natural language processing tasks (Dai and Le, 2015; Peters et al., 2017; Howard and Ruder, 2018). More recent uses of pre-training adapt transfer learning by first training a network on a language modeling task and then fine-tuning (retraining) that model for a supervised problem of interest (Dai and Le, 2015; Howard and Ruder, 2018; Radford et al., 2018). Pre-training, in this way, has the advantage that the model can build on previous parameters to reduce the amount of information it needs to learn for a specific downstream task. Conceptually, the model can be viewed as applying what it has already learned from the language model task when learning the downstream task.

BERT (Bidirectional Encoder Representations from Transformers) is a pre-trained neural network that has been shown to obtain state-of-the-art results on eleven natural language processing tasks after fine-tuning (Devlin et al., 2018). BERT relies on two pre-training objectives: (1) a variant of language modeling called *Cloze* (originally proposed in Taylor 1953) where-in 20 % of the words in a sentence are masked, and the model must unmask them and (2) a next sentence prediction task where-in the model is given two pairs of sentences and must decide if the second sentence immediately follows the first. Despite its strong empirical performance, the architecture of BERT is relatively simple: four layers of transformers (Vaswani et al., 2017) are stacked to process each sentence.

In terms of injecting knowledge into pre-training, Zhang et al. (2019) explored injecting entity information into BERT using multi-head attention. However, their approach requires explicitly indicating entity boundaries or relation constituents with special input tokens for down-stream fine-tuning. By contrast, OSCR requires no modification of input formats in the host network. Sun et al. (2019) explored modifying BERT's pre-training by masking entire entities and phrases extracted from external knowledge. Meanwhile, Xie et al. (2019) explored projecting propositional knowledge using Graph Convolutional Networks (GCNs). OSCR, instead, introduces a regularization term that can be added to any natural language pre-training objectives, without modifying the architecture of the network or the pre-training objectives themselves.

3   The Data

Incorporating OSCR into pre-training requires an embedded ontology (or knowledge) graph, and one or more natural language pre-training objectives to regularize – in our case, BERT's *Cloze* and next-sentence prediction tasks. These objectives, in turn, require a document collection.

3.1   The Ontology

ConceptNet 5 is a semantic network containing relational knowledge contributed to Open Mind Common Sense (Singh et al., 2002) and to DB-Pedia (Auer et al., 2007), as well as dictionary knowledge from Wiktionary, the Open Multilingual WordNet (Singh et al., 2002; Miller, 1995), the high-level ontology from OpenCyc[1], and knowledge about word associations from "Games with a Purpose" (von Ahn, 2006). In our experiments we used ConceptNet 5 as our ontology relying on an embedded representation of the ontology known as ConceptNet NumberBatch (Speer et al., 2017),

---

[1] http://www.cyc.com/opencyc/

in which embeddings for all entities in ConceptNet were built using an ensemble of (a) data from ConceptNet, (b) word2vec (Mikolov et al., 2013), (c) GloVe (Pennington et al., 2014), and (d) OpenSubtitles 2016[2] using retrofitting.

3.2 The Documents

Our text corpus was a 2019 dump of English Wikipedia articles with templates expanded as provided by Wikipedia's Cirrus search engine[3]. Preprocessing relied on NLTK's Punkt sentence segmenter[4] (Loper and Bird, 2002), and the WordPiece subword tokenizer provided with BERT.

4 The Approach

Virtually all neural networks designed for natural language processing represent language as a sequence of words, subwords, or characters. By contrast, Ontologies and knowledge bases encode semantic information about *entities*, which may correspond to individual nouns (e.g., "badge") or multiword phrases ("police officer"). Consequently, injecting world and domain knowledge from a knowledge base into the network requires *semantically decomposing* the information about an entity into the supporting information about its constituent words. For example, injecting the semantics of "Spanish Civil War" into the network requires learning what information the word "Spanish" introduces to the nominal "Civil War" and what information "Civil" adds to the word "War". To do this, OSCR is implemented using a three-step approach illustrated in Figure 2:

Step 1. entities are recognized in a sentence using a Finite State Transducer (FST);

Step 2. the sequence of subwords corresponding to each entity are semantically composed to produce an entity-level encoding; and

Step 3. the average energy between the composed entity encoding and the pre-trained entity encoding from the ontology is used as a regularization term in the pre-training loss function.

By training the model to compose sequences of subwords into entities, during back-propagation, the semantics of each entity are decomposed and

---

[2] http://opus.nlpl.eu/OpenSubtitles-v2016.php

[3] https://www.mediawiki.org/wiki/Help:CirrusSearch

[4] https://www.nltk.org/_modules/nltk/tokenize/punkt.html

injected into the network based on the neural activations associated with its constituent words.

4.1 Entity Detection

We designed OSCR to require as few modifications to the underlying host network (e.g., BERT) as possible. We recognized entities during training and inference online by (1) tokenizing each entity in our ontology using the same tokenizer used to prepare the BERT pre-training data, and (2) compiling a Finite State Transducer to detect sequences of subword IDs corresponding to entities. The FST, illustrated in Figure 3, allowed us to detect entities on-the-fly without hard coding a specific ontology and without inducing any discernible change in training or inference time. Although we did not explore it in this work, this potentially allows for multiple ontologies to be injected through OSCR during pre-training. In these experiments, due to the simplicity of ConceptNet entities, we relied on exact string matching to detect entities. Formally, let $X = x_1, x_2, \cdots, x_N$ represent the sequence of words in a sentence. The FST processes X and returns three sequences: $s_1, s_2, \cdots, s_M$; $l_1, l_2, \cdots, l_M$; and $e_1, e_2, \cdots, e_M$ representing the start offset, length, and the pretrained embedded representation of every mention of any entity in the Ontology.

Entity Subsumption. When detecting entities, it is often the case that multiple entities may correspond to the same span of text. As illustrated in Figure 2, the entity "Spanish Civil War" contains the subsumed entities "Spanish", "Civil War", "Civil", and "War". Likewise, because BERT masks 20 % of the words in each sentence, it is possible for entities to involve masked words. Note: including or excluding subsumed and de-masked entities (as illustrated in Figure 2) provided no discernible effect in our experiments.

Entity Demasking. Because BERT masks tokens when pre-training, we evaluated the impact of (a) de-masking words before detecting entities and (b) ignoring all entity mentions involving masked words.

4.2 Semantic Composition

The role of semantic composition in OSCR, is to learn a composed representation $c_1, c_2, \cdots, c_M$ for each entity detected in X such that $c_i = compose\left(x_{s_i}, x_{s_i+1}, \cdots, x_{s_i+l_i}\right)$. As pre-training in

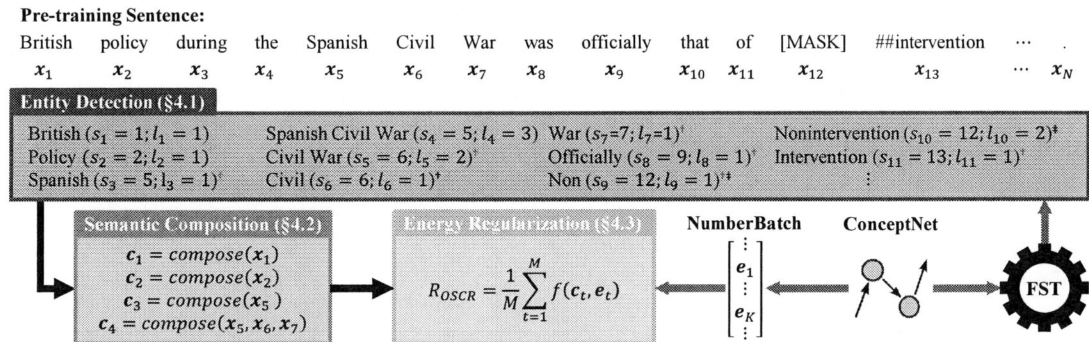

Figure 2: Architecture of OSCR when injecting ontology knowledge from ConceptNet into BERT where '†' indicates subsumed entities, '‡' indicates de-masked entities, N is the length of the input sentence, M is the number of entities detected in the sentence, and K is the number of entities with embeddings in ConceptNet.

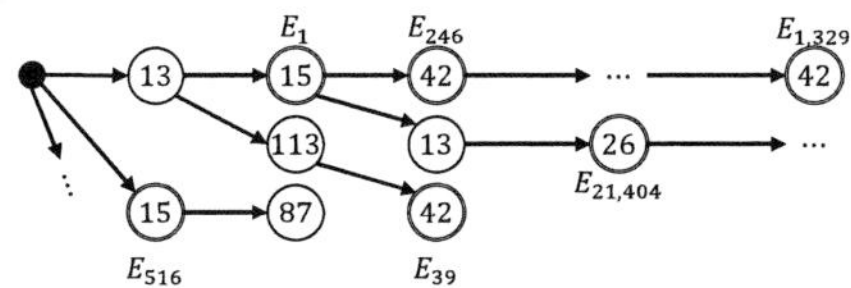

Figure 3: Finite State Transducer (FST) used to detect entities during pretraining; each node corresponds to a word ID, double circles represent terminal states, and e_i indicates the ith pretrained entity embedding in ConceptNet's NumberBatch.

BERT is computationally expensive, we considered three computationally-efficient methods for composing words and subwords into entities.

Recurrent Additive Networks (RANs) are a simplified alternative to LSTM- or GRU-based recurrent neural networks that use only additive connections between successive layers and have been shown to obtain similar performance with 38% fewer learnable parameters (Lee et al., 2017).

Given a sequence of words $x_1, x_2, \cdots, x_L$ we use the following layers to accumulate information about how the semantics of each word in an entity contribute to the overall semantics of the entity:

$$\widetilde{m}_t = W_m x_t \tag{1a}$$

$$i_t = \sigma \left(W_i \left[h_{t-1}, x_t \right] + b_i \right) \tag{1b}$$

$$f_t = \sigma \left(W_f \left[h_{t-1}, x_t \right] + b_f \right) \tag{1c}$$

$$m_t = i_t \circ \widetilde{m}_t + f_t \circ m_{t-1} \tag{1d}$$

$$h_t = g \left(m_t \right) \tag{1e}$$

where $[\bullet]$ represents vector concatenation, $\widetilde{m}_t$ represents the content layer which encodes any new semantic information provided by word x_t, $\circ$ indicates an element-wise product, i_t represents the input gate, f_t represents the forget gate, m_t represents the internal memories about the entity, and h_t is the output layer encoding accumulated semantics about word x_t. We define the composed entity $c_i := h_{s_i + l_i}$ (i.e., the content vector of the RAN after processing the last token in the entity) for the sequence beginning with x_{s_i}.

Linear Recurrent Additive Networks To further reduce model complexity, we considered a second, simpler version of a RAN omits the content and output layers (i.e., Equations 1a and 1e) and Equation 1d is updated to depend on x_t directly: $m_t = i_t \circ x_t + f_t \circ m_{t-1}$. As above, we define the composed entity $c_i := m_{s_i + l_i}$ for the sequence of subwords beginning with x_{s_i}.

Linear Interpolation Finally, we considered a third, even simpler form of semantic composition. Inspired by Goodwin and Harabagiu (2016), we represented the semantics of an entity as an unordered linear combination of the semantics of its constituent words, i.e.: $c_i := W_e \left(x_{s_i} + x_{s_i+1} + \cdots + x_{s_i+l_i} \right) + l_i \cdot b_e$.

4.3 Energy Regularization

We project the composed entities into the same vector space as the pretrained entity embeddings from the Ontology, and measure the average energy across all entities detected in the sentence:

$$\mathcal{R}_{\text{OSCR}} = \frac{1}{M} \sum_{i=1}^{M} f \left(W_p c_i + b_p, e_i \right) \tag{2}$$

where f is an *energy function* capturing the energy between the composed entity c_i and the pretrained entity embedding e_i. We considered three energy functions: (1) the Euclidean distance, (2) the absolute distance, and (3) the angular distance, which can handle negative values.

5 Experiments

5.1 Experimental Setup

Hyper-parameter Tuning For each fine-tuning task, we used a greedy approach to hyper-parameter tuning by incrementally and independently optimizing: batch size $\in \{8, 16, 32\}$; initial learning rate $\in \left\{1 \times 10^{-5}, 2 \times 10^{-5}, 3 \times 10^{-5}\right\}$; whether to include subsumed entities $\in$ {yes, no}; and whether to include masked entities $\in$ {yes, no}.

For CoPA, the Story Cloze task, and RQE, we found an optimal batch size of 16 and an optimal learning rate of 2×10^{-5}. We also found that including subsumed entities and masked was optimal (at a net performance improvement of $< 1\%$ accuracy).

Pretraining We pretrained BERT using a 2019 Wikipedia dump formatted for Wikipedia's Cirrus search engine.[5] Preprocessing relied on NLTK's Punkt sentence segmenter[6] (Loper and Bird, 2002), and the WordPiece subword tokenizer provided with BERT. We used the vocabulary from BERT base (not large) and a maximum sequence size of 384 subwords, training 64 000 steps, with an initial learning rate of 2×10^{-5}, and 320 warm-up steps.

BERT Modifications We used a modified version of BERT, allowing for mixed-precision training. This necessitated a number of minor changes to improve numerical stability around softmax operations. Training was performed using a single node with 4 Tesla P100s each (multiple variants of OSCAR were trained simultaneously using five such nodes at a time). Non-TPU multi-GPU support was added to BERT based on Horovod[7] and relying on Open MPI.

5.2 Results

We evaluated the impact of OSCR on three question answering tasks requiring world or domain knowledge and causal reasoning.

Choice of Plausible Alternatives a SemEval 2012 shared task, (CoPA) presents 500 training and 500 testing sets of two-choice questions and requires to choose the most plausible cause or effect entailed by the premise, as illustrated in Figure 1 (Roemmele et al., 2011). The topics of these questions were drawn from two sources: (1) personal stories taken from a collection of blogs (Gordon and Swanson, 2009); and (2) subject terms from the Library of Congress Thesaurus for Graphic Materials, while the incorrect alternatives were created so as to penalize "purely associative methods".

Premise: Gina misplaced her phone at her grandparents. It wasn't anywhere in the living room. She realized she was in the car before. She grabbed her dad's keys and ran outside.

Ending A: She found her phone in the car.

Ending B: She didn't want her phone anymore.

Figure 4: Example of a Story Cloze question (correct answer is A).

Consumer Health Question: Can sepsis be prevented. Can someone get this from a hospital?

FAQ A: Who gets sepsis?

FAQ B: What is the economic cost of sepsis?

Figure 5: Example of a Recognizing Question Entailment (RQE) question (correct answer is A).

The Story Cloze Test evaluates story understanding, story generation, and script learning and requires a system to choose the correct ending to a four-sentence story, as illustrated in Figure 4 (Mostafazadeh et al., 2016). In our experiments, we used only the 3,744 labeled stories.

Recognizing Question Entailment Healthcare questions can be highly complex compared to general open-domain questions, potentially involving accounting for family, social, and medical history. A proposed solution to healthcare question complexity is to decompose the question into simpler subquestions, which can be more easily answered. Recognizing Question Entailment (RQE, Ben Abacha and Demner-Fushman 2016) consists of 8588 training and 302 testing pairs of consumer health questions (CHQs) and frequently asked questions (FAQs) with labels indicating whether answering the FAQ

[5] https://www.mediawiki.org/wiki/Help:CirrusSearch

[6] https://www.nltk.org/_modules/nltk/tokenize/punkt.html

[7] https://eng.uber.com/horovod/

Model	CoPA	Cloze	RQE
Cirrus BERT	55.2	74.200	74.834
Cirrus BERT + OSCR	**73.6**	**87.974**	**77.815**
Composition: RAN	60.6	85.890	**77.815**
Composition: Attention	**73.6**	**87.974**	75.497
Composition: Linear	72.8	85.516	76.490
Energy: Absolute	**72.0**	83.431	75.497
Energy: Euclidean	60.6	85.890	75.497
Energy: Angular	59.2	**86.264**	**77.815**

Table 1: Accuracy of fine-tuned BERT after pretraining on the Cirrus Wikipedia data with and without OSCR.

entails answering the CHQ, as illustrated in Figure 5.

Table 1 presents the results of BERT when pretrained on Wikipedia with and without OSCR, the state-of-the-art, and the average performance of different semantic composition methods and energy functions when calculating OSCR.

6 Discussion

6.1 The Impact of External Knowledge.

It is clear from Table 1 that incorporating OSCR provided a significant improvement in accuracy for both common sense causal reasoning tasks, indicating that OSCR was able to inject useful world knowledge into the network. We also evaluated the impact of OSCR on the Stanford Question Answering Dataset (SQuAD), version 1.1, and observed no discernable change in performance (an Accuracy of 86.6% without and 86.5% with OSCR). The lack of impact of SQuAD is unsurprising, as the vast majority of SQuAD questions can be answered directly by surface-level information in the text, but it shows that injecting world knowledge with OSCR does not come at the expense of model performance for tasks that require little outside knowledge.

6.2 The Impact of Domain Knowledge.

While less pronounced than the general domain, for the clinical domain, OSCR provided a modest improvement over standard BERT, and both improved over the state-of-the-art.

6.3 The Impact of Entity Masking

Entity Subsumption We evaluated the impact of including subsumed entities when calculating OSCR and found it provided, on average, only a minor increase in accuracy (< 1% average relative improvement) at a 10% increase in total training

time. Consequently, we recommend ignoring all subsumed entities.

Entity De-masking De-masking entities had little over-all impact on model performance (< 1% average relative improvement) and no discernible effect on training time. This may be explained by the fact that Wikipedia sentences are typically much longer than standard English sentences, so the likelihood of an important entity being masked is relatively small.

6.4 The Role of Semantic Composition

When comparing semantic composition methods, the Linear method had the most consistent performance across both domains; the Recurrent Additive Network (RAN) obtained the lowest performance on the general domain and the highest performance on medical texts, while the Linear RAN exhibited the opposite behavior. While this suggests more complex domains require more complex representations of semantic composition, we recommend Linear composition as it exhibits consistent performance and requires 50% less training time than the RAN and 40% less than the Linear RAN.

6.5 The Impact of the Energy Functions

In terms of energy functions, the Euclidean distance was the most consistent, the Angular distance was the best for the Story Cloze and RQE tasks, and the Absolute difference was the best for CoPA. The Angular distance (being scale-invariant) is least affected by the number of subwords constituting an entity while the Absolute distance is most affected. Consequently, we believe the Absolute distance was only effective on the CoPA evaluation because the entities in CoPA are typically very short (single words or subwords). We recommend selecting the energy function based on the average length of entities in the fine-tuning tasks: Angular distance with long entities, Absolute distance with short entities, and Euclidean distance with varied entities.

Finally, we compared the impact of including and excluding subsumed and masked entities and found that neither resulted in any substantial change in model improvements (< 1% change in accuracy), while ignored masked and subsumed entities lead to a 20% average reduction in training time.

6.6 Limitations and Future Work

In this study, we only considered ConceptNet as our ontology because we were primarily interested in injecting common-sense world knowledge. However, OSCR is not specific to any Ontology. Likewise, we considered only one type of pretrained entity embeddings: ConceptNet NumberBatch (Speer et al., 2017), despite the availability of other, more sophisticated approaches for knowledge graph embedding including, TransE (Bordes et al., 2013), TranR (Lin et al., 2015), TransH (Wang et al., 2014), RESCAL (Nickel et al., 2011) and OSRL(Xiong et al., 2018). In future work, we hope to explore the impact of incorporating different Ontologies and knowledge graphs as well as alternative types of entity embeddings (Bordes et al., 2013; Lin et al., 2015; Wang et al., 2014; Nickel et al., 2011; Xiong et al., 2018).

7   Conclusions

In this paper we presented OSCR (Ontology-based Semantic Composition Regularization), a learned regularization method for injecting task-agnostic knowledge from an Ontology or knowledge graph into a neural network during pretraining. We evaluated the impact of including OSCR when pretraining BERT with Wikipedia articles by measuring the performance when fine-tuning on two question answering tasks involving world knowledge and causal reasoning and one requiring domain (healthcare) knowledge and obtained 33.3 %, 18.6 %, and 4 % improved accuracy compared to pre-training BERT without OSCR.

Reproducibility

All code, data, and experiments are available on GitHub at `https://github.com/h4ste/oscar`.

Acknowledgments

This work was supported by the intramural research program at the U.S. National Library of Medicine, National Institutes of Health, and utilized the computational resources of the NIH HPC Biowulf cluster (`http://hpc.nih.gov`).

References

Sören Auer, Christian Bizer, Georgi Kobilarov, Jens Lehmann, Richard Cyganiak, and Zachary Ives. 2007. Dbpedia: A nucleus for a web of open data. In *Proceedings of the 6th International The Semantic Web and 2Nd Asian Conference on Asian Semantic Web Conference*, ISWC'07/ASWC'07, pages 722–735, Berlin, Heidelberg. Springer-Verlag.

Asma Ben Abacha and Dina Demner-Fushman. 2016. Recognizing question entailment for medical question answering. In *AMIA 2016, American Medical Informatics Association Annual Symposium, Chicago, IL, USA, November 12-16, 2016*.

Antoine Bordes, Nicolas Usunier, Alberto Garcia-Duran, Jason Weston, and Oksana Yakhnenko. 2013. Translating embeddings for modeling multi-relational data. In C. J. C. Burges, L. Bottou, M. Welling, Z. Ghahramani, and K. Q. Weinberger, editors, *Advances in Neural Information Processing Systems 26*, pages 2787–2795. Curran Associates, Inc.

Andrew M Dai and Quoc V Le. 2015. Semi-supervised sequence learning. In C. Cortes, N. D. Lawrence, D. D. Lee, M. Sugiyama, and R. Garnett, editors, *Advances in Neural Information Processing Systems 28*, pages 3079–3087. Curran Associates, Inc.

Jacob Devlin, Ming-Wei Chang, Kenton Lee, and Kristina Toutanova. 2018. Bert: Pre-training of deep bidirectional transformers for language understanding. *arXiv preprint arXiv:1810.04805*.

Travis Goodwin and Sanda Harabagiu. 2016. Embedding open-domain common-sense knowledge from text. In *Proceedings of the Tenth International Conference on Language Resources and Evaluation (LREC 2016)*, pages 4621–4628, Portorož, Slovenia. European Language Resources Association (ELRA).

Andrew Gordon and Reid Swanson. 2009. Identifying personal stories in millions of weblog entries. In *Third International Conference on Weblogs and Social Media, Data Challenge Workshop, San Jose, CA*, volume 46.

H Paul Grice. 1975. Logic and conversation. *1975*, pages 41–58.

Jeremy Howard and Sebastian Ruder. 2018. Universal language model fine-tuning for text classification. In *Proceedings of the 56th Annual Meeting of the Association for Computational Linguistics (Volume 1: Long Papers)*, pages 328–339. Association for Computational Linguistics.

Kenton Lee, Omer Levy, and Luke Zettlemoyer. 2017. Recurrent additive networks. *arXiv preprint arXiv:1705.07393*.

Yankai Lin, Zhiyuan Liu, Maosong Sun, Yang Liu, and Xuan Zhu. 2015. Learning entity and relation embeddings for knowledge graph completion. In *Proceedings of the Twenty-Ninth AAAI Conference on Artificial Intelligence*, AAAI'15, pages 2181–2187. AAAI Press.

Edward Loper and Steven Bird. 2002. Nltk: The natural language toolkit. In *Proceedings of the ACL-02 Workshop on Effective Tools and Methodologies for Teaching Natural Language Processing and Computational Linguistics - Volume 1*, ETMTNLP '02, pages 63–70, Stroudsburg, PA, USA. Association for Computational Linguistics.

Christopher D Manning. 2015. Computational linguistics and deep learning. *Computational Linguistics*, 41(4):701–707.

Tomas Mikolov, Kai Chen, Greg Corrado, and Jeffrey Dean. 2013. Efficient estimation of word representations in vector space. *arXiv preprint arXiv:1301.3781*.

George A Miller. 1995. Wordnet: a lexical database for english. *Communications of the ACM*, 38(11):39–41.

Nasrin Mostafazadeh, Nathanael Chambers, Xiaodong He, Devi Parikh, Dhruv Batra, Lucy Vanderwende, Pushmeet Kohli, and James Allen. 2016. A corpus and cloze evaluation for deeper understanding of commonsense stories. In *Proceedings of the 2016 Conference of the North American Chapter of the Association for Computational Linguistics: Human Language Technologies*, pages 839–849. Association for Computational Linguistics.

Maximilian Nickel, Volker Tresp, and Hans-Peter Kriegel. 2011. A three-way model for collective learning on multi-relational data. In *Proceedings of the 28th International Conference on International Conference on Machine Learning*, ICML'11, pages 809–816, USA. Omnipress.

Jeffrey Pennington, Richard Socher, and Christopher Manning. 2014. Glove: Global vectors for word representation. In *Proceedings of the 2014 Conference on Empirical Methods in Natural Language Processing (EMNLP)*, pages 1532–1543. Association for Computational Linguistics.

Matthew Peters, Waleed Ammar, Chandra Bhagavatula, and Russell Power. 2017. Semi-supervised sequence tagging with bidirectional language models. In *Proceedings of the 55th Annual Meeting of the Association for Computational Linguistics (Volume 1: Long Papers)*, pages 1756–1765. Association for Computational Linguistics.

Alec Radford, Karthik Narasimhan, Time Salimans, and Ilya Sutskever. 2018. Improving language understanding with unsupervised learning. Technical report, Technical report, OpenAI.

Pranav Rajpurkar, Jian Zhang, Konstantin Lopyrev, and Percy Liang. 2016. SQuAD: 100,000+ questions for machine comprehension of text. In *Proceedings of the 2016 Conference on Empirical Methods in Natural Language Processing*, pages 2383–2392. Association for Computational Linguistics.

Melissa Roemmele, Cosmin Adrian Bejan, and Andrew S Gordon. 2011. Choice of plausible alternatives: An evaluation of commonsense causal reasoning. In *2011 AAAI Spring Symposium Series*.

Push Singh, Thomas Lin, Erik T. Mueller, Grace Lim, Travell Perkins, and Wan Li Zhu. 2002. Open mind common sense: Knowledge acquisition from the general public. In *On the Move to Meaningful Internet Systems, 2002 - DOA/CoopIS/ODBASE 2002 Confederated International Conferences DOA, CoopIS and ODBASE 2002*, pages 1223–1237, Berlin, Heidelberg. Springer-Verlag.

Robyn Speer, Joshua Chin, and Catherine Havasi. 2017. Conceptnet 5.5: An open multilingual graph of general knowledge. In *AAAI Conference on Artificial Intelligence*, pages 4444–4451.

Yu Sun, Shuohuan Wang, Yukun Li, Shikun Feng, Xuyi Chen, Han Zhang, Xin Tian, Danxiang Zhu, Hao Tian, and Hua Wu. 2019. Ernie: Enhanced representation through knowledge integration.

Ole Tange. 2018. *GNU Parallel 2018*. Ole Tange.

Wilson L. Taylor. 1953. "cloze procedure": A new tool for measuring readability. *Journalism Bulletin*, 30(4):415–433.

Ashish Vaswani, Noam Shazeer, Niki Parmar, Jakob Uszkoreit, Llion Jones, Aidan N Gomez, Ł ukasz Kaiser, and Illia Polosukhin. 2017. Attention is all you need. In I. Guyon, U. V. Luxburg, S. Bengio, H. Wallach, R. Fergus, S. Vishwanathan, and R. Garnett, editors, *Advances in Neural Information Processing Systems 30*, pages 5998–6008. Curran Associates, Inc.

L. von Ahn. 2006. Games with a purpose. *Computer*, 39(6):92–94.

Q. Wang, Z. Mao, B. Wang, and L. Guo. 2017. Knowledge graph embedding: A survey of approaches and applications. *IEEE Transactions on Knowledge and Data Engineering*, 29(12):2724–2743.

Zhen Wang, Jianwen Zhang, Jianlin Feng, and Zheng Chen. 2014. Knowledge graph embedding by translating on hyperplanes. In *Proceedings of the Twenty-Eighth AAAI Conference on Artificial Intelligence*, AAAI'14, pages 1112–1119. AAAI Press.

Yaqi Xie, Ziwei Xu, Mohan S Kankanhalli, Kuldeep S Meel, and Harold Soh. 2019. Embedding symbolic knowledge into deep networks. In H. Wallach, H. Larochelle, A. Beygelzimer, F. d'Alché-Buc, E. Fox, and R. Garnett, editors, *Advances in Neural Information Processing Systems 32*, pages 4233–4243. Curran Associates, Inc.

Wenhan Xiong, Mo Yu, Shiyu Chang, Xiaoxiao Guo, and William Yang Wang. 2018. One-shot relational learning for knowledge graphs. In *Proceedings of the 2018 Conference on Empirical Methods in Natural Language Processing*, pages 1980–1990. Association for Computational Linguistics.

Zhengyan Zhang, Xu Han, Zhiyuan Liu, Xin Jiang, Maosong Sun, and Qun Liu. 2019. ERNIE: Enhanced language representation with informative entities. In *Proceedings of the 57th Annual Meeting of the Association for Computational Linguistics*, pages 1441–1451, Florence, Italy. Association for Computational Linguistics.

Target Concept Guided Medical Concept Normalization in Noisy User-Generated Texts

Katikapalli Subramanyam Kalyan
Department of Computer Applications
NIT Trichy, India
kalyan.ks@yahoo.com

Sivanesan Sangeetha
Department of Computer Applications
NIT Trichy, India
sangeetha@nitt.edu

Abstract

Medical concept normalization (MCN) i.e., mapping of colloquial medical phrases to standard concepts is an essential step in analysis of medical social media text. The main drawback in existing state-of-the-art approach (Kalyan and Sangeetha, 2020b) is learning target concept vector representations from scratch which requires more training instances. Our model is based on RoBERTa and target concept embeddings. In our model, we integrate a) target concept information in the form of target concept vectors generated by encoding target concept descriptions using SRoBERTa, state-of-the-art RoBERTa based sentence embedding model and b) domain lexicon knowledge by enriching target concept vectors with synonym relationship knowledge using retrofitting algorithm. It is the first attempt in MCN to exploit both target concept information as well as domain lexicon knowledge in the form of retrofitted target concept vectors. Our model outperforms all the existing models with an accuracy improvement up to 1.36% on three standard datasets. Further, our model when trained only on mapping lexicon synonyms achieves up to 4.87% improvement in accuracy.

1 Introduction

Medical concept normalization (MCN) involves learning a model which can assign medical concept from a standard lexicon for the given health related mention. Table 1 shows few examples of concept mentions and corresponding standard concepts from SNOMED-CT lexicon. Normalizing medical concepts finds application in tasks like questions answering, pharmacovigilance, knowledge graph construction etc. In this work, we deal with medical concept normalization in noisy user-generated texts like tweets and online discussion forum posts. With the rising popularity of social media platforms, common public are using these

platforms to share information. For example, in twitter people share their health experiences and in websites like AskAPatient.com, public post reviews for the drugs they consume. This valuable health information available in social media platforms can be exploited in applications like pharmacovigilance, public health monitoring etc (Kalyan and Sangeetha, 2020c). In general, most of the common public express their health related concerns in an informal way using colloquial language. For example, *'dizziness'* is expressed as *'head spinning a little'* and *'diarrhoea'* is expressed as *'bathroom with runs'* (Limsopatham and Collier, 2016; Lee et al., 2017). As social media text is highly noisy with irregular grammar and colloquial words, medical concept normalization in social media text is more challenging.

Concept Mention	Standard Concept
lowering of energy	lack of energy (SNOMED ID: 248274002)
felt weak	asthenia (SNOMED ID: 13791008)
very severe pain in arms	pain in upper limb (SNOMED ID: 102556003)
only wanted to sleep	hypersomnia (SNOMED ID: 77692006)

Table 1: Examples of concept mentions and corresponding standard concepts from Systematized Nomenclature of Medicine – Clinical Terms (SNOMED CT) lexicon.

1.1 Motivation

Most of the existing work in medical concept normalization in social media text ignore valuable target concept knowledge (Limsopatham and Collier, 2016; Lee et al., 2017; Han et al., 2017; Belousov et al., 2017). Recently researchers (Tutubalina et al., 2018; Miftahutdinov and Tutubalina, 2019; Pattisapu et al., 2020; Kalyan and Sangeetha, 2020b) focused on exploiting target concept knowledge in normalizing concepts. The drawbacks in these recent works in integrating target concept

Proceedings of Deep Learning Inside Out (DeeLIO):
The First Workshop on Knowledge Extraction and Integration for Deep Learning Architectures, pages 64–73
Online, November 19, 2020. ©2020 Association for Computational Linguistics

knowledge in deep learning based medical concept normalization systems are

- Tutubalina et al. (2018) and Miftahutdinov and Tutubalina (2019) exploit target concept knowledge in the form of cosine similarity between tf-idf based vector representations of concept mentions in social media text and concept descriptions from UMLS. However, tf-idf based cosine similarity features between concept mentions and concept descriptions are not effective as concept mentions are noisy, descriptive and colloquial in nature while concept descriptions are expressed in formal language.

- Pattisapu et al. (2020) choose appropriate target concept based on cosine similarity between concept mention and graph embedding based target concept vectors. Here concept mentions are encoded using RoBERTa and then transformed to target concepts embedding space using two fully connected layers. However, a) the quality of graph embedding based target concept vectors depends on the comprehensiveness of mapping lexicon which limits the application of this approach (e.g., MedDRA is less comprehensive compared to SNOMED-CT (Bodenreider, 2009)) b) graph embedding methods used by Pattisapu et al. (2020) generate target concept vectors based on network structure only and completely ignore other information like concept text description and c) when mapping lexicon used is different across datasets, it requires more time and resources to generate target concept vectors using graph embedding methods for each dataset (Kalyan and Sangeetha, 2020b).

- Kalyan and Sangeetha (2020b) learn the vector representations of concept mentions and concepts jointly. The authors randomly assign values to target concept vectors and update them at the time of training. However, learning concept vectors from scratch requires more number of training instances. With less number of training instances, this approach results in poor performance which we illustrate in Section 6.1. This is the current state-of-the-art approach in medical concept normalization in social media text.

Our proposed model overcomes the drawbacks in existing work in utilizing target concept knowledge and answers the following two research questions.

- RQ1 - How to effectively integrate target concept knowledge in deep learning based medical concept normalization system?

- RQ2 - How to utilize domain lexicon knowledge in medical concept normalization?

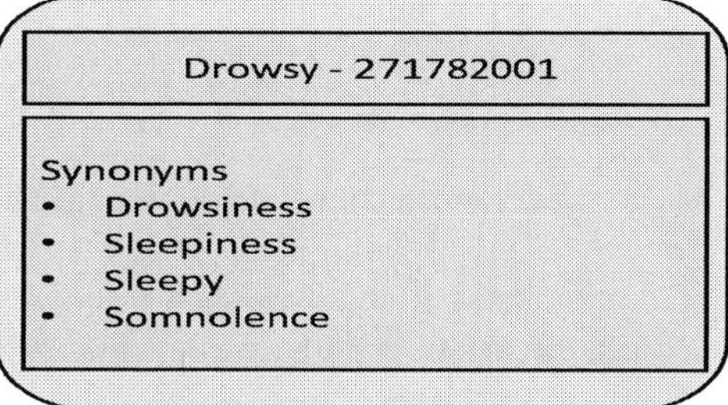

Figure 1: SNOMED-CT Concept and its synonyms. Here, '*Drowsy*' is concept description and '*271782001*' is concept-id.

As shown in Figure 1, every concept has concept-id, description and set of synonyms. To address RQ1, we represent each target concept using fixed length dense vector which is generated by encoding target concept description using SRoBERTa. SRoBERTa (Reimers and Gurevych, 2019) is Siamese network based Sentence RoBERTa model trained on NLI+Multi NLI and STS datasets. It is state-of-the-art sentence embedding model which encodes sequence of words into dense fixed length vectors in a way that sequences which are in close meaning are also close in embedding pace . To address RQ2, we retrofit target concept vectors produced by SRoBERTa using synonyms from mapping lexicon. Retrofitting algorithm (Faruqui et al., 2015) enriches concept vectors with synonym relationship knowledge from domain lexicon.

In our model we encode a) input concept mentions using RoBERTa and b) target concepts using SRoBERTa and enrich them with synonym relationship knowledge. We compute similarity vector in which each value is equal to cosine similarity between vectors of concept mentions and all the target concepts. Finally, the cosine similarity values are normalized and the target concept with maximum similarity is chosen. During training, the vectors of target concepts are not updated. We evaluate our model on three standard MCN datasets CADEC, PsyTAR and SMM4H2017 and achieve accuracy improvements up to 1.36%. Further, our model when trained only using mapping lexicon synonyms achieves up to 4.87% improvement in accuracy. The key aspects of our work are

- A simple approach to integrate both target concept information and domain lexicon knowledge in medical concept normalization in the form of retrofitted target concept vectors.

- Our model achieves state-of-the-art performance on three standard medical concept normalization datasets.

- Our model when trained using mapping lexicon synonyms only, achieves up to 4.87% improvement in accuracy which shows that our approach to generate target concept vectors is better than graph embedding based approach (Pattisapu et al., 2020) or learning from scratch (Kalyan and Sangeetha, 2020b).

2 Related Work

2.1 Medical Concept Normalization

Traditional concept normalization systems used string matching (Aronson, 2001; McCallum et al., 2005; Tsuruoka et al., 2007) or machine learning approaches (Leaman et al., 2013; Leaman and Lu, 2014). These methods perform poorly in case of instances with no words in common between concept mention and concept description. With the introduction of embedding models like Word2vec (Mikolov et al., 2013) and ELMo (Peters et al., 2018) which can encode syntactic and semantic information, researchers focused on exploiting embeddings in normalizing medical concepts. For example, Limsopatham and Collier (2016) used CNN and RNN models with word2vec embeddings. Subramanyam and Sangeetha (2020) proposed a model based on BiLSTM and clinical ELMo embeddings. Han et al. (2017) used hierarchical character LSTM on the top of character embeddings while Belousov et al. (2017) used Multinomial Logistic Regression classifier on the top of embeddings inferred from various corpora.

In recent times, unsupervised pre-trained models like BERT (Devlin et al., 2019), RoBERTa (Liu et al., 2019) achieved significant improvements in most of the natural language processing tasks. Most of the recent work in medical concept normalization (Miftahutdinov and Tutubalina, 2019; Kalyan and Sangeetha, 2020a; Pattisapu et al., 2020; Kalyan and Sangeetha, 2020b) in social media text is based on BERT and RoBERTa. Miftahutdinov and Tutubalina (2019) experimented with BERT and cosine similarity based semantic features, Kalyan and Sangeetha (2020a) experimented with various general and domain specific BERT models combined with highway network layer. Pattisapu et al. (2020) normalize medical concepts using RoBERTa and graph embedding based concept vectors while approach of Kalyan and Sangeetha (2020b) involves learning the vectors representations of target concepts along with input concept mentions. Our approach is similar to (Kalyan and Sangeetha, 2020b) by choosing target concept which has maximum cosine similarity with the input concept mention. However unlike Kalyan and Sangeetha (2020b) method which learns target concept vectors from scratch, we use retrofitted target concept vectors which are generated using SRoBERTa and then enriched with synonym relationship knowledge from domain lexicon. It is the first work to exploit both target concept information and domain lexicon knowledge effectively in MCN in the form of retrofitted target concept vectors.

2.2 Sentence Embeddings

Sentence embeddings encode sequence of words into dense fixed size vector. Some of the popular approaches are averaging word vectors, encoder-decoder based skip thought (Kiros et al., 2015), InferSent (Conneau et al., 2017) which is Siamese BiLSTM+max pooling trained on SNLI, transformer based Universal Sentence Encoder (Cer et al., 2018). Recently, Reimers and Gurevych (2019) proposed SRoBERTa, Siamese network based Sentence RoBERTa model and it is trained on NLI + MultiNLI datasets followed by STS dataset. It is a state-of-the-art sentence embedding model which encodes sequence of words into dense fixed length vector in a way that sequences which are close in meaning are also close in embedding pace.

2.3 Retrofitting algorithm

Vector representations generated by neural embedding models are rich in syntactic and semantic information but lack valuable relationship knowledge from semantic lexicons. To enrich vector representations with relationship knowledge, Faruqui et al. (2015) proposed retrofitting algorithm. It is simply a post-processing step and can be applied to vectors generated using any embedding model. It learns retrofitted concept vectors $\{v_1, v_2, v_3, .., v_n\}$ from concept vectors $\{\hat{v_1}, \hat{v_2}, \hat{v_3}, ..., \hat{v_n}\}$ by iteratively minimizing distance between (i) retrofitted vector v_i and its counterpart $\hat{v_i}$ and (ii) retrofitted vector v_i and all its neighbors v_j. The objective function is

$$\sum_{i=1}^{n} \left[\alpha_i \left\| v_i - \hat{v_i} \right\|^2 + \sum_{(i,j) \in E} \beta_{ij} \left\| v_i - v_j \right\|^2 \right] \quad (1)$$

Here retrofitted vectors v_i are initialized with values of concept vectors $\hat{v_i}$ and then updated iteratively by minimizing the objective function.

3 Datasets

Our proposed model is evaluated on three standard MCN datasets of noisy user-generated texts. Out of these, CADEC (Karimi et al., 2015) and PsyTAR (Zolnoori et al., 2019) datasets contain concept mentions gathered from user-generated AskAPatient.com reviews and SMM4H2017 (Sarker et al., 2018) contains adverse drug reaction (ADR) mentions extracted from twitter.

CADEC: Karimi et.al released CSIRO Adverse Drug Event Corpus (CADEC) having user posted drug reviews gathered from AskAPatient (Karimi et al., 2015). The annotators manually identified concept mentions and mapped them to SNOMED-CT concepts which resulted in a corpus of 6754 concept mentions and 1029 SNOMED-CT codes. As 66% of instances are common in train and test splits in the random folds of this dataset released by Limsopatham and Collier (2016), Tutubalina et al. (2018) split this dataset into five folds[1] with no overlap.

PsyTAR: Zolnoori et al. (2019) released PsyTAR corpus which includes 887 user generated psychiatric drug reviews collected from AskAPatient. This dataset includes manually identified 6556 concept phrases which are mapped to 618 concepts in SNOMED-CT. Zolnoori et al. (2019) released random folds of this dataset. However, 56% of instances are common in train and test in these folds. So, Miftahutdinov and Tutubalina (2019) create custom folds of this dataset[2] to reduce the overlap between train and test sets.

SMM4H017: Sarker et al. (2018) released this dataset[3] of ADR mentions for subtask3 of SMM4H2017 shared task organized by Health Language Processing Lab @ University of Pennsilvaniya. Initially, twets containing generic and trade names of drugs were collected. Then, ADR mentions were manually identified and mapped to MedDRA concepts. In this corpus, train set consists of 6500 ADR phrases and 472 unique MedDRA codes, test set consists of 2500 ADR phrases and 254 MedDRA codes.

The significant overlap between train and test sets in random folds of CADEC and PsyTAR datasets can result in bias and contribute to high performance of model (Lee et al., 2017; Kalyan and Sangeetha, 2020a). So, we evaluate our approach on custom folds of PsyTAR and CADEC datasets in addition to SMM4H2017 dataset, like the recent previous works (Pattisapu et al., 2020; Kalyan and Sangeetha, 2020b)

4 Methodology

4.1 Model Description

Our model is based on RoBERTa and target concept embeddings. Initially we compute vector representations of input phrase and concepts in standard lexicon using RoBERTa and SRoBERTa respectively. We further enrich target concept vectors with synonym relationship from domain lexicon using retrofitting algorithm. Then, we find cosine similarity between vectors of concept mention and all the target concepts. Finally, the concept mention is mapped to concept with maximum similarity. Figure 2 gives an overview of our proposed model.

Target Concept Representation

We use SRoBERTa, state-of-the-art sentence embedding model to compute target concept representations and then inject synonym relationship using retrofitting algorithm to get target concept vector $e_c \in \mathbb{R}^h$.

$$e_c = Retrofit(SRoBERTa(concept)) \quad (2)$$

Concept Mention Representation

Learning quality representation of concept mentions is a key step in medical concept normalization. We use RoBERTa, which is an improved version of BERT with large training batch sizes and more

---

[1]https://cutt.ly/Gi6kka6
[2]https://doi.org/10.5281/zenodo.3236318

[3]https://data.mendeley.com/datasets/rxwfb3tysd/2

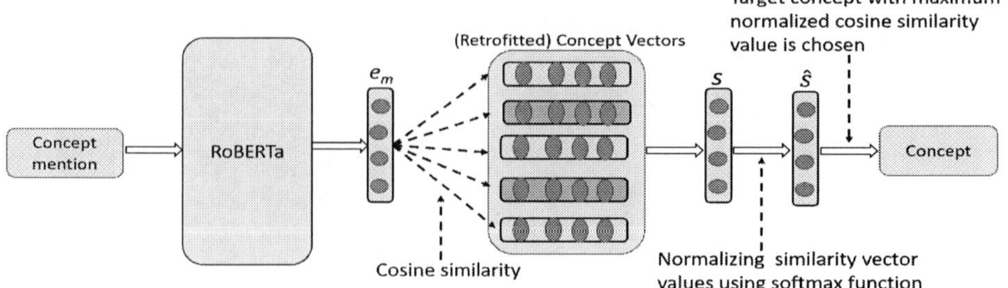

Figure 2: Overview of our proposed model for medical concept normalization in noisy user-generated texts. e_m - RoBERTa encoded input concept mention, s - similarity vector computed based on cosine similarity between the vectors of input phrase and concepts in standard lexicon, $\hat{s}$ - normalized cosine similarity vector.

training corpus, to compute input concept mention representation $e_m \in \mathbb{R}^h$.

$$e_m = RoBERTa(mention) \quad (3)$$

We find similarity vector based on cosine similarity between vectors of input pharse and concepts in standard lexicon. Finally, we normalize all the cosine similarity values using softmax which result in normalized similarity vector $\hat{s} \in \mathbb{R}^C$.

$$\hat{s} = [\hat{s_i}]_{i=1}^{C} \quad (4)$$

Here C represents total number of unique target concepts in the dataset, $\hat{s_i} = Softmax(f(e_m, e_{ci}))$ where the function f() represents cosine similarity and e_{ci} represents vector of the concept c_i. We train the model using AdamW optimizer (Loshchilov and Hutter, 2019) which minimize cross entropy loss (L_{CE}) between normalized similarity vector $\hat{s}$ and the ground truth vector s. During training, we freeze the vectors of target concepts.

$$L_{CE} = -\frac{1}{K} \sum_{i=1}^{K} \sum_{j=1}^{C} s_j^i log(\hat{s}_j^i) \quad (5)$$

4.2 Implementation Details

We do basic pre-processing steps like lower-casing, removing non-ASCII and special characters in concept mention and concept descriptions. We remove unnecessary words like 'nos', 'unspecified' and 'finding' in concept descriptions. In case of concept mentions, we do additional pre-processing steps like removing repeating characters (e.g., sooo much → so much) , replacing medical acronyms[4]

---

[4]Gathered from UMLS Methathesaurus, Wikipedia and https://www.acronymslist.com/cat/medical-acronyms.html

('ra' → 'rheumatoid arthritis') and contractions (isn't → is not) with full forms.

Pattisapu et al. (2020) treat synonyms in mapping lexicon as concept mention and augment the training set with the labeled instances generated from synonyms. However, we augment training set with synonyms of less frequently occurring concepts only. In case of CADEC and Psy-TAR datasets, we use synonyms from the mapping lexicon SNOMED-CT. In case of SMM4H2017 dataset, we use synonyms from UMLS Metathesaurus as synonyms are very few in number in Med-DRA. For each concept in MedDRA, we find the corresponding concept unique identifier(CUI) in UMLS and then gather all the associated synonyms excluding non-English synonyms.

In case of retrofitting algorithm, we choose number of iterations = 10 as suggested by the authors. Further, we use the implementation[5] provided by the authors. As there is no official validation set in case of all the three datasets, we use 10% of the augmented training set for validation. We find optimal hyperparameter values by performing random search over the range of hyperparameter values. During training, we freeze target concept vectors. We implement all our models in PyTorch using transformers package from huggingface (Wolf et al., 2019).

4.3 Evaluation Metrics

In case of all the three datasets, standard evaluation metric is accuracy (Miftahutdinov and Tutubalina, 2019; Pattisapu et al., 2020; Kalyan and Sangeetha, 2020b). In case of CADEC and PsyTAR datasets which are multi-fold, reported accuracy is average accuracy across all five folds.

---

[5]https://github.com/mfaruqui/retrofitting

4.4 Comparison with existing methods

Here, we compare our approach with the following existing methods.

Hierarchical Character-LSTM Han et al. (2017) use hierarchical character level LSTM to normalize the concept mentions. Intially, they generate character level word representations using LSTM over embeddings of characters and their classes and then apply bidirectional LSTM over these word representations to generate contextual word vectors. Finally, vector obtained by max-pooling of contextual word vectors is given to fully connected softmax layer.

Multinomial LR Belousov et al. (2017) generate concept mention vector representation as average of three weighted vectors of words in the concept mention. Here, word weights are based on inverse document frequencies of words and word vectors are obtained as average of GoogleNews, twitter and drugtwitter embeddings. With these mention representations as input, Multinomial Logistic Regression classifier assigns the concepts.

BERT + Cosine Semantic Features Miftahutdinov and Tutubalina (2019) generate representation of concept mention using BERT. To integrate target concept knowledge , the authors generate semantic features based on cosine similarity between tf-idf vector representations of concept mention and all the target concepts in the dataset. Finally, the output of BERT and cosine semantic features are concatenated and given to fully connected softmax layer which assigns the concepts.

BERT + Highway Network Layer Kalyan and Sangeetha (2020a) experiment with various general and domain specific BERT models for medical concept normalization. The output of BERT model is passed through highway network layer to eliminate the unnecessary information and then passed through fully connected softmax layer to get the target concept.

RoBERTa + Graph based Concept Vectors Pattisapu et al. (2020) generate target concept vectors using graph embedding algorithms. They train RoBERTa based model which embeds input concept mention into the embedding space of target concept vectors. For a given input phrase, the nearest standard concept in embedding space is assigned.

RoBERTa + Random Concept Vectors Kalyan and Sangeetha (2020b) propose a model based on RoBERTa which jointly learns the representations of concept mention and the standard concepts. The authors randomly initialize the target concept vectors and then they are updated during training. The standard concept with maximum cosine similarity with input phrase is chosen.

4.5 Models

RoBERTa We generate the representations of input concept mention using RoBERTa. We experiment with both variants of RoBERTa namely RoBERTa-base and RoBERTa-large. In both the cases, the size of concept mention vector is equal to the hidden vector size i.e., 768 in case of RoBERTa-base and 1024 in case of RoBERTa-large.

+ Concept Vectors (CV) We generate target concept vectors by encoding their descriptions using SRoBERTa. In case of a) RoBERTa-base model, we use target concept vectors generated by 'roberta-base-nli-stsb-mean-tokens' and b) RoBERTa-large model, we use target concepts generated by 'roberta-large-nli-stsb-mean-tokens'.

+ Retrofitted Concept Vectors(RCV) We enrich target concepts generated by SRoBERTa with synonym relationship knowledge from mapping lexicon using retrofitting algorithm.

5 Results

Our proposed model is evaluated on the standard MCN datasets CADEC, PsyTAR and SMM4H2017. The performance of our model and existing models is presented in Table 2. From Table 2, we notice that our proposed model achieves the best results of 86.40%, 85.04% and 91.73% across CADEC, PsyTAR and SMM4H2017 datasets. Our model outperforms existing methods with accuracy improvement up to 1.36%. The existing state-of-the-art model Kalyan and Sangeetha (2020b) learns target concept vectors from scratch and so it requires more number of training instances. Our model outperforms the approach of Kalyan and Sangeetha (2020b) (i) up to 1.9% in case of base version and (ii) up to 1.36% in case of large version. The use of retrofitted concept vectors improved performance only in case of SMM4H2017. The performance of retrofitted concept vectors depends on the number of available synonyms for each concept.

Method	CADEC	PsyTAR	SMM4H2017
Existing Methods			
(Han et al., 2017)	-	-	87.20
(Belousov et al., 2017)	-	-	87.70
(Miftahutdinov and Tutubalina, 2019)	79.83	77.52	89.28
(Kalyan and Sangeetha, 2020a)	82.62	-	-
(Pattisapu et al., 2020)	83.18	82.42	-
(Kalyan and Sangeetha, 2020b)$^{\pi}$	82.60	81.90	90.15
(Kalyan and Sangeetha, 2020b)$^{\Pi}$	85.49	83.68	90.84
Our Method			
RoBERTa-base+ CV$^{\gamma}$	84.53	82.41	91.34
RoBERTa-base+ RCV$^{\delta}$	84.11	82.34	91.19
RoBERTa-large + CV$^{\gamma}$	**86.40**	**85.04**	91.19
RoBERTa-large+ RCV$^{\delta}$	86.04	85.02	**91.73**

Table 2: Performance of our mdoel and existing methods on CADEC, PsyTAR and SMM4H2017 datasets. π - model based on Roberta-base and Π - model based on Roberta-large. γ - concept vectors generated using SRoBERTa and δ - concept vectors generated using SRoBERTa and then retrofitted using synonym relationship from domain lexicon.

The synonyms for SMM4H2017 are gathered from UMLS Metathesaurus and as they are more number in number compared to SNOMED-CT synonyms, retrofitted concept vectors improve accuracy only in case of SMM4H2017 (Roberta-large). In future, we would like to see whether using UMLS synonyms instead of SNOMED-CT synonyms improve performance in case of CADEC and PsyTAR datasets also.

6 Analysis and Discussion

6.1 Training only on mapping lexicon synonyms

There will be a set of synonyms for each concept in mapping lexicon. Table 3 shows some of the concepts and corresponding synonyms from SNOMED-CT lexicon. We consider each synonym as user-generated concept mention and generate labeled instances from mapping lexicon synonyms.

To show the performance of our model in the absence of human annotated instances in training set, we train our model using labeled instances generated from mapping lexicon synonyms and then evaluate our model on the corresponding test set. Tabel 4 shows the performance of our model and existing models across three datasets. As reported in the table, our model outperforms existing methods with accuracy improvement up to 4.46% and 4.87% across CADEC and PsyTAR datasets respectively.

From Table 4, we infer that among the three approaches, Kalyan and Sangeetha (2020b) achieved the lowest performance in case of CADEC and PsyTAR datasets. When compared to Kalyan and Sangeetha (2020b), the performance of a) Pattisapu et al. (2020) is 9.42% and 9.87% higher b) our approach is 13.88% and 14.74% higher across CADEC and PsyTAR datasets respectively. Kalyan and Sangeetha (2020b) learn the vector representations of concept mentions and concepts jointly. The authors randomly assigned values to target concepts and then updated them during training. However, learning concept vectors from scratch requires more number of training instances. As the number of training instances generated from synonyms is less in number, this approach results in poor performance.

In case of SMM4H2017, Kalyan and Sangeetha (2020b) achieved the best performance of 63.28% which is 2.55% more than our approach. Here as the number of training instances generated from synonyms is more in number, Kalyan and Sangeetha (2020b) outperformed our approach. This shows that learning target concept vectors from scratch is effective only when training instances are more in number.

6.2 Failure Analysis

Here we analyse the reasons for the wrong predictions given by our best performing model. For this, we check all the failure cases in CADEC dataset.

Our model failed to handle the concept mentions which are misspelled words of ground truth con-

Concept-ID	Concept Description	Concept Synonyms
60119000	Exhaustion	Washed out, Worn out
278040002	Loss of hair	Thinning hair, Falling hair
386705008	Lightheadedness	Feels light headed, Dizziness light headed , Lightheaded
131148009	Bleeding	Haemorrhage, Hemorrhage
247640008	Unable to think clearly	Muddled thought , Muddled thinking
102897001	Feeling intoxicated	Feeling drunk, Feeling groggy

Table 3: Concepts and their synonyms from SNOMED-CT lexicon

Method	CADEC	PsyTAR	SMM4H2017
Existing Methods			
(Pattisapu et al., 2020)	64.80	58.4	-
(Kalyan and Sangeetha, 2020b)$^{\pi}$	51.55	45.77	55.75
(Kalyan and Sangeetha, 2020b)$^{\Pi}$	55.38	48.53	**63.28**
Ours			
Roberta-base + CV$^{\gamma}$	62.44	59.47	58.78
Roberta-base + RCV$^{\delta}$	63.73	60.14	57.31
Roberta-large + CV$^{\gamma}$	**69.26**	63.06	58.82
Roberta-large + RCV$^{\delta}$	69.14	**63.27**	60.73

Table 4: Performance of our model and existing methods when trained only on mapping lexicon synonyms. π - model based on Roberta-base and Π - model based on Roberta-large. γ - concept vectors generated using SRoBERTa. δ - concept vectors generated using SRoBERTa and then retrofitted using synonym relationship from domain lexicon.

cepts. For example, the concept mention *'insomina* is mapped to *'nausea - 422587007 '* instead of the ground truth concept *'insomnia - 193462001'*. Similarly, the concept mentions *'naseua'*, *'fatique'*, *'insommnia'*, *'diziness'*, *'nausia'* and *'diarreah'* are not mapped to the ground truth concepts *'nausea - 422587007'*, *'fatigue - 84229001 '*, *'insomnia - 193462001 '*, *'dizziness - 404640003'*, *'nausea - 422587007'* and *'diarrhea - 62315008'* respectively. Here, all the concept mentions are misspelled words of the ground truth concepts.

In some of the cases, our model assigned concepts which are more specific than the ground truth concepts. For example, our model mapped the concepts mentions *'pain so bad'*, *'so much pain'*, *'worse pain'* and *'pain bad'* to the concept *'severe pain - 76948002'* rather than the ground truth *'pain - 22253000'*. Here we observe that in case of all these concept mentions, the concept *'severe pain'* is more specific and hence appropriate compared to the ground truth *'pain'*.

In few cases, our model assigned concepts which are closely related to the ground truth concept. For example, the concept mention *'difficult to concentrate* is assigned to the concept *'unable to con-*centrate - 60032008'* instead of the ground truth concept *'poor concentration - 26329005'*. Here the predicted and ground truth concepts are closely related. Similarly, *'could not walk across the room'* is assigned to *'unable to walk - 282145008'* instead of *'walking disability - 228158008'*.

One more case in which our model failed is when the concept mention is an abbreviation of the ground truth concept. For example, the concept mention *'ibu'* is assigned to the concept *'ubidecarenone'* and the ground truth concept is *'ibuprofen'*. Here, *'ibu'* is an abbreviation of *'ibuprofen'*.

6.3 Limitations

In case of SMM4H2017 dataset, we find the corresponding CUI for each MedDRA concept and include all the associated synonyms excluding non-English synonyms. Here the limitation is that, some CUIs can be mapped to more than one MedDRA concept. For example, *'C0020649 (Hypotension)'* can be mapped to both the MedDRA concepts *'10021097 (Hypotension)'* and *'10005734 (Blood pressure decreased)'*. Similarly, *'C0036974 (Shock)'* can be mapped to both the MedDRA concepts *'10009192 (Circulatory collapse)'* and

'10034567 (Peripheral circulatory failure)'.

7 Conclusion

Here, we propose a model based on RoBERTa and target concept embeddings to normalize concepts in medical related user-generated texts. Our model integrates target concept knowledge as well domain lexicon knowledge in a simple and novel way. The existing state-of-the-art approach (Kalyan and Sangeetha, 2020b) exploits target concept knowledge by learning vector representations of target concepts from scratch. As target concept vectors are learned from scratch, this approach requires more training instances and it performs poorly with less number of training instances. Our model exploits target concept information and domain lexicon knowledge in the form of retrofitted target concept vectors. We encode target concepts using SRoBERTa and enrich these concept vectors with synonym relationship knowledge from standard lexicon using retrofitting algorithm. Our model outperforms all the existing methods and achieves significant improvements on three standard datasets.

References

Alan R Aronson. 2001. Effective mapping of biomedical text to the umls metathesaurus: the metamap program. In *Proceedings of the AMIA Symposium*, page 17. American Medical Informatics Association.

Maksim Belousov, William Dixon, and Goran Nenadic. 2017. Using an ensemble of generalised linear and deep learning models in the smm4h 2017 medical concept normalisation task. In *SMM4H@ AMIA*, pages 54–58.

Olivier Bodenreider. 2009. Using snomed ct in combination with meddra for reporting signal detection and adverse drug reactions reporting. In *AMIA Annual Symposium Proceedings*, volume 2009, page 45. American Medical Informatics Association.

Daniel Cer, Yinfei Yang, Sheng-yi Kong, Nan Hua, Nicole Limtiaco, Rhomni St John, Noah Constant, Mario Guajardo-Cespedes, Steve Yuan, Chris Tar, et al. 2018. Universal sentence encoder for english. In *Proceedings of the 2018 Conference on Empirical Methods in Natural Language Processing: System Demonstrations*, pages 169–174.

Alexis Conneau, Douwe Kiela, Holger Schwenk, Loïc Barrault, and Antoine Bordes. 2017. Supervised learning of universal sentence representations from natural language inference data. In *Proceedings of the 2017 Conference on Empirical Methods in Natural Language Processing*, pages 670–680.

Jacob Devlin, Ming-Wei Chang, Kenton Lee, and Kristina Toutanova. 2019. Bert: Pre-training of deep bidirectional transformers for language understanding. In *Proceedings of the 2019 Conference of the North American Chapter of the Association for Computational Linguistics: Human Language Technologies, Volume 1 (Long and Short Papers)*, pages 4171–4186.

Manaal Faruqui, Jesse Dodge, Sujay Kumar Jauhar, Chris Dyer, Eduard Hovy, and Noah A Smith. 2015. Retrofitting word vectors to semantic lexicons. In *Proceedings of the 2015 Conference of the North American Chapter of the Association for Computational Linguistics: Human Language Technologies*, pages 1606–1615.

Sifei Han, Tung Tran, Anthony Rios, and Ramakanth Kavuluru. 2017. Team uknlp: Detecting adrs, classifying medication intake messages, and normalizing adr mentions on twitter. In *SMM4H@ AMIA*, pages 49–53.

Katikapalli Subramanyam Kalyan and S Sangeetha. 2020a. Bertmcn: Mapping colloquial phrases to standard medical concepts using bert and highway network. Technical report, EasyChair.

Katikapalli Subramanyam Kalyan and S Sangeetha. 2020b. Medical concept normalization in user generated texts by learning target concept embeddings. *arXiv preprint arXiv:2006.04014*.

Katikapalli Subramanyam Kalyan and S Sangeetha. 2020c. Secnlp: A survey of embeddings in clinical natural language processing. *Journal of biomedical informatics*, 101:103323.

Sarvnaz Karimi, Alejandro Metke-Jimenez, Madonna Kemp, and Chen Wang. 2015. Cadec: A corpus of adverse drug event annotations. *Journal of biomedical informatics*, 55:73–81.

Ryan Kiros, Yukun Zhu, Russ R Salakhutdinov, Richard Zemel, Raquel Urtasun, Antonio Torralba, and Sanja Fidler. 2015. Skip-thought vectors. In *Advances in neural information processing systems*, pages 3294–3302.

Robert Leaman, Rezarta Islamaj Doğan, and Zhiyong Lu. 2013. Dnorm: disease name normalization with pairwise learning to rank. *Bioinformatics*, 29(22):2909–2917.

Robert Leaman and Zhiyong Lu. 2014. Automated disease normalization with low rank approximations. In *Proceedings of BioNLP 2014*, pages 24–28.

Kathy Lee, Sadid A Hasan, Oladimeji Farri, Alok Choudhary, and Ankit Agrawal. 2017. Medical concept normalization for online user-generated texts. In *2017 IEEE International Conference on Healthcare Informatics (ICHI)*, pages 462–469. IEEE.

Nut Limsopatham and Nigel Collier. 2016. Normalising medical concepts in social media texts by learning semantic representation. Association for Computational Linguistics.

Yinhan Liu, Myle Ott, Naman Goyal, Jingfei Du, Mandar Joshi, Danqi Chen, Omer Levy, Mike Lewis, Luke Zettlemoyer, and Veselin Stoyanov. 2019. Roberta: A robustly optimized bert pretraining approach. *arXiv preprint arXiv:1907.11692*.

Ilya Loshchilov and Frank Hutter. 2019. Decoupled weight decay regularization. In *International Conference on Learning Representations*.

Andrew McCallum, Kedar Bellare, and Fernando Pereira. 2005. A conditional random field for discriminatively-trained finite-state string edit distance. In *Proceedings of the Twenty-First Conference on Uncertainty in Artificial Intelligence*, pages 388–395.

Zulfat Miftahutdinov and Elena Tutubalina. 2019. Deep neural models for medical concept normalization in user-generated texts. In *Proceedings of the 57th Annual Meeting of the Association for Computational Linguistics: Student Research Workshop*, pages 393–399.

Tomas Mikolov, Kai Chen, Greg Corrado, and Jeffrey Dean. 2013. Efficient estimation of word representations in vector space. In *1st International Conference on Learning Representations, ICLR 2013, Scottsdale, Arizona, USA, May 2-4, 2013, Workshop Track Proceedings*.

Nikhil Pattisapu, Sangameshwar Patil, Girish Palshikar, and Vasudeva Varma. 2020. Medical Concept Normalization by Encoding Target Knowledge. In *Proceedings of the Machine Learning for Health NeurIPS Workshop*, volume 116 of *Proceedings of Machine Learning Research*, pages 246–259. PMLR.

Matthew E Peters, Mark Neumann, Mohit Iyyer, Matt Gardner, Christopher Clark, Kenton Lee, and Luke Zettlemoyer. 2018. Deep contextualized word representations. In *Proceedings of NAACL-HLT*, pages 2227–2237.

Nils Reimers and Iryna Gurevych. 2019. Sentence-bert: Sentence embeddings using siamese bert-networks. In *Proceedings of the 2019 Conference on Empirical Methods in Natural Language Processing and the 9th International Joint Conference on Natural Language Processing (EMNLP-IJCNLP)*, pages 3973–3983.

Abeed Sarker, Maksim Belousov, Jasper Friedrichs, Kai Hakala, Svetlana Kiritchenko, Farrokh Mehryary, Sifei Han, Tung Tran, Anthony Rios, Ramakanth Kavuluru, et al. 2018. Data and systems for medication-related text classification and concept normalization from twitter: insights from the social media mining for health (smm4h)-2017

shared task. *Journal of the American Medical Informatics Association*, 25(10):1274–1283.

Kalyan Katikapalli Subramanyam and S Sangeetha. 2020. Deep contextualized medical concept normalization in social media text. *Procedia Computer Science*, 171:1353 – 1362. Third International Conference on Computing and Network Communications (CoCoNet'19).

Yoshimasa Tsuruoka, John McNaught, Jun'i; chi Tsujii, and Sophia Ananiadou. 2007. Learning string similarity measures for gene/protein name dictionary look-up using logistic regression. *Bioinformatics*, 23(20):2768–2774.

Elena Tutubalina, Zulfat Miftahutdinov, Sergey Nikolenko, and Valentin Malykh. 2018. Medical concept normalization in social media posts with recurrent neural networks. *Journal of biomedical informatics*, 84:93–102.

Thomas Wolf, Lysandre Debut, Victor Sanh, Julien Chaumond, Clement Delangue, Anthony Moi, Pierric Cistac, Tim Rault, Rémi Louf, Morgan Funtowicz, et al. 2019. Huggingface's transformers: State-of-the-art natural language processing. *ArXiv*, pages arXiv–1910.

Maryam Zolnoori, Kin Wah Fung, Timothy B Patrick, Paul Fontelo, Hadi Kharrazi, Anthony Faiola, Yi Shuan Shirley Wu, Christina E Eldredge, Jake Luo, Mike Conway, et al. 2019. A systematic approach for developing a corpus of patient reported adverse drug events: a case study for ssri and snri medications. *Journal of biomedical informatics*, 90:103091.

Incorporating Commonsense Knowledge Graph in Pretrained Models for Social Commonsense Tasks

Ting-Yun Chang[1], Yang Liu[2], Karthik Gopalakrishnan[2], Behnam Hedayatnia[2],
Pei Zhou[3], Dilek Hakkani-Tür[2] *

[1] Academia Sinica, Taiwan;
[2] Alexa AI, Amazon, USA;
[3] USC, USA

r06922168@ntu.edu.tw, {yangliud,karthgop,behnam,hakkanit}@amazon.com

Abstract

Pretrained language models have excelled at many NLP tasks recently; however, their social intelligence is still unsatisfactory. To enable this, machines need to have a more general understanding of our complicated world and develop the ability to perform commonsense reasoning besides fitting the specific downstream tasks. External commonsense knowledge graphs (KGs), such as ConceptNet, provide rich information about words and their relationships. Thus, towards general commonsense learning, we propose two approaches to *implicitly* and *explicitly* infuse such KGs into pretrained language models. We demonstrate our proposed methods perform well on SocialIQA, a social commonsense reasoning task, in both limited and full training data regimes.

1 Introduction

Empowering machines with commonsense has become a hot topic recently. Past research efforts for this problem include the construction of various data sets and models. Several commonsense data sets have been commonly used in past work to develop machines' commonsense capability (Talmor et al., 2019; Huang et al., 2019; Zellers et al., 2019; Sap et al., 2019b; Sakaguchi et al., 2019; Gordon et al., 2012; Rajani et al., 2019). In particular, SocialIQA (Sap et al., 2019b) is a multiple-choice QA data set for probing machine's emotional and social intelligence in a variety of everyday situations, which is the data set used in this study. To improve the modeling approaches for the SocialIQA and other commonsense tasks, Shwartz et al. (2020) and Bosselut and Choi (2019) focused on zero-shot setting using pretrained language models. Khashabi et al. (2020) reformulated the multi-choice setup used in most data sets as a generation task and

---

‡ Work was done while Ting-Yun Chang and Pei Zhou were interns at Amazon.

achieved impressive performance by fine-tuning T5 (Raffel et al., 2019). Recently there is an increasing effort to utilize external knowledge bases to incorporate commonsense information underlying the text (Shwartz et al., 2020; Mitra et al., 2019; Ji et al., 2020a,b).

While most prior work on SocialIQA utilized large pretrained language models (Devlin et al., 2019; Liu et al., 2019; Radford et al., 2018, 2019; Raffel et al., 2019), we argue that such a challenging task requires commonsense reasoning of social events, and simply fine-tuning the model to fit the task is insufficient. We believe it would be beneficial if the model can learn from knowledge-rich resources such as ConceptNet (Liu and Singh, 2004), and thus have a broader and deeper understanding of the information not present in the provided context and answer candidates.

In this paper, we propose two approaches tailored to large pretrained language models to utilize existing knowledge graph (KGs) for downstream commonsense tasks. The first approach leverages the KGs *implicitly* by pretraining on the relevant tuples to the SocialIQA task, while the second one maintains a dynamic knowledge base during fine-tuning, utilizing KGs *explicitly* via an attention mechanism. Our experiments demonstrate the effectiveness of both approaches on SocialIQA under limited and full training data regimes, and the critical role of relevant knowledge.

2 Problem Formulation and Baseline

In SocialIQA, given a context C of an event and a corresponding question Q, the goal is to select the correct choice from the answer set $A = (A_1, A_2, A_3)$. An example is shown in Figure 1, with the provided context, question, and three answer candidates.

A typical approach (as used in   Sap et al.

Proceedings of Deep Learning Inside Out (DeeLIO):
The First Workshop on Knowledge Extraction and Integration for Deep Learning Architectures, pages 74–79
Online, November 19, 2020. ©2020 Association for Computational Linguistics

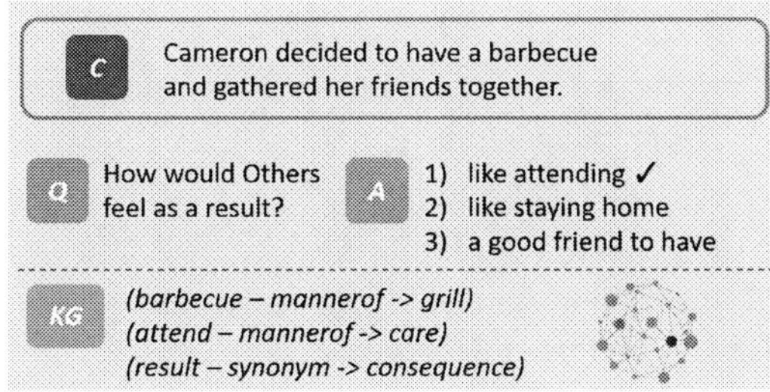

Figure 1: An instance in SocialIQA and our retrieved tuples from ConceptNet.

(2019b)) for solving this kind of multiple-choice problems with a pretrained Transformer-based language model is by concatenating C, Q, and A_i with a separator token, and then letting the model output a score via a multi-layer perceptron (MLP) built on top of the final hidden representation of the classifier token $[CLS]$. Finally, scores for each data point are normalized across all (C, Q, A_i) instances with softmax, and cross-entropy loss is applied for model training.

Since RoBERTa (Liu et al., 2019) has shown competitive performance on the SocialIQA task, we use it as a baseline model in this study. Furthermore, in addition to multiple-choice classification, we perform masked language modeling (MLM) (Devlin et al., 2019), masking 15% tokens in the concatenation of C, Q, and the correct answer A_{y^*}, when fine-tuning on the SocialIQA task.

3 Incorporating Commonsense Knowledge Graph

In this section, we introduce two methods to incorporate a given KG into our pretrained model. We experiment with both ATOMIC (Sap et al., 2019a) and ConceptNet (Liu and Singh, 2004) as our KGs.

- **ATOMIC** focuses on inferential knowledge of everyday situations. Each node in ATOMIC is a social event, containing 9 *if-then* relation types. Note that though SocialIQA is derived from ATOMIC, it has been rewritten by crowd workers (Sap et al., 2019b).

- **ConceptNet** represents general words and phrases that people use and the commonsense relationships between them, such as *IsA, At-Location, Desires, Synonym*.

3.1 Querying Knowledge Graph

For both methods, we first extract keywords in the input data to query ConceptNet using only the lemmatized *noun, verb, adjective* words in (C, Q, A) as queries, with stop words excluded. First, we find the node corresponding to each query in the KG, and retrieve all the connected tuples *(query, relation with weight, tail)* within one hop. We then sort all the retrieved tuples by their $relation\ weight \times query's\ idf$, and keep the top-$k$ tuples for each data point.[1] In Figure 1, the bottom shows examples of retrieved tuples from ConceptNet for an instance in the SocialIQA data. Note that since ATOMIC highly overlaps with SocialIQA, we do not extract keywords to query the KG but pretrain the model on the entire KG.

3.2 Pretraining Language Models on Retrieved Concepts

In the first approach, we leverage the KG via infusing it into the pretraining step. Using the SocialIQA data as queries, we first retrieve tuples from the KGs as described above, and then convert them to textual forms. To enable this conversion, we hand-crafted templates for different relations. For example, a tuple in ConceptNet *(barbecue, hascontext, cooking)* would be converted into "*barbecue is a word used in the context of cooking.*" When using ATOMIC, because there are some blanks and unknown names such as "*PersonX meets _ for lunch*", we replace *PersonX* and *PersonY* with two different common *last names* to avoid gender bias, and following Mitra et al. (2019), we utilize the pretrained BERT-large's MLM head to fill in the blanks. After these steps, we build a corpus derived from concepts in the KGs relevant to the SocialIQA task.

We then train our RoBERTa-based models using such a corpus with the MLM loss (Devlin et al., 2019), masking either the head or tail entities, e.g., *barbecue* or *cooking*. Further training the pretrained models on such a corpus is expected to implicitly learn commonsense knowledge in the KGs that is relevant to SocialIQA. Finally, we continue to fine-tune the model on the SocialIQA task, similar to the baseline described in Section 2.

---

[1]Initially, we tried to extract the shortest path between keywords in the KG similar to Shwartz et al. (2020). However, as ConceptNet does not disambiguate word senses, we observed that such paths usually deviate from the original semantics. For example, consider "*C: Cameron decided to have a barbecue and gathered her friends together. A_1: like attending.*" The path we found between *barbecue* and *attend* is: *barbecue–isa→dish–synonym→serve←synonym–attend*. Similarly, since we found that some of the retrieved tuples within one hop are already irrelevant, we did not use more hops to retrieve relevant tuples.

3.3 Modeling Concepts Via Attention

In the second approach, we treat the retrieved tuples as items in a cached external knowledge base (KB), which dynamically changes based on every input instance. The model can then decide the importance of each item and leverage them accordingly.

KG Attentive Representations Motivated by previous work on question answering (Seo et al., 2017; Zhu et al., 2018; Wang et al., 2018; Huang et al., 2019), which uses attention among different segments of the input, here we treat the knowledge tuples as a new segment. Specifically, we concatenate the top-k retrieved tuples and map them into the space of RoBERTa's final hidden representations as an additional segment, and then attend to it using RoBERTa's last hidden representation to generate a new KG-attentive sentence representation.

Formally, let d be the hidden dimension, l be the sequence length of the input, $H_R \in \mathbb{R}^{l \times d}$ be RoBERTa's final hidden representation for the SocialIQA input sequence for a given candidate, and $H_{KG} \in \mathbb{R}^{k \times d}$ is the representation of the k encoded tuples. We attend to H_{KG} from H_R:

$$\hat{H}_R = H_R W_1 + \mathbf{1} * b_1^T,$$
$$\hat{H}_{KG} = H_{KG} W_1 + \mathbf{1} * b_1^T,$$
$$H_R^{KG} = Softmax(\frac{\hat{H}_R \hat{H}_{KG}^T}{\sqrt{d}}) H_{KG} \quad (1)$$

where $W_1 \in \mathbb{R}^{d \times d}$, $\mathbf{1} \in \mathbb{R}^l$ (a vector of all-ones), $b_1 \in \mathbb{R}^d$, and $H_R^{KG} \in \mathbb{R}^{l \times d}$ is the KG-attentive sentence representation.

Encoding Knowledge Tuples To obtain H_{KG}, we need to represent the tuples and project them to the RoBERTa's hidden representation space. We first convert the tuples into fixed embeddings with three different approaches:

- Pretrained KG embeddings based on ConceptNet via TransE (Bordes et al., 2013; Zhou et al., 2018).

- Pretrained word embeddings retrofitted by ConceptNet (Speer et al., 2017), where its training adjusts a word's embeddings to be close to those of its neighbors in the graph.

- Encoded tuple-converted text with templates and pretrained universal sentence encoder (USE) (Cer et al., 2018), a Transformer-based

sentence encoder that transforms text into vectors that can be used for text classification and semantic similarity.

Then we transform these embeddings of the top-k tuples using a linear transformation that is learned during training, and then concatenate all of them to form the knowledge representation $H_{KG} \in \mathbb{R}^{k \times d}$.

Fusion Layer We then combine H_R and H_R^{KG} with a *fusion layer*. Formally,

$$\tilde{H}_R = [H_R \oplus H_R^{KG}] W_2 + \mathbf{1} * b_2^T,$$
$$\tilde{h}_R = max\{\tilde{H}_R\},$$
$$S = MLP(\tilde{h}_R), \quad (2)$$

where we first transform the concatenation (denoted by $\oplus$) of H_R and H_R^{KG} to $\tilde{H}_R \in \mathbb{R}^{l \times d}$, and then perform max-pooling along the sequence dimension to obtain the condensed representation $\tilde{h}_R \in d$ for classification. Finally, we get the score $S \in \mathbb{R}^1$ for each answer via a multilayer perceptron (MLP). The model architecture is illustrated in Figure 2.

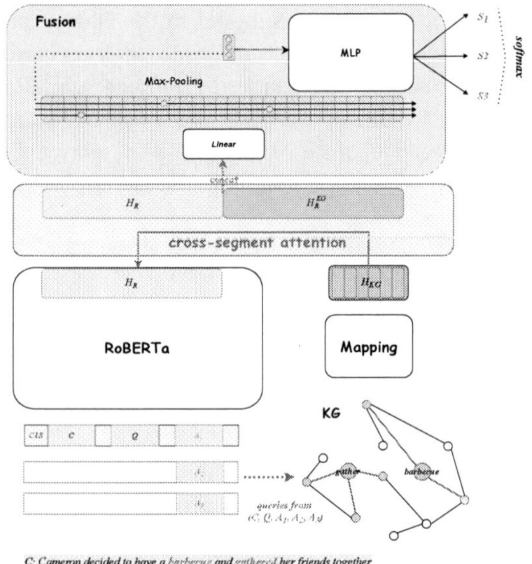

Figure 2: Illustration of the proposed model incorporating external KGs for SocialIQA.

4 Experiments and Results

4.1 Experimental Setup

We use Hugging Face's `transformers` toolkit[2] and train our models on the 33k SocialIQA training

[2]https://huggingface.co/transformers/

instances, running hyper-parameters search over the learning rate in $\{5e-6, 1e-5, 2.5e-5\}$, and the *effective batch size* (number of GPUs $\times$ batch size per GPU $\times$ gradient accumulation steps) in $\{8, 16, 32\}$ for the proposed models and baselines respectively, and report their best performance on the dev set. We set the maximum returned tuples of each instance to $k = 30$.

4.2 Results

Table 1 shows the results on the dev set using different methods. We can see the first pretraining method using ATOMIC performs well, which is not surprising since it is the partial source of SocialIQA, and it is likely that the model may have seen related information about dev/test set during pretraining. On the other hand, the performance of ConceptNet-pretrain suggests that without a sophisticated design, exposing too many irrelevant tuples from ConceptNet in pretraining may compromise the model's performance on the downstream task. This finding is consistent with Gururangan et al. (2020). In our analysis, we did find that some of the extracted tuples are noisy, mainly because ConceptNet is comprehensive, but it does not contain annotations for different word senses.

Model	Accuracy (%)
Baseline Sap et al. (2019b)	78.0
ConceptNet-pretrain	76.8
ATOMIC-pretrain	**79.1**
ConceptNet-attention-TransE	78.5
ConceptNet-attention-Retrofit	78.7
ConceptNet-attention-USE	**79.2**

Table 1: Comparison of different models on the SocialIQA dev set.

The second method, however, seems promising. Among its three variants (see Section 3.3), the one using TransE as knowledge embeddings performed the worst, possibly because of its much smaller dimension of the pretrained TransE embeddings ($\in \mathbb{R}^{100}$) we adopted[3], compared to the other two variants (300 and 512) and RoBERTa-large's hidden dimension $d = 1024$. These results indicate that the second method of using ConceptNet is less sensitive to the noisy tuples because of the explicit attention mechanism, which allows the model to utilize the items in the KG selectively.

4.3 Few-Shot Learning

To demonstrate the effective utilization of external KGs, we now investigate performance in the limited training data regime. We fine-tuned our model on 5%, 10%, and 20% of SocialIQA's training instances, respectively. We compare both the explicit method, ConceptNet-attention-USE, and the implicit method, ATOMIC-pretrain, with the typical implementation of RoBERTa as the baseline. We apply MLM on SocialIQA fine-tuning (Section 2) in all the three models, since we have found it helps stabilize the training.

The results in Table 2 show that ATOMIC-pretrain performs especially well, even though it only relies on the pretraining phase to infuse the ATOMIC graph, reaching 72.9% when only 5% of training instances are used. ConceptNet-attention-USE performs the worst on the 5% setting, but better than the baseline on the other two settings. Note that a BERT-base model trained on the full training set only achieves 63.3% (Sap et al., 2019b), showing that RoBERTa model may already learn some commonsense in its pretraining phase. Furthermore, our proposed methods demonstrate that with the external knowledge graphs on relevant domains, we can obtain even better results when only a small number of annotated training instances for the downstream task are available.

	5%	10%	20%
RoBERTa + MLM	70.3	72.3	73.0
ATOMIC-pretrain	72.9	73.3	76.0
ConceptNet-attn-USE	69.7	73.3	74.6

Table 2: Results (accuracy %) when using few training instances for model fine-tuning.

5 Conclusion

In this paper, we propose two methods to introduce KGs into pretrained language models for commonsense tasks. The first one implicitly infuses relevant knowledge into MLM pretraining, while the second method uses the attention mechanism to allow pretrained language models to explicitly utilize the dynamic query tuples. Our experiments on the SocialIQA task show that leveraging external KGs via attention outperforms the baseline pretrained language models, and the quality of the relevant graphs matters for downstream task performance. Our work can be further improved by designing better algorithms for KG retrieval in the future. Although our experiments have focused on SocialIQA with ConceptNet and ATOMIC, our method can be generalized to other similar tasks to leverage knowledge graphs.

References

Antoine Bordes, Nicolas Usunier, Alberto Garcia-Duran, Jason Weston, and Oksana Yakhnenko. 2013. Translating embeddings for modeling multi-relational data. In *Advances in neural information processing systems*, pages 2787–2795.

Antoine Bosselut and Yejin Choi. 2019. Dynamic knowledge graph construction for zero-shot commonsense question answering. *arXiv preprint arXiv:1911.03876*.

Daniel Cer, Yinfei Yang, Sheng-yi Kong, Nan Hua, Nicole Limtiaco, Rhomni St John, Noah Constant, Mario Guajardo-Cespedes, Steve Yuan, Chris Tar, et al. 2018. Universal sentence encoder for english. In *Proceedings of the 2018 Conference on Empirical Methods in Natural Language Processing: System Demonstrations*, pages 169–174.

Jacob Devlin, Ming-Wei Chang, Kenton Lee, and Kristina Toutanova. 2019. BERT: Pre-training of deep bidirectional transformers for language understanding. In *Proceedings of the 2019 Conference of the North American Chapter of the Association for Computational Linguistics (NAACL)*, pages 4171–4186.

Andrew Gordon, Zornitsa Kozareva, and Melissa Roemmele. 2012. Semeval-2012 task 7: Choice of plausible alternatives: An evaluation of commonsense causal reasoning. In * SEM 2012: The First Joint Conference on Lexical and Computational Semantics–Volume 1: Proceedings of the main conference and the shared task, and Volume 2: Proceedings of the Sixth International Workshop on Semantic Evaluation (SemEval 2012)*, pages 394–398.

Suchin Gururangan, Ana Marasović, Swabha Swayamdipta, Kyle Lo, Iz Beltagy, Doug Downey, and Noah A Smith. 2020. Don't stop pretraining: Adapt language models to domains and tasks. *arXiv preprint arXiv:2004.10964*.

Lifu Huang, Ronan Le Bras, Chandra Bhagavatula, and Yejin Choi. 2019. Cosmos qa: Machine reading comprehension with contextual commonsense reasoning. In *Proceedings of the 2019 Conference on Empirical Methods in Natural Language Processing and the 9th International Joint Conference on Natural Language Processing (EMNLP-IJCNLP)*, pages 2391–2401.

Haozhe Ji, Pei Ke, Shaohan Huang, Furu Wei, and Minlie Huang. 2020a. Generating commonsense explanation by extracting bridge concepts from reasoning paths. *AACL-IJCNLP*.

Haozhe Ji, Pei Ke, Shaohan Huang, Furu Wei, Xiaoyan Zhu, and Minlie Huang. 2020b. Language generation with multi-hop reasoning on commonsense knowledge graph. In *Proceedings of the 2020 Conference on Empirical Methods in Natural Language Processing (EMNLP)*.

Daniel Khashabi, Tushar Khot, Ashish Sabharwal, Oyvind Tafjord, Peter Clark, and Hannaneh Hajishirzi. 2020. Unifiedqa: Crossing format boundaries with a single qa system. *arXiv preprint arXiv:2005.00700*.

Hugo Liu and Push Singh. 2004. Conceptnet—a practical commonsense reasoning tool-kit. *BT technology journal*, 22(4):211–226.

Yinhan Liu, Myle Ott, Naman Goyal, Jingfei Du, Mandar Joshi, Danqi Chen, Omer Levy, Mike Lewis, Luke Zettlemoyer, and Veselin Stoyanov. 2019. Roberta: A robustly optimized bert pretraining approach. *arXiv preprint arXiv:1907.11692*.

Arindam Mitra, Pratyay Banerjee, Kuntal Pal, Swaroop Mishra, and Chitta Baral. 2019. How additional knowledge can improve natural language commonsense question answering? *arXiv preprint arXiv:1909.08855*.

Alec Radford, Karthik Narasimhan, Tim Salimans, and Ilya Sutskever. 2018. Improving language understanding by generative pre-training.

Alec Radford, Jeffrey Wu, Rewon Child, David Luan, Dario Amodei, and Ilya Sutskever. 2019. Language models are unsupervised multitask learners.

Colin Raffel, Noam Shazeer, Adam Roberts, Katherine Lee, Sharan Narang, Michael Matena, Yanqi Zhou, Wei Li, and Peter J Liu. 2019. Exploring the limits of transfer learning with a unified text-to-text transformer. *arXiv preprint arXiv:1910.10683*.

Nazneen Fatema Rajani, Bryan McCann, Caiming Xiong, and Richard Socher. 2019. Explain yourself! leveraging language models for commonsense reasoning. In *Proceedings of the 57th Annual Meeting of the Association for Computational Linguistics*, pages 4932–4942.

Keisuke Sakaguchi, Ronan Le Bras, Chandra Bhagavatula, and Yejin Choi. 2019. Winogrande: An adversarial winograd schema challenge at scale. In *Proceedings of the AAAI Conference on Artificial Intelligence*, pages 8732–8740.

Maarten Sap, Ronan Le Bras, Emily Allaway, Chandra Bhagavatula, Nicholas Lourie, Hannah Rashkin, Brendan Roof, Noah A Smith, and Yejin Choi. 2019a. Atomic: An atlas of machine commonsense for if-then reasoning. In *Proceedings of the AAAI Conference on Artificial Intelligence*, volume 33, pages 3027–3035.

Maarten Sap, Hannah Rashkin, Derek Chen, Ronan Le Bras, and Yejin Choi. 2019b. Social iqa: Commonsense reasoning about social interactions. In *Proceedings of the 2019 Conference on Empirical Methods in Natural Language Processing and the 9th International Joint Conference on Natural Language Processing (EMNLP-IJCNLP)*, pages 4453–4463.

Minjoon Seo, Aniruddha Kembhavi, Ali Farhadi, and Hannaneh Hajishirzi. 2017. Bidirectional attention flow for machine comprehension. In *International Conference on Learning Representations*.

Vered Shwartz, Peter West, Ronan Le Bras, Chandra Bhagavatula, and Yejin Choi. 2020. Unsupervised commonsense question answering with self-talk. *arXiv preprint arXiv:2004.05483*.

Robyn Speer, Joshua Chin, and Catherine Havasi. 2017. Conceptnet 5.5: An open multilingual graph of general knowledge. In *Proceedings of the AAAI Conference on Artificial Intelligence*.

Alon Talmor, Jonathan Herzig, Nicholas Lourie, and Jonathan Berant. 2019. CommonsenseQA: A question answering challenge targeting commonsense knowledge. In *Proceedings of the 2019 Conference of the North American Chapter of the Association for Computational Linguistics (NAACL)*, pages 4149–4158.

Liang Wang, Meng Sun, Wei Zhao, Kewei Shen, and Jingming Liu. 2018. Yuanfudao at semeval-2018 task 11: Three-way attention and relational knowledge for commonsense machine comprehension. In *Proceedings of The 12th International Workshop on Semantic Evaluation*, pages 758–762.

Rowan Zellers, Ari Holtzman, Yonatan Bisk, Ali Farhadi, and Yejin Choi. 2019. HellaSwag: Can a machine really finish your sentence? In *Proceedings of the 57th Annual Meeting of the Association for Computational Linguistics*, pages 4791–4800.

Hao Zhou, Tom Young, Minlie Huang, Haizhou Zhao, Jingfang Xu, and Xiaoyan Zhu. 2018. Commonsense knowledge aware conversation generation with graph attention. In *IJCAI*.

Haichao Zhu, Furu Wei, Bing Qin, and Ting Liu. 2018. Hierarchical attention flow for multiple-choice reading comprehension. In *Proceedings of the AAAI Conference on Artificial Intelligence*.

Commonsense Statements Identification and Explanation with Transformer-based Encoders

Sonia-Teodora Cibu
Department of Computer Science
Technical University of Cluj-Napoca
Cluj-Napoca, Romania
sonia.teodora94@gmail.com

Anca Marginean
Department of Computer Science
Technical University of Cluj-Napoca
Cluj-Napoca, Romania
anca.marginean@cs.utcluj.ro

Abstract

In this work, we present our empirical attempt to identify the proper strategy of using Transformer Language Models to identify sentences consistent with commonsense. We tackle the first two tasks from the ComVE (Wang et al., 2020a) competition. The starting point for our work is the BERT assumption according to which a large number of NLP tasks can be solved with pre-trained Transformers with no substantial task-specific changes of the architecture. However, our experiments show that the encoding strategy can have a great impact on the quality of the fine-tuning. The combination between cross-encoding and multi-input models worked better than one cross-encoder and allowed us to achieve comparable results with the state-of-the-art without the use of any external data.

1 Introduction

For human beings, the answer to the question "Can we consider a statement consistent with commonsense?" comes natural even in the absence of a certain context. It is not only about understanding the words in the statement, but also about reasoning based on commonsense knowledge. Until recently, this was considered difficult for the machines (Ostermann et al., 2018), since it was considered that it requires a formal representation of an extremely large knowledge base equipped with a general inference mechanism.

In the Transformers era, the machines' deeper understanding of text has gained increasing attention. Transformers brought reduction of losses of semantics and connections in long text through the extensive use of attention mechanisms and the elimination of the recurrent connections and convolutions. Their good performance in recognizing complex semantic relations offered a faster starting point for the upcoming stacked layers of Transformers capable of generalizing with impressive results on downstream tasks.

SemEval-2020 Task 4, Commonsense Validation and Explanation (ComVE) (Wang et al., 2020a) addresses commonsense understanding in the problem of identifying the sentences which are inconsistent with commonsense and the reason for which they are inconsistent. On the basis of transfer learning using Transformers, our experiments explored the power of different Transformer models offered by huggingface PyTorch library on the data set provided in this competition. During our experiments, answers to the following questions were searched:

- Are Language Models strong enough to deliver a good result on commonsense understanding after having been fine-tuned with a significantly small amount of data comparable to the one used in the pre-training phase?

- Is freezing the Language Model a solution for better accuracy on a downstream task?

- Does a powerful encoder require a powerful decoder to perform sentence classification?

Our contribution is in identifying a suitable Transformer for these specific commonsense tasks, together with the suitable encoding and decoding strategies. Our conclusions are supported by empirical experiments, but the deeper understanding behind these conclusions requires further qualitative analysis which is not yet included.

2 Related Work

Pre-trained Transformer Language Models (LM) are the foundation of our work. Given a sequence of words, an LM estimates the probability distribution of the next word, where the latter can be any word from the vocabulary. Furthermore, given a fixed sentence, or succession of words, an LM can

Proceedings of Deep Learning Inside Out (DeeLIO):
The First Workshop on Knowledge Extraction and Integration for Deep Learning Architectures, pages 80–88
Online, November 19, 2020. ©2020 Association for Computational Linguistics

assign a probability to the whole sentence. Being trained on large sets of unlabeled text, LMs aim to capture the context dependent semantics of words and phrases.

ELMo (Peters et al., 2018) would be the first to look at from the historical point of view. It runs the input through a BiLSTM network gathering left and right context. The drawback stands in risking to derive mistaken context from the misplaced expressions.

BERT (Devlin et al., 2019) is a multi-layer bidirectional Transformer encoder with integrated self-attention mechanism. The volume of text on which BERT was pre-trained, totalling to 16GB of text, prepared the model for numerous NLP tasks, such as question answering and language understanding.

For solving the commonsense tasks, we looked for an LM which takes into consideration both ELMo and BERT advantages. XLNet (Yang et al., 2019) is a generalized autoregressive method (AR). The autoregressive language model is a contextualized method of predicting the next word considering either a forward or backward factorized context. The main flaw of the autoregressive method is that long-distance context is lost in detriment of close surroundings. XLNet solves this by maximizing the expected log-likelihood of a sequence thanks to the token's permutation operation providing context from both the left and right context. Reflecting on BERT's autoencoding technique and avoiding the [MASK] token impediment, XLNet uses the AR bidirectional context to offer meaning to the current token.

RoBERTa (Liu et al., 2019) is a replication of BERT. It is trained on $10\times$ bigger text corpus with larger batches and for a longer period, with elimination of the next sentence prediction objective and a dynamically change in the masking pattern. The vocabulary size is increased by using Byte-Pair-Encoding (Radford et al., 2018) instead of character-level encoding.

The majority of the participants in the ComVE competition (Wang et al., 2020a) used pre-trained LM. The top performing systems used also external knowledge either through the use of formal commonsense knowledge-bases, like ConceptNet, either through a second pre-training of the LM on text relevant for commonsense understanding.

We obtained comparable results with the top performing systems for the first two of the three tasks of the competition without any external sources. Our approach relies on a proper encoding strategy for the sentences or pairs of sentences-explanations.

3 Data Set

The ComVE data set was inspired by existing commonsense corpora, like Choice of Plausible Alternatives (COPA) (Roemmele et al., 2011) and Winograd Schema Challenge (WSC) (Levesque, 2011). The first two ComVE tasks involved two balanced corpora, consisting of a total of 10.000 train sentences and 997 dev sentences each.

In *Task A* of ComVE, the validation one, two statements that differ by one or several words are given without any other context (e.g. *He was sent to a (restaurant)/(hospital) for treatment after a car crash;*, or *Bob looks up a words in a (dictionary)/(shopping list)*). Besides the fact that no context is given, the strong resemblance of the inputs increases the request for a good understanding of the subtle meaning of words.

In *Task B*, the explanation one, a nonsense premise is given together with three possible explanations and it is asked to identify the most plausible explanation for the fact that the premise is inconsistent with commonsense. The premises are the statements classified as nonsense on the validation task. We give here an example:

- Premise: *Bob looks up a word in a shopping list.*

- Alternative explanations which justify the fact that the premise is inconsistent with commonsense:

    1. *words are too expensive to be listed on a shopping list,*
    2. *shopping lists don't tell the meaning of words,*
    3. *Bob doesn't know what to buy.*

A few preprocessing steps were done: we converted all the sentences into lowercase and final punctuation was added where it was missing, more specifically a '.' for statements and a '?' for the nonsense sentences in the second task.

4 Encoder/Decoder Architectures

In order to solve the commonsense tasks, we chose to focus on the final mission rather than on developing a brand-new model trained from scratch

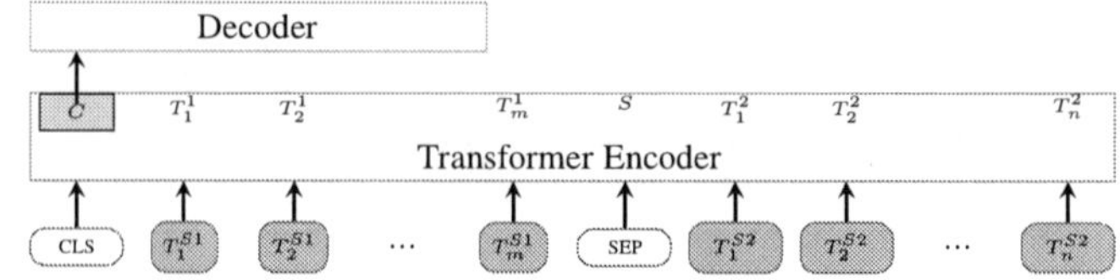

Figure 1: Task A: One single Model for 2 statements packed together

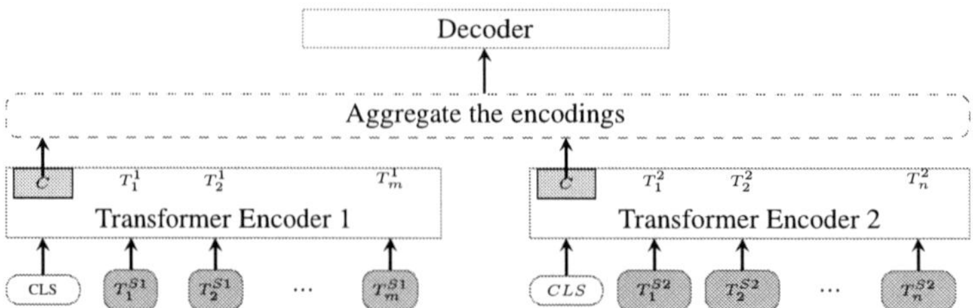

Figure 2: Task A: Two Models, one for each statement

on an enormous corpus of text. Therefore, our involvement stands in locating and perfecting an existing Transformer using only the ComVE data set, without any external knowledge base or additional dataset for a two phase training.

Transformers were built to generalize well over multiple NLP tasks. The common practice involves adding the right decoder on top of the Transformer encoder and fine tuning with a proper amount of data. The encoder extracts the semantics and the features from the inputs, while the decoder performs the classification.

Our first experiments targeted identification of the Transformer Language Model that is capable to extract the most relevant aspects for the classification of text into *consistent with commonsense* and *inconsistent*. The rest of the experiments targeted architectures which instead of including only one encoder for all the statements, include two or three encoders, one for each statement in case of *Task A*, respectively one for each pair of (Premise, Explanation) for *Task B*. *Task A* was reduced to a binary classification problem in which the model must decide the gibberish statement. As for *Task B*, selecting the good explanation was considered a multi-class classification. In the rest of this section, we detail the proposed architectures, while the corresponding experiments are described in section 5.

4.1 Encoding with a Single Language Model

For *Task A*, the input consists of two statements. When using only one LM to encode a sequence which packs both statements (see Fig. 1), the output representation is a result of the entire input.

An LM, used with an encoding objective and processing multiple sentences packed together into a single sequence, is called cross-encoder since it performs a full self-attention over the entire sequence (Humeau et al., 2020).

Interference in representations of the composed input is beneficial when there are cause-effect or similar relations between the phrases. But for both targeted tasks (*Task A* and *Task B*), we need to emphasize the differences in the semantics. Despite the fact that for some NLP multi-sentence tasks, cross-encoders work better than bi-encoders (Humeau et al., 2020), according to our experiments, detailed in section 5, a single LM was not able to perceive well enough the disparities. We assume that this happens due to the intrinsic interference present when encoding simultaneously two very similar statements (in terms of number of common words), but extremely different in their degree of consistency with commonsense. Consequently, we moved to a multi LMs approach for the encoding part.

4.2 Encoding with Multiple Language Models

In multi LMs approach, two (or three for the second task) similar language models are seen as the encoder (see Fig. 2, 3).

4.2.1 Multiple simple encoders

For *Task A*, each LM is processing an input statement. The encoding for all the special classification tokens CLS is aggregated through simple concatenation or other aggregation function, and fed into

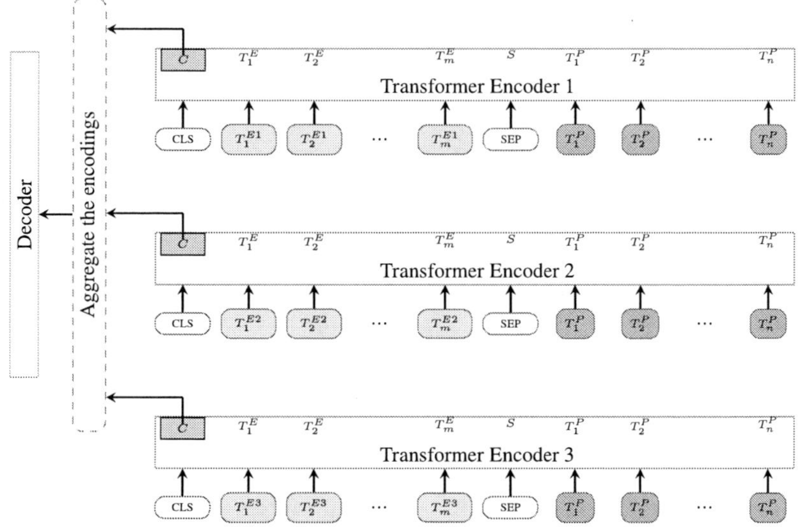

Figure 3: Task B: Three Models, one for each pair (Premise, Explanation)

the decoder (see Fig. 2). The weights of the two encoders are initialised with the same values, but during the train they have separate evolution, even though not completely independent, since they depend on the same loss function.

With this approach, distinct instances of one type of LM encode very similar or extremely different phrases. Therefore, the built representations capture unique features and semantics specific to the input. The disparities and the inconsistencies are easily depicted throughout the decoder. Two LMs separately encoding different statements are perceived as a bi-encoder (Humeau et al., 2020).

After observing the benefits and the drawbacks of bi-encoders and cross-encoders for the task at hand, we decided to rely the solution for the explanation task on a beneficial combination of them in the form of a multiple cross-encoders approach.

4.2.2 Multiple cross-encoders

The input data of the explanation task (*Task B*) is composed of four statements: one nonsense premise and three possible explanations. In order to decide which explanation is the most plausible for the nonsense premise, a strong explanation-relation must be captured among the premise and the explanation.

Capturing the justification relation between the phrases is accomplished by feeding the concatenation of each pair (premise-explanation) into a cross-encoder. Establishing which is the most intense relation is done by making use of three distinct

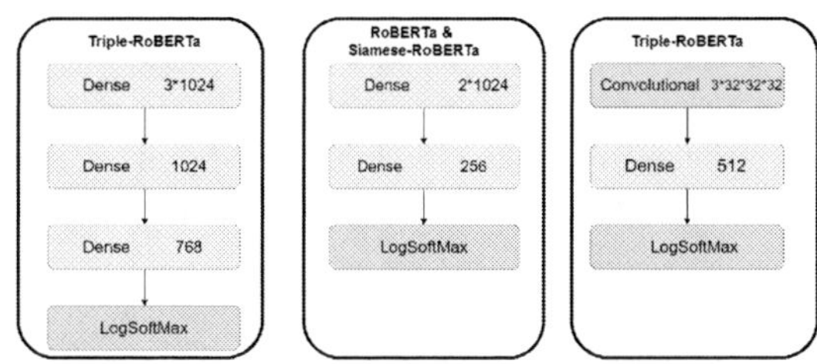

Figure 4: Structure of the decoder for Multi LMs

cross-encoders, one for each such pair (see Fig 3).

4.3 Decoder

Throughout the development stages, a reoccurring question was: how much of an improvement will a more complex decoder bring? Figure 4 depicts, from left to right, the structure of the tested decoders for *Task B* with multi LMs, for *Task A* with multi LMs, respectively for *Task B* with multi LMs. For the first two, the aggregation of the outputs for the 3 or 2 LMs is a simple concatenation, while convolution based concatenation is attempted in the last one.

Advancing from the Dense layers classifier to a basic Convolutional one (the right of Fig. 4), did not bring any increase in performance. The attempt was trivial and further experiments in this area are left for future research.

5 Experiments

For all the described architectures, we give details about the run experiments. For single LM encoding, we tested several language models, including BERT, XLNet and RoBERta. For multiple LMs encoding, we preferred RoBERTa due to the results obtained on the single LM approach. As future work, we plan to repeat all the multiple LMs experiments for other LMs than RoBERTa. This is needed in order to support our current conclusion that for the task at hand, multiple LMs encoding work better.

5.1 Experiments for Task A with a Single LM

5.1.1 BERT as single LM for task A

The first Transformer integrated as a unique LM as the encoder was BERT large uncased, which accepts as an input:

- a sequence of tokens, as follows: CLS ⟨ tokens of sentence 1 ⟩ [SEP] ⟨tokens of sentence 2⟩ [SEP].

- the classification token CLS is added in the first position to prepare the model for a classification task; the hidden state of this token is an aggregate representation of the classification task.

- token_type_ids specifies to which sentence each token belongs; this seems redundant after adding the separation token.

- attention_mask specifies which are input tokens and which are padding.

BERT's constraints specify that: i) all the inputs must have the same length, ii) the maximum input length is 512 tokens. In the data set, the sentences vary and the longest one has 27 tokens. Therefore, the used length will be:

- $27 * 2$ {two maximum length sentences}

- $+3$ {1*[CLS] + 2*[SEP] must have tokens}

- $+2$ {'.' *2, bonus token if needed}

- $+5$ {[PAD] until a power of 2 size} $= 64$

Model's documentation recommends [2, 4] Epoch, $[2e - 5, 5e - 5]$ constant learning rate and optimizer's epsilon $1e - 6$. We trained in batches of 32 for 4 Epochs using the AdamW optimizer as regularization mechanism, scoring a maximum of 0.89 accuracy on the dev set (Table 1).

On top of the LM were added two Dense layers activated by a TanH function. The investigation

Epoch	Max lr	Epsilon	Batch size	Accuracy
4	$2e - 5$	$1e - 8$	32	0.86
3	$5e - 5$	$1e - 6$	32	0.87
3	$5e - 5$	$1e - 6$	16	0.86
5	**$5e - 5$**	**$1e - 6$**	**32**	**0.89**
5	$2e - 5$	$1e - 8$	32	0.85
10	**$2e - 5$**	**$1e - 8$**	**32**	**0.89**

Table 1: Results for Task A with BERT as single LM.

Ep.	Max lr	Epsilon	Batch size	Accuracy
5	$5e - 5$	$1e - 6$	32	0.79
10	$2e - 5$	$1e - 8$	32	0.85
10	**$2e - 5$**	**$1e - 8$**	**64**	**0.86**

Table 2: Results for Task A with XLNet as single LM.

went further, training for more Epochs, adding a learning rate decay, but without any improvements to accuracy. Models' size is a limitation and the 16GB of text may not suffice for the model to gather all the meanings and contexts of the words.

5.1.2 XLNet as single LM for task A

Despite applying all the improvements made to BERT for the XLNet large, the latter did not outperform the former (see Table 2). The reason may be the fact that the context for a word is formed by factorizing the rest of the tokens. In case of mistaken tokens, the factorized permutation contributes to current token corrupting its meaning.

Nevertheless, this should elevate a sentence's probability of being nonsense, but the model is not strong enough yet.

5.1.3 RoBERTa as single LM for Task A

RoBERTa outperformed BERT and XLNET in almost all NLP tasks while offering a good generalization. The pre-training over the 160GB of text may be the reason for its performance.

In our case, using RoBERTa large with all the previous settings, running for 10 Epochs, resulted in a 0.91 accuracy (see Table 3).

The reported performances obtained by BERT, XLNET and RoBERTa used in the single model approach led us to the conclusion that all three are capable of building encodings which capture aspects related to the text's consistency with commonsense . We underline again that no additional dataset or knowledge base were included and the accuracy still reached values of 0.9. The rest of the experiments switched to the multi model approach.

Max lr	Eps	Batch size	Act. func.	Acc	F1
$2e{-}5$	$1e{-}8$	32	TanH	0.89	0.85
$2e{-}5$	**$1e{-}8$**	**32**	**ReLU**	**0.91**	**0.87**

Table 3: Results for Task A with RoBERTa as single LM.

Ep.	Max lr	Batch size	Act. func.	Acc	Hid. size	F1
10	$2e{-}5$	100	TanH	0.90	1024	0.90
30	$2e{-}5$	100	ReLU	0.94	1024	0.93
30	$5e{-}6$	128	ReLU	0.94	128	0.93
30	$5e{-}6$	128	SeLU	0.94	512	0.93
30	$5e{-}6$	**128**	**SeLU**	**0.95**	**256**	**0.95**

Table 4: Results for Task A with two instances of RoBERTa.

Ep.	Max lr	Batch size	Act. func.	Acc.	Hid. size	F1
30	$1e{-}5$	128	SeLU	0.95	256	0.95
30	$5e{-}6$	128	**SeLU**	0.96	**256**	**0.96**
30	$5e{-}6$	128	SeLU	0.96	256	0.95
30	$5e{-}6$	180	SeLU	0.95	256	0.94

Table 5: Results for Task A with two instances of RoBERTa with Symmetric Update.

5.2 Experiments for Task A and Task B with Multiple LMs

5.2.1 RoBERTa as multi LMs for Task A

In all previous experiments for single model, the LM was used as a cross-encoder, meaning that for the two input sentences each token will consider not only the phrase it belongs to, but also tokens from the other phrase. It is worth mentioning that each token will see itself in similar context twice.

When using cross-encoders, out of the two sentences, a wrong token has no other tokens to pay attention to. At the same time, a correct token, but placed in the wrong sentence, might look for meaning inside the correct sentence. We use here the term "wrong" as similar to "inconsistent with commonsense".

Given this condition and aspiring to evaluate the sentences independently from one another, we used the multiple models approach. This is similar to Siamese-RoBERTa (Reimers and Gurevych, 2019) but used in an almost bi-encoder fashion. As described in Fig. 3, two RoBERTa models are trained together for *Task A*. Each is fed with one sentence; the output of the CLS token is concatenated and then passed through two Dense layers, using TanH activation function, or ReLU or SeLU, with a dropout of 0.1. Our multi LMs encoding do not work as full bi-encoders, as for the later, the forward propagation is performed separated. Furthermore, in our case, the backpropagation depends on the concatenation of the encoders results, while in case of bi-encoders it is done independently for both included LMs.

We observe that the size of the classifier and the size of the mini batches influence the convergence speed of the network (see Table 4). By analysing the results, the transition from a single cross-encoder LM to multi LMs confirms that observing the input statements independently works better since each LM assembles context only from within.

We observed that the TanH activation function provides significantly lower accuracy than ReLU. The size of the classifier appears to have a strong impact on the convergence speed. With a small hidden size, the model converges slower and hits a higher accuracy score than with a larger size, which converges rapidly but stops improving. On the contrary, a larger size for the mini batches improves the results.

The used optimizer was AdamW with a linear learning rate decay and no warm-up steps. An early stopping mechanism was integrated which ends the fine-tuning after 10 Epochs if the F1 score did not improve. Choosing the F1 score as the monitored metric is the consequence of observing that the loss value increases after reaching a minimum, but the evaluation metrics are not very much affected.

For this setup, a RoBERTa large model was used, on an NVIDIA V100 32GB running at most for 38 minutes, 1 minute per Epoch with batch sizes varying from 32 to 128, and classifier's hidden size ranging from 128-2048.

5.2.2 RoBERTa as multi LMs with Symmetric Update for Task A

In the previous experiment, each RoBERTa encoder would see only one half of the statements pair during the training and the evaluation. For the models to work as Siamese, their weights update should be much more similar. To solve this inconsistency problem, we integrated a mechanism in which, during an Epoch, both permutations of the statements pair are consecutively fed into the model.

The convergence speed was greatly improved in some cases because of the double weight update during an Epoch. This method increased the met-

Ep.	Max lr	Warm-up Steps.	Act. Func.	Acc./F1
30	$1e-5$	1570	SeLU	0.89 / 0.89
30	$2e-5$	2000	SeLU	0.88 / 0.88

Table 6: Results for Task B with three instances of RoBERTa using RMSProb.

Max lr	Warm-up steps	Act. Func.	Acc.	Hid. size	F1
$5e-6$	2000	SeLU	0.89	768	0.89
$1e-5$	1570	SeLU	0.91	768	0.91

Table 7: Results for Task B with three instances of RoBERTa using AdamW.

Max lr	Warm-up steps.	Kernel size	Acc.	Hid. size	F1
$5e-6$	2000	3	0.89	768	0.89
$1e-5$	2000	9	0.90	768	0.90

Table 8: Results for Task B with three instances of RoBERTa using Convolution.

rics to 0.96 as seen in Table 5, but it also confirmed that the concatenation of the representations suffices for the network to update its parameters in an almost symmetric manner.

5.2.3 Three RoBERTa as multi LMs for Task B

The encoder for the explanation task was influenced by the results on the validation task with single/multi LMs. Since cross-encoding worked well, but multiple LMs improved the obtained performance, for Task B we employed multiple cross-encoders. For this task, the system should not only derive semantics from the sentences, but also evaluate its relatedness with the premise's context. As detailed in Fig. 3, we used a cross-encoder for each pair premise-explanation. The four sentences were turned into three pairs fed in a parallel manner into the network. For the moment, the encoder consists of three RoBERTa models processing each pair.

Observing from the previous experiment that a similar weights update does not bring an impressive improvement, each model will see only a pair through the fine-tuning and evaluation process.

The optimizers used for these experiments were RMSProb (Table 6, with batch size = 64) and AdamW (Table 7, with batch size = 32), with learning rate decay and warm-up steps. The integrated decoders consisted of three Dense Layers activated by a SeLU function, as the previous experiments, or a Convolutional Layer (Table 8). Similar to *Task A*, the convolutional based decoder did not improve the results, although further experiments are needed. The most important hyperparameter was the order of the statements inside the pairs. RoBERTa is a bidirectional Language Model, hence the relation inference appears to be emphasised better when the justification comes first.

6   Discussions

The results revealed the importance of the amount of text on which the LMs were pre-trained. The model's size also has significance, as larger models are better at generalizations.

A single Transformer Language Model delivers good results after fine-tuning on a comparable small amount of data. Additionally, the fine-tuning does not seem to alter the previous knowledge accumulated by the model.

This raised the question whether it is necessary to fine-tune the model on a specific task if the LM was already trained on a large text corpus, or is it possible to freeze the model. Consequently, we used a RoBERTa Large model, added a classifier on top and trained only the classifier on the provided corpus. Freezing the model obstructed LM's capabilities and it delivered poor results, similar to random guessing.

Even when we worked with two RoBERTa Large models coupled as Siamese but with complete freeze, the results were close to randomness, confirming that the LM adjusts its behaviour based on the task. It implies that a Transformer may be considered as a good encoder, but it needs adjustments in the form of fine-tuning.

Another observation regards the needed decoder. A 2 RoBERTa Large model is a formidable model with powerful generalization capabilities, but it does not incorporate enough knowledge to correctly classify a sentence as nonsense or consistent with commonsense if on top of it a very simple two layers classifier is added.

As the results showed, the LMs, especially bidirectional LMs are an excellent starting point in solving commonsense tasks (at least as they are formulated in the ComVE tasks). From our current experiments, multiple model approach works better than single one. Multiple cross-encoders with RoBERTa Large is a capable architecture which combines and leverages the benefits of both encoder (cross/bi) techniques. Our results show that it can be further improved, but it still provides good enough performance.

When using the same decoder, freezing the LM resulted in extremely low performance, while fine tuning the LM reached accuracy values higher than 0.9. In the same time, with the same LM, but different decoders, the performance changed. Consequently, we could assert that we need a good encoding, which can be attained even with a small dataset from the pre-trained LM, but we also need a good decoder. However, the set of the experiments need to be extended in order to check the presumption that multiple LMs work better than single LMs not only in case of RoBERTa, but also other LMs.

6.1 Comparison with Related Findings

According to the results of the competition (Wang et al., 2020a), making use of pre-trained Language Models seems to be the logical direction in solving an NLP task which requires commonsense reasoning. The techniques in which the advantages of LMs are leveraged and the patience in finding the optimum set of hyperparameters appear to dictate the position of the result on the ComVE competition leaderboard.

In Table 9 all the architectures are based on Transformer LMs, either BERT or RoBERTa (Saeedi et al., 2020); other LMs were tested as well, but poor results were delivered. Either multiple LMs were introduced in the architecture(Dash et al., 2020), together with knowledge bases such as ConceptNet (Zhao et al., 2020) or prolonged pre-training of LMs for the network to benefit from additional knowledge (Xing et al., 2020). In (Wang et al., 2020b), (Wan and Huang, 2020), extra-words were added in the input.

An impressive approach was the use of the trained model and knowledge for the task of validation in the scope of helping the explanation model in making its choice and vice-versa, in the process of subtask level transfer learning (Liu et al., 2020).

When comparing the obtained results, even without the addition of extra knowledge from Concept-Net or the prolonged training, with reproducible results accompanied by papers from the competition leaderboard, it appears that the ones obtained through our approach manage to score a place among the best ones.

6.2 Future Work

Background Knowledge As mentioned, the knowledge of our solutions relies only on the information congregated in the RoBERTa pre-training

Rank TaskA	Rank TaskB	Team Name	Acc. Dev A	Acc. Dev B
1	2	ECNU	96.7	94.68
1	3	IIE-NLP-NUT	96.7	94.5
2	5	KaLM	96.3	93.2
3	**6**	**Ours**	**96.1**	**91.11**
4	-	CS-NLP	96.08	-
5	1	LMVE	95.91	96.39
6	7	CS-NET	95.2	89.7
7	4	CUHK	95.1	93.5

Table 9: Comparison with related findings

stage and the targeted data set. RoBERTa's expertise can be enlarged, adding background knowledge from lexical bases as WordNet and knowledge bases as ConceptNet. We consider that offering a larger bag of meaning for each token may associate the current context with one of its definitions, contributing to a stronger connection between the context and the token.

A similar situation may occur when the bloomer token is evaluated. The definitions supplied by the additional bases might establish an erroneous binding with the current context. It might happen that delivering all the connotations for a word will not necessarily improve the results.

Strong Classifier Our architectures have on top two or three Dense layers as a decoder which performs the classification task. It has been suggested in the paper (Devlin et al., 2019) that a complex decoder is not necessary for the model to deliver a good outcome.

The encoder's capabilities are still limited by the classifier's simplicity. Aggregating information from a sequence of tokens and using only the output of the [CLS] restricts the LMs generalization over the input. Feeding into decoder all the outputs from the last hidden states might improve the outcome.

7 Conclusions

In this paper we evaluated three Transformer Language Models, BERT, XLNet, and RoBERTa, for the commonsense validation and explanation problems proposed in Sem-Eval 2020 ComVE. The experiments have shown that the self-attention mechanism used by BERT and RoBERTa models is more suited for the commonsense tasks.

We also leveraged the complexity of the model by using two Language Models to capture the independent sense for each input sentence. Two separate models are more capable to emphasize the subtle disparities from the input sentences.

Furthermore, in order to select the the right explanation for the inconsistency of the premise with commonsense, we used an architecture with three RoBERTa, each one working as a cross-encoder for pairs (premise, explanation).

References

Soumya Ranjan Dash, Sandeep Routray, Prateek Varshney, and Ashutosh Modi. 2020. CS-NET at SemEval-2020 Task 4: Siamese BERT for ComVE. *CoRR*, abs/2007.10830.

Jacob Devlin, Ming-Wei Chang, Kenton Lee, and Kristina Toutanova. 2019. BERT: Pre-training of deep bidirectional transformers for language understanding. In *Proceedings of the 2019 Conference of the North American Chapter of the Association for Computational Linguistics: Human Language Technologies, Volume 1 (Long and Short Papers)*, pages 4171–4186, Minneapolis, Minnesota. Association for Computational Linguistics.

Samuel Humeau, Kurt Shuster, Marie-Anne Lachaux, and Jason Weston. 2020. Poly-encoders: Architectures and Pre-training Strategies for Fast and Accurate Multi-sentence Scoring. In *8th International Conference on Learning Representations, ICLR 2020, Addis Ababa, Ethiopia, April 26-30, 2020*. OpenReview.net.

Hector J. Levesque. 2011. The Winograd Schema Challenge. In *Logical Formalizations of Commonsense Reasoning, Papers from the 2011 AAAI Spring Symposium, Technical Report SS-11-06, Stanford, California, USA, March 21-23, 2011*. AAAI.

Shilei Liu, Yu Guo, Bochao Li, and Feiliang Ren. 2020. LMVE at SemEval-2020 Task 4: Commonsense Validation and Explanation using Pretraining Language Model. *CoRR*, abs/2007.02540.

Yinhan Liu, Myle Ott, Naman Goyal, Jingfei Du, Mandar Joshi, Danqi Chen, Omer Levy, Mike Lewis, Luke Zettlemoyer, and Veselin Stoyanov. 2019. RoBERTa: A Robustly Optimized BERT Pretraining Approach. *CoRR*, abs/1907.11692.

Simon Ostermann, Michael Roth, Ashutosh Modi, Stefan Thater, and Manfred Pinkal. 2018. SemEval-2018 Task 11: Machine Comprehension Using Commonsense Knowledge. In *Proceedings of The 12th International Workshop on Semantic Evaluation*, pages 747–757, New Orleans, Louisiana. Association for Computational Linguistics.

Matthew Peters, Mark Neumann, Mohit Iyyer, Matt Gardner, Christopher Clark, Kenton Lee, and Luke Zettlemoyer. 2018. Deep Contextualized Word Representations. In *Proceedings of the 2018 Conference of the North American Chapter of the Association for Computational Linguistics: Human Language Technologies, Volume 1 (Long Papers)*, pages 2227–2237, New Orleans, Louisiana. Association for Computational Linguistics.

Alec Radford, Jeffrey Wu, Rewon Child, David Luan, Dario Amodei, and Ilya Sutskever. 2018. Language models are unsupervised multitask learners.

Nils Reimers and Iryna Gurevych. 2019. Sentence-BERT: Sentence Embeddings using Siamese BERT-Networks. In *Proceedings of the 2019 Conference on Empirical Methods in Natural Language Processing and the 9th International Joint Conference on Natural Language Processing (EMNLP-IJCNLP)*, pages 3982–3992, Hong Kong, China. Association for Computational Linguistics.

Melissa Roemmele, Cosmin Adrian Bejan, and Andrew S. Gordon. 2011. Choice of Plausible Alternatives: An Evaluation of Commonsense Causal Reasoning. In *Logical Formalizations of Commonsense Reasoning, Papers from the 2011 AAAI Spring Symposium, Technical Report SS-11-06, Stanford, California, USA, March 21-23, 2011*. AAAI.

Sirwe Saeedi, Aliakbar Panahi, Seyran Saeedi, and Alvis C. Fong. 2020. CS-NLP team at SemEval-2020 Task 4: Evaluation of State-of-the-art NLP Deep Learning Architectures on Commonsense Reasoning Task. *CoRR*, abs/2006.01205.

Jiajing Wan and Xinting Huang. 2020. KaLM at SemEval-2020 Task 4: Knowledge-aware Language Models for Comprehension And Generation. *CoRR*, abs/2005.11768.

Cunxiang Wang, Shuailong Liang, Yili Jin, Yilong Wang, Xiaodan Zhu, and Yue Zhang. 2020a. SemEval-2020 Task 4: Commonsense Validation and Explanation. *CoRR*, abs/2007.00236.

Hongru Wang, Xiangru Tang, Sunny Lai, and Kwong-Sak Leung. 2020b. CUHK at SemEval-2020 Task 4: CommonSense Explanation, Reasoning and Prediction with Multi-task Learning. *CoRR*, abs/2006.09161.

Luxi Xing, Yuqiang Xie, Yue Hu, and Wei Peng. 2020. IIE-NLP-NUT at SemEval-2020 Task 4: Guiding PLM with Prompt Template Reconstruction Strategy for ComVE. *CoRR*, abs/2007.00924.

Zhilin Yang, Zihang Dai, Yiming Yang, Jaime Carbonell, Russ R Salakhutdinov, and Quoc V Le. 2019. XLNet: Generalized Autoregressive Pretraining for Language Understanding. In H. Wallach, H. Larochelle, A. Beygelzimer, F. dAlché-Buc, E. Fox, and R. Garnett, editors, *Advances in Neural Information Processing Systems 32*, pages 5753–5763. Curran Associates, Inc.

Qian Zhao, Siyu Tao, Jie Zhou, Linlin Wang, Xin Lin, and Liang He. 2020. ECNU-SenseMaker at SemEval-2020 Task 4: Leveraging Heterogeneous Knowledge Resources for Commonsense Validation and Explanation. *CoRR*, abs/2007.14200.

On the Complementary Nature of Knowledge Graph Embedding, Fine Grain Entity Types, and Language Modeling

Rajat Patel and **Francis Ferraro**

University of Maryland, Baltimore County

{rpatel12, ferraro}@umbc.edu

Abstract

We demonstrate the complementary natures of neural knowledge graph embedding, fine-grain entity type prediction, and neural language modeling. We show that a language model-inspired knowledge graph embedding approach yields both improved knowledge graph embeddings and fine-grain entity type representations. Our work also shows that jointly modeling both structured knowledge tuples and language improves both.

1 Introduction

The surge in large knowledge graphs—e.g., Freebase (Bollacker et al., 2008), DBpedia (Auer et al., 2007), YAGO (Suchanek et al., 2007)—has induced knowledge graph-based applications. Properly making use of this structured knowledge is a prime challenge. Knowledge graph embedding [KGE] (Bordes et al., 2013; Socher et al., 2013) addresses this problem by representing the nodes (entities) and their edges (relations) in a continuous vector space. Learning these representations deduces new facts from and identifies dubious entries in the knowledge base. It also improves relation extraction (Weston et al., 2013), knowledge base completion (Bordes et al., 2013) and entity resolution (Nickel et al., 2011).

Entity typing can provide crucial constraints and information on the knowledge contained in a KG. While historically this has been modeled as explicitly structured knowledge, and recent work has modeled the contextual language in order to make in-context entity type classifications, we argue that language modeling techniques provide an effective approach for modeling both the explicit and implicit constraints found in both structured resources and free-form contextual language.

Meanwhile, while language modeling [LM] has historically been a core problem within natural language processing (Rosenfeld, 1994), recent deep

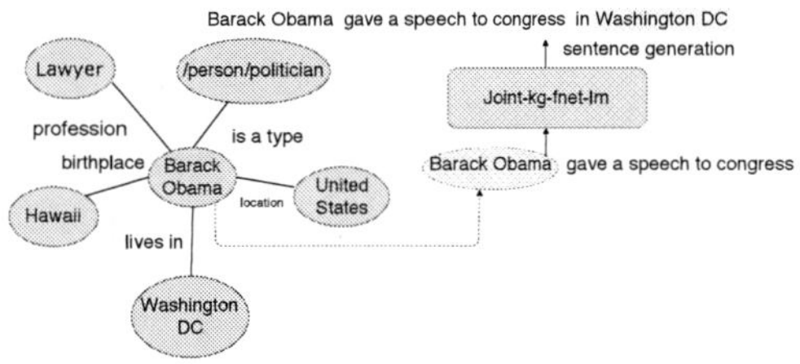

Figure 1: Our joint learning framework learns the representation for the entity "Barack Obama's" in the same embedding space as that of the given input contextual description, "Barack Obama gave a speech to Congress." Further, by learning the entity type of '/person/politician', the model provides a better contextual understanding of the underlying entity.

learning advances have been very successful in convincing the community of the power and flexibility of language modeling (Peters et al., 2018; Devlin et al., 2019; Yang et al., 2019, i.a.).

Building off of insights and advances in knowledge graph embedding, entity typing, and language modeling, we identify and advocate for leveraging the complementary nature of knowledge graphs, entity typing, and language modeling. In it, we introduce a comparatively simple framework that uses powerful, yet well-known, neural building blocks to (jointly) learn representations that simultaneously capture (1) explicit facts and information stored in a knowledge base, (2) explicit constraints on facts (exemplified by entity typing), and (3) *implicit* knowledge and constraints communicated via natural language and discourse. Figure 1 provides an overview of the joint learning framework proposed in this work: an entity ("*Barack Obama*") along with its relations are represented in a continuous vector space. The framework also understands the underlying type ("*/person/politician*") for the given entity by learning the entity representation with contextual understanding ("*Barack Obama*

Proceedings of Deep Learning Inside Out (DeeLIO):

The First Workshop on Knowledge Extraction and Integration for Deep Learning Architectures, pages 89–99

Online, November 19, 2020. ©2020 Association for Computational Linguistics

gave a speech to Congress"). By using the type and the factual information the framework enhances the comprehension of the focus entity in downstream applications like language modeling.[1]

We note that others have explored what KG facts *have already been learned* by *specific*, advanced/contemporary LMs (Petroni et al., 2019). That work utilized a pre-trained BERT model and queried what types of KG facts it contains. In addition, our primary goal is not broad, state-of-the-art performance—though we demonstrate that very strong performance is achievable. Rather, our goal is to examine what the complementary strengths, and evident limitations, of language modeling techniques for knowledge and entity type representation are. In doing so, we show that our joint framework yields empirical benefits for individual tasks. Our models leverage context-independent word embeddings, and we specifically eschew language models pre-trained on web-scale data.[2] Our results further suggest that schema-free approaches to knowledge graph construction/embedding and fine grained entity typing should be studied in greater detail, and competitive, if not state-of-the-art, performance can be obtained with comparatively simpler, resource-starved language models. This has promising implications for low-resource, few-shot, and/or domain-specific information extraction needs.

Using publicly available data, our work has four main contributions. (1) It advocates for a language-modeling based knowledge graph embedding architecture that achieves state-of-the-art performance on knowledge graph completion/fact prediction against comparable methods. (2) It introduces a neural-based technique based on both knowledge graph embedding and language modeling to predict fine-grain entity types, which yields competitive through state-of-the-art performance against comparable methods. (3) It proposes the joint learning of factual information with the underlying entity types in a shared embedding space. (4) It demonstrates that learning a knowledge graph embedding

model and language model in a shared embedding space are symbiotic, yielding strong KGE performance and drastic perplexity improvements.[3]

2   Background

The underlying information in the knowledge bases is difficult to comprehend and manipulate (Wang et al., 2014). A vast number of knowledge graph embeddings techniques have been proposed over the years to mirror the entities and relations in the knowledge graphs. RESCAL (Krompaß et al., 2013) is one of the first semantic-based embedding technique that captures the latent interaction between the entities and the relation. A model such as RESCAL can use graph properties to improve the underlying entity and relation representations (Padia et al., 2019; Balazevic et al., 2019; Minervini et al., 2017). A more simplified approach is defined in DistMult (Yang et al., 2014) by restricting the relation matrix to a diagonal matrix.

Neural Tensor Network (NTN) (Socher et al., 2013) is one such technique that combines the relation specific tensors with head and tail vector representation over non-linear activation function mapped to hidden layer representation. Translational methods like TransE (Bordes et al., 2013) use distanced based models to represent entities and the relationships in the same vector space R^d. TransH (Wang et al., 2014) overcomes the shortcomings of TransE by modeling the vector representation with relations specific hyperplane. TransR (Lin et al., 2015), TransD (Ji et al., 2015) model the representation similar to TransH by having relation specific spaces and decomposing the relation specific projection matrix as a product of two vector representations respectively.

Recognition of entity types into coarse grain types has been explored by researchers over the past two decades. Neural approaches have brought advances in extending the prediction problem from coarse grain entity types to fine-grain entity types. Work by Ling and Weld (2012) was one of the first attempts in predicting the fine-grain entity types. The work framed the problem as multi-class multi-label classification. This work also led to an important contribution of a labeled dataset FIGER, widely used as a benchmark dataset in measuring the performance of fine-grain entity type prediction architectures. Ren et al. (2016a) introduced the

---

[1]Though the entity typing examples here could be interpreted as being hierarchical, our method neither assumes nor requires any type hierarchy.

[2]We do not deny that current pre-trained language models can be effective for other language-based tasks beyond language modeling. However, the reason we do not use transformer LMs like BERT or GPT-2 is because the amount of data they are pre-trained with can make it difficult to (a) fairly compare to previous work (is it the modeling approach, or the underlying, large-scale data at work?), and (b) identify and track the benefits of learning our tasks jointly.

[3]Our code is available at https://github.com/rajathpatel23/joint-kge-fnet-lm.

method of automatic fine-grain entity typing by using hierarchical partial label embedding. Shimaoka et al. (2016) introduced a neural fine-grain entity type prediction architecture that uses semantic context with self-attention and handcrafted features to capture semantic context needed for fine-grain type prediction. Xin et al. (2018b) showed that analyzing sentences with a pre-trained language model enhanced prediction performance. Zhang et al. (2018a) introduced a document level context and signifies the importance of mention level attention mechanism along with the sentence-level context in enhancing the performance of fine-grain entity prediction. Xu and Barbosa (2018) enhanced neural fine-grain entity typing by penalizing the cross-entropy loss with hierarchical context loss for the fine-grain type prediction.

Language modeling has seen great progress in recent times. Bengio et al. (2000) pioneered the renewed use of distributed representation for dealing with the dimensionality curse imposed by the statistical methods. Their language model used recurrent neural networks for dealing with long sequences of text. Mikolov et al. (2010) extended the idea of building the recurrent neural network-based language models with an improved feedback mechanism of backpropagation in time.

We are not the first to examine the intersection of knowledge graph embedding and language modeling. Ristoski and Paulheim (2016); Cochez et al. (2017) directly embed RDF graphs using language-modeling based techniques. Ahn et al. (2017) and Logan IV et al. (2019) have more recently leveraged information from a knowledge base to improve language modeling. However, in addition to knowledge graphs and language modeling, we additionally consider fine-grain entity typing.

With the success of contextualized vector representations and the availability of large-scale, pre-trained language models, there have been a number of efforts aimed at improving the knowledge implicitly contained in word and sentence representations. For example, Bosselut et al. (2019) introduce COMET, which describes a framework to learn and generate rich and diverse common-sense descriptions via language models (e.g., the autoregressive GPT-2). Similarly, Zhang et al. (2019) and Peters et al. (2019) provide insights into aspects of LM on downstream NLP tasks. While we share the overall goal of improving knowledge representation within language modeling, the short-term goals are dif-

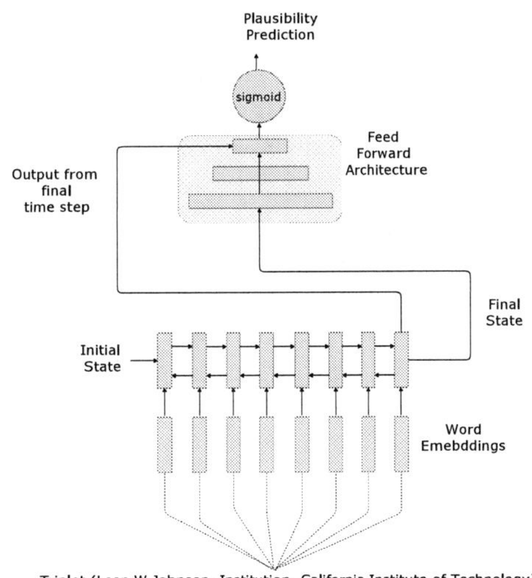

Figure 2: Knowledge Graph Embedding as language modeling, where triples are "tokenized" into word embeddings and the computed, sequential output states are used to predict triple correctness.

ferent, as we focus on individual facts, rather than traditional background/commonsense knowledge, and demonstrating the complementary nature of KGE, entity typing, and LM.

3 Methodology

This section introduces the framework for jointly learning knowledge graph embedding (KGE), fine grain entity types (ET) and language models (LM). It uses a multi-task learning architecture built over baseline architectures for all three tasks. We begin by introducing LM-inspired knowledge graph embedding and fine grain entity typing architectures; we describe the joint learning architectures in §5. Fundamentally, our approach relies on appropriate and select parameter sharing across the KGE, ET, and LM tasks in order to learn these models jointly. While joint learning or multi-task learning through shared parameters have been examined before for a number of tasks, we argue that this parameter sharing is a very effective way to improve KGE, ET, and/or LM (for a particular baseline). Its simplicity is a core benefit.

3.1 Knowledge Graph Embedding as a Language Model

The architecture in Figure 2 embeds the factual entities and the relations. Let G be a knowledge graph (KG) with nodes V and edge E, where V is a set of entities $e_1, \ldots, e_{|V|}$ which are connected to each other by edges E. E is a set of K relations $r_1, \ldots, r_k$. The architecture learns to embed the entities and relations into a (traditionally dense) vector space. Given the head entity e_i, relation r_k and tail entity e_j, we predict whether a given triplet $x_i = (e_i, r_k, e_j)$ is true (in the KG).

The model is a combination of a bi-LSTM (Hochreiter and Schmidhuber, 1997; Schuster and Paliwal, 1997) and a feed-forward architecture. In the spirit of language modeling, we represent each triple x_i input to the architecture as a sequence of n tokens $(x_{i_1}, x_{i_2}, .., x_{i_n})$. These tokens are represented in a continuous vector space by vector v_{i_t} with dimension d, where $v_{i_d} \in R^d$. The bi-LSTM layer produces a learned representation of each token by maintaining two hidden states for each word: the forward state $\overrightarrow{h_{i_t}}$ learns representation from left to right (Eq. (1)) and the backward state $\overleftarrow{h_{i_t}}$ learns the representation from right to left (Eq. (2)):

$$\overrightarrow{h_{i_t}} = \text{bi-LSTM}(W_{\overrightarrow{h}} x_{i_t} + V_{\overrightarrow{h}} \overrightarrow{h}_{i_{t-1}} + b_{\overrightarrow{h}}) \quad (1)$$

$$\overleftarrow{h_{i_t}} = \text{bi-LSTM}(W_{\overleftarrow{h}} x_{i_t} + V_{\overleftarrow{h}} \overleftarrow{h}_{i_{t+1}} + b_{\overleftarrow{h}}) \quad (2)$$

$$h_{i_t} = \text{concat}[\overrightarrow{h_{i_t}}, \overleftarrow{h_{i_t}}]. \quad (3)$$

The forward and the backward states of the bi-LSTM layer are concatenated to produce a sequentially encoded representation h_i for each time step t given the input sequence x_i. The bi-LSTM weight matrices W and V and b are learned during training. In principle the bi-LSTMs can be stacked, though we found not stacking to be empirically effective.

Though the bi-LSTM produces a sequence of hidden states, we summarize the information captured by it in a single, "final" state C_{final}. This state is then used to represent the information encoded by the whole sequence for the subsequent classification task. We let the rightmost state represent the "final" state, i.e., $C_{\text{final}} = h_{i_n}$.[4]

The feed-forward architecture is a multi-layer perceptron with $L = 3$ rectified linear hidden layers (ReLU). The input to the feed-forward layer is a learned final cell state representation C_{final} from the bi-LSTM sequence encoder. The feed-forward process captures the information from the learned sequence encoder and outputs a transformed representation z_l from the final output layer:

$z_l = \text{ReLU}(W_l z_{l-1} + b_l)$, with $z_0 = C_{\text{final}}$, and layer-specific weights W_l and biases b_l.

The output representation z_L is then used to calculate the semantic matching score for the factual input x_t. This score is calculated by incorporating the learned representation z_L with the sequentially encoded final sequence step representation h_t. The product is then passed through a sigmoid activation function, $f(x_t; \theta) = \sigma(z_l^T h_t)$, where θ is a collection of network parameters used for training the language model-inspired knowledge graph embedding architecture. These parameters are jointly learned by minimizing a weighted cross-entropy loss with ℓ_2 regularization (Eq. (4)):

$$J(\theta) = -\frac{1}{N} \sum_{i=0}^{N} k \cdot y_i \cdot \log(f(x_t; \theta)) +$$
$$(1 - y_i) \cdot \log(1 - f(x_t; \theta)) + \lambda ||\theta||^2 \quad (4)$$

where k is the weight assigned to the positive samples during the training, y_i represents the original labels, and λ is the regularization parameter.

As a result of our KGE method, we do not produce or store single, canonical representations of entities and relations. We argue that the lack of a canonical entity embedding is a large benefit of our model. First, it is consistent with the push for contextualized embeddings. Second, we believe that, even in a KG, an entity's precise meaning or representation should depend on the fact/tuple that is being considered.[5]

3.2 Neural-Fine Grain Entity Type Prediction

Recognizing the type of the given entity has been an integral part of tasks like knowledge base completion (Bordes et al., 2013), question answering and co-reference resolution. Ling and Weld (2012) extended the problem of entity type prediction to fine-grain entity types. Given an input vector V_x for entity x, type embedding matrix θ, the function g predicts all the possible entity types t for given entity x as $g(V_x; \theta) = \theta^T V_x$. The model learns the parameters θ by optimizing the hinge loss to classify a given entity into all the possible types T:

$$J(\theta) = \sum_{t=0}^{T} \max(0, 1 - y_t \cdot g(V_x; \theta)). \quad (5)$$

---

[4]In early experiments we tried other approaches, such as averaging all hidden representation to compute the final state ($C_{\text{final}} = \frac{1}{n} \sum_t h_{i_t}$. These caused neither large improvements nor decreases in performance. As a result, we advocate here for the simpler computation of $C_{\text{final}} = h_{i_n}$.

[5]If a single representation is needed, note that because we tokenize entity, types, relations, and arguments into words, we could generate a single representation by combining the, e.g., entity's individual word embeddings according to the LM.

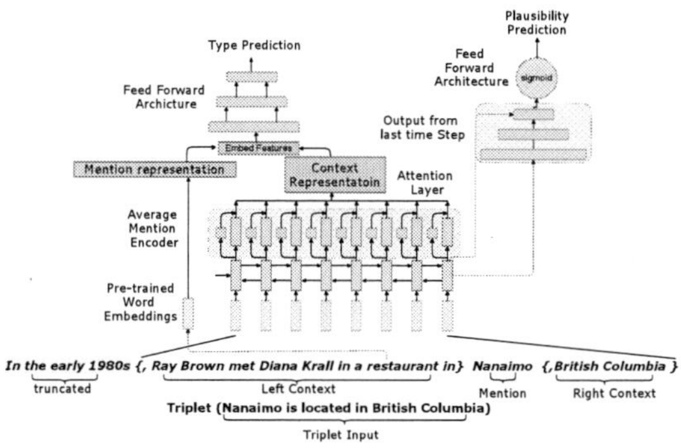

Figure 3: The joint learning architecture for training KGE and entity typing takes in both factual triplets and context information for an entity. Parameters of the architecture are trained to learn both the factual information as well the corresponding entity types.

An entity is predicted to be of type t if $g(x; \theta)$ is greater than a given threshold value τ (typically, $\tau = 0.5$, though it can be set empirically).

The architecture in Figure 3 shows different sets of embedding-based features used to predict the entity type t. Word-level features and context level features—word spans to the left and right of the entity—are taken into consideration. The feature design used here is similar to the design of the features introduced by Shimaoka et al. (2016). We note that our method neither assumes nor requires any type hierarchy, though including a type hierarchy is an avenue for future exploration.

Mention Encoder We encode a mention representation m as the average of word embedding vectors u_i for all words i present in the given entity e: $m = \frac{1}{|n|} \sum_{i=0}^{n} u_i$.

Context Encoder The contextual representation for the given mention e is performed by dividing into left context l_c and right context r_c, where the left context is all the words present on the left of the given entity e, and the right context contains all the words present to the right of the given entity e. The left and right context are encoded by passing the context through a bi-LSTM sequence encoder (Hochreiter and Schmidhuber, 1997; Schuster and Paliwal, 1997). The sequence encoder is similar to the one used by Zhang et al. (2018a). The outputs of the bi-LSTM sequence encoder are the sequential vector representation from both forward (left-to-right) and backward pass (right-to-left), $(l_f, l_b) = \text{BiLSTM}(l_c, h, h_{t-1})$ and $(r_f, r_b) = \text{BiLSTM}(r_c, h, h_{t-1})$, where (l_f, l_b) are the sequential output for the left context from forward and backward passes, (r_f, r_b) are the sequential outputs from the right context from forward and backward passes, h and h_{t-1} are the current and the previous hidden states for forward and backward passes respectively. Left outputs are concatenated to form a left-looking encoding $L_c = \text{concat}[l_f, l_b]$, while right outputs are concatenated to form a right-looking encoding $R_c = \text{concat}[r_f, r_b]$. The complete contextual representation C of the context is the concatenation of the left context and right context representations, $C = \text{concat}[L_c, R_c]$.

Attention We use an attention mechanism to reweight contextualized token embeddings. The attention layer, similar to that of Shimaoka et al. (2016), is a 2 layer feed forward neural architecture where the attention weight for each time step of the context representation is learned given the parameter matrix W_a and W_s: $a_i = \text{softmax}(W_s \tanh(C_i \cdot W_a))$. The context representation is a weighted sum of attention and the context representation, $C_{rep} = \sum_{i=0}^{t} a_i \cdot C_i$.

The attention mechanism used here differs from Shimaoka et al. (2016) such that in our work the contextual embeddings share the same attention parameters. The features extracted from the mention encoder m and attention weighted context encoder C_r are concatenated to form a learned representation $V = \text{concat}(m_i, C_{rep})$ that is passed to the feed-forward architecture for classification.

The feed-forward architecture is a 3-layer neural architecture with a batch normalization layer (Ioffe and Szegedy, 2015) present between the first and the second layers with a ReLU activation (Nair and Hinton, 2010). The input to the feed-forward layer is a concatenated representation from the context and mention encoders. The feed-forward process captures the information from the learned features and outputs a transformed representation $q_l = \max(0, V_l \cdot q_{l-1} + d_l)$ from the final output layer to classify the given mention into the corresponding entity types, where V_l, d_l are the weights and bias for the hidden layer unit l respectively. We initialize $q_0 = C_r$.

3.3 Language Model

The language model predicts the next possible word based on the previous inputs, as $p(w_n | w_1, w_2, ... w_{n-1}) = \prod_i P(w_n | w_{n-k}, ... w_{n-1})$. We use a simple

Method	WN11	FB13	Avg
NTN (Socher et al., 2013)	86.2	90.0	88.1
TransE (Bordes et al., 2013)	75.9	81.5	78.7
TransH (Wang et al., 2014)	78.8	83.3	81.1
TransR (Lin et al., 2015)	85.9	82.5	84.2
TransD (Ji et al., 2015)	86.4	89.1	87.8
TEKE (Wang and Li, 2016)	86.1	84.2	85.2
TransG (Xiao et al., 2016)	87.4	87.3	87.4
TranSparse (Ji et al., 2016)	86.4	88.2	87.4
DistMult (Yang ct al., 2014)	87.1	86.2	86.7
DistMult-HRS (Zhang et al., 2018b)	**88.9**	89.0	89.0
AATE (An et al., 2018)	88.0	87.2	87.6
ConvKB (Nguyen et al., 2017)	87.6	88.8	88.2
DOLORES (Wang et al., 2018)	87.5	89.3	88.4
Proposed method: LM-inspired KGE	88.3	**90.21**	**89.44**

Table 1: Comparison of previous approaches with proposed method on triple classification task.

Methods	Strict F1	Loose Micro	Loose Macro
Ling and Weld (2012)	52.30	69.30	69.90
Ren et al. (2016b)	49.44	68.75	68.75
Ma et al. (2016).	53.54	66.53	68.06
Ren et al. (2016a)	53.30	66.40	69.30
Shimaoka et al. (2016) (w/o Hand-Crafted features)	54.53	71.58	74.76
Shimaoka et al. (2016) (w/ Hand-Crafted features)	59.68	75.36	78.97
Zhang et al. (2018a)	60.05	75.52	78.67
Proposed Method (w/o Hand-Crafted features)	**61.10**	**75.70**	**78.95**
Proposed Method (w/ Hand-Crafted features)	**62.16**	**76.12**	**79.69**

Table 2: The performance of the proposed fine grain entity architecture to previous approaches on FIGER.

LSTM to learn the sequential structure of the text.

4 Experimental Settings

The input to the joint learning architectures are the pre-trained GloVe embedding vectors trained on 840 billion words (Pennington et al., 2014). The parameters of the baseline and the joint learning architecture are learned with Stochastic Gradient Descent and Adam (Kingma and Ba, 2014) as a learning rate optimizer. The training of the joint learning networks is performed with alternating optimization. The loss functions of the respective tasks are optimized at each alternate epoch/ interval. The hyper-parameters for training these joint architecture are chosen manually for the best-performing models on validation sets.

Data For a direct comparison of the performance as possible, we use previously studied datasets. We evaluate KG triple classification using the standard datasets of WordNet 11 (WN11) and Freebase 13 (FB13). WN11 (Strapparava and Valitutti, 2004) is a publicly available lexical graph of *synsets* (synonyms). Freebase (Bollacker et al., 2008) is a collaborative ontology consisting of factual tuples of entities related to each other through semantic relation. While recent work has advocated for examining variants and other derivatives of these datasets such as FB15k-237 and WN18RR (Toutanova and Chen, 2015; Dettmers et al., 2018; Padia et al., 2019, i.a.), there is a relative lack of previous experimental work on these newer datasets. Given space limitations, and in order to compare to the vast majority of previous work, we chose to report on the more common WN11 and FB13.

We evaluate fine grain entity type prediction on the well-studied OntoNotes (Hovy et al., 2006) and FIGER (Ling and Weld, 2012) datasets. The OntoNotes dataset used here is a manually curated dataset by Gillick et al. (2014), consisting of 89 different entity types. FIGER consists of 113 entity types, occuring in sentences from 780k Wikipedia articles and 434 news reports. We evaluate the joint KGE and Entity Typing model on WikiAuto and WikiMan, both introduced by Xin et al. (2018a). WikiAuto is curated by distant supervision, with Freebase entities and types and sentence descriptions from Wikipedia articles. WikiMan is a manually curated dataset from Wikipedia articles with Freebase entities.

Lastly, we evaluate the joint KGE and LM on WikiFact (Ahn et al., 2017), built using the facts from Freebase and Wikipedia descriptions. The content of the dataset is limited to *Film/Actor/* from Freebase. Further the anchor fact defined in the text of the dataset are not used for training the joint model. The description of the entities in the original dataset contain both the summary and the body from Wikipedia. The current study is performed by using the description from the summary section defined in the dataset. The joint model is trained and evaluated with the split of 80/10/10 for train, validation and test sets, respectively.

Metrics KGE triple classification is evaluated through accuracy. The entity type model's performance is evaluated based on three common entity typing metrics—Strict F1, Loose Macro F1 and Loose Micro F1 (Ling and Weld, 2012)—while language modeling is measured by perplexity.

Previous Work as Baselines When possible, we directly compare our model's performance to that of previously published work.

Methods	Strict F1	Macro F1	Micro F1
AFET (Ren et al., 2016a)	20.32	54.51	52.61
KB only (Xin et al., 2018a)	35.12	70.49	63.36
HNM (Dong et al., 2015)	34.88	64.37	68.39
SA (Shimaoka et al., 2016)	42.77	72.40	74.91
MA (KNET) (Xin et al., 2018a)	41.58	72.66	75.72
KA (KNET) (Xin et al., 2018a)	45.49	72.46	**76.22**
Joint Model-Proposed	**46.18**	**72.78**	76.02

Table 3: We compare previous techniques on the WIKI-AUTO dataset for fine-grain typing. The proposed method outperforms all previous, comparable techniques. While techniques that utilize disambiguation to improve the results on the knowledge attention (e.g., KA + D (KNET) from Xin et al. (2018a)) can yield very modest improvements, e.g., to 77 micro F1, due to the extra information used, those results are not directly comparable to the proposed model.

Methods	Strict F1	Macro F1	Micro F1
AFET (Ren et al., 2016a)	18.00	56.33	56.52
KB only (Xin et al., 2018a)	17.00	63.00	40.52
HNM (Dong et al., 2015)	15.00	64.75	65.30
SA (Shimaoka et al., 2016)	18.00	69.44	70.14
MA (KNET) (Xin et al., 2018a)	**26.00**	71.19	72.08
KA (KNET) (Xin et al., 2018a)	23.00	71.10	71.67
Joint Model- Proposed	25.00	**73.40**	**74.43**

Table 4: We compare previous techniques on Wiki-MAN dataset for fine-grain entity type classification.

5 Results and Discussion

This section presents the results of our basic KGE, entity typing models, and the joint learning architecture and their comparison to previous methods. The models were trained using either a 16GB V100 or 11GB 2080 TI GPU (single GPU training only).

5.1 The Effectiveness of a LM-inspired KGE

The proposed knowledge graph embedding architecture (§3.1) is trained for triple classification task: given an input triple x_i, predict whether the fact it represents is true or not. Table 1 provides an overview of performance of our architecture in comparison to previously studies approaches, obtained from the corresponding paper.

Examining the results on WN11 and FB13, we see that in all but one case our approach improves upon the state of the art performance on triple classification task; in that one case (DistMult-HRS on WN11) our model was very competitive. These strong results support our hypothesis that language modeling principles can be an effective knowledge graph embedding technique. In examining per-relation performance on both WN11 and FB13, we observed an increase in the lower bound of accuracy results for relationships on both WordNet and

Freebase, compared to Socher et al. (2013). We see a rise in accuracy from Socher et al. (2013)'s 75.5% to 81% for the *(domain region)* relation from WordNet. On Freebase, we see performance for the *institution* relation goes from 77.2% to 80.9% with the current architecture.

Recently, Yao et al. (2019) presented KG-BERT, which uses a pretrained BERT model to encode and classify triples. While this approach is empirically powerful, and surpasses our approach, we note that due to the limited training context of the current architecture, directly comparing those triple classification results with ours would be mischaracterizing the strengths and limitations of both approaches. Considering the training complexity and costs of transformer networks, our model presents an appealing balance between efficacy and efficiency.

5.2 The Effectiveness of Entity Typing with KGE-Inspired Models

Our novel neural fine grain entity type prediction techniques is compared with previous approaches in Table 2. The neural architecture provides an improvement on FIGER in F1. To have a direct comparison, whe datasets used for the experiments are same as used by Shimaoka et al. (2016) and Zhang et al. (2018a). Our method uses a margin based loss function to learn entity types, and outperforms all the previous methods (Abhishek et al., 2017; Ren et al., 2016a,b) that learn fine grain entity type prediction through margin base loss functions and evaluated on the same datasets.

5.3 The Effectiveness of Joint KGE and Entity Typing

Building on the baseline models, the joint model (Figure 3) addresses the implicit constraint given in the knowledge graph. The architecture learns to correlate the mention entities with the entities present in the context to addresses the problems of "context-entity separation" and "text knowledge separation," as defined by Xin et al. (2018a). The joint architecture is evaluated on the WikiAuto and WikiMan datasets. The model is trained with combination of FB15K dataset and WikiAuto to learn the both the factual information along with the entity typing structure. Tabs. 3 and 4 provide an overview of results from current method and it comparisons with the previous techniques.

We trained and tested the joint model on a combination of datasets for KGE and FNER; see Table 5. The results show the complementary nature

Dataset KGE	Dataset FNER	Strict F1	Macro F1	Micro -F1	Accuracy	AUROC	AUCPR	F1	Precision	Recall
FB13 (our baseline)		-	-	-	90.21	0.96	0.95	0.9	0.89	0.91
WN11 (our baseline)		-	-	-	88.3	0.94	0.93	0.88	0.85	0.91
FB15K (our baseline)		-	-	-	94.73	0.98	0.97	0.94	0.92	0.97
	OntoNotes (our baseline)	53.22	69.36	61.65	-	-	-	-	-	-
FB15k	OntoNotes	53.33	70.47	62.95	93.43	0.97	0.97	0.93	0.9	0.97
WN11	OntoNotes	52.79	69.12	61.62	87.61	0.93	0.94	0.88	0.83	0.94
FB13	OntoNotes	53.34	70.81	63.44	89.79	0.96	0.96	0.9	0.87	0.93

Table 5: We show the changes in performance we observe when training joint fine-grain entity type prediction and triple classification models (bottom portion) vs. single-objective models (top portion). Joint training can lead to improvements on both KGE and FNER.

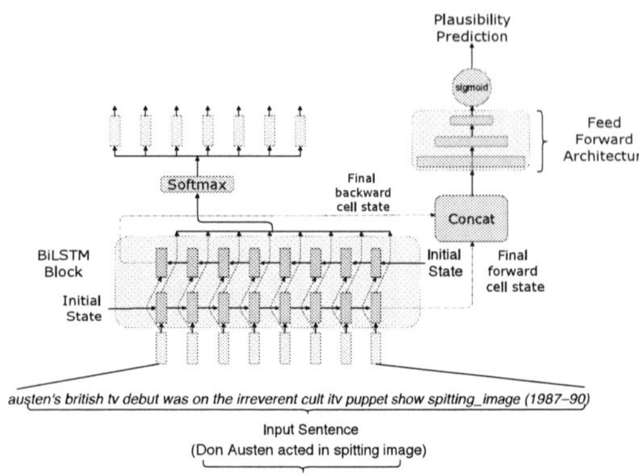

Figure 4: The architecture for joint learning of knowledge graph embedding with language model. We use an LSTM for the LM component, and a bi-LSTM for the KGE component. The LM LSTM and the forward portion of the bi-LSTM are the same, allowing the transfer of knowledge. The architecture takes in as input the whole sentence and the triplet to learn the semantic structure and factual information from the knowledge base.

of learning fine-grain entity types and knowledge graph embedding jointly with steady performances on either task with respect to their baselines.

5.4 The Effectiveness of Joint KGE and Language Modeling

We examine the complementary nature of LM and KGE on the WikFacts dataset introduced by Ahn et al. (2017), which contains both sentences and KGE-style tuples. Figure 4 shows the architecture for jointly learning to embed a KG and model language. We use a single-layer LSTM (unidirectional: left-to-right) for language modeling, though the core KGE architecture relies on an bi-LSTM. We unify these by ensuring that the LM LSTM and the left-to-right portion of the KGE bi-LSTM use the same weights. We compare this joint approach to the same models trained separately and inde-

Model	Perplexity ($\downarrow$)	Acc ($\uparrow$)
LSTM LM (baseline)	440.72	-
bi-LSTM KGE (baseline)	-	**94.22**
Joint LSTM LM + bi-LSTM KGE	**299.17**	93.73

(a) Performance of jointly learning an LSTM LM and bi-LSTM KGE.

Model	Perplexity ($\downarrow$)	Acc ($\uparrow$)
LSTM LM (baseline)	437.22	-
LSTM KGE (baseline)	-	90.66
Joint LSTM LM + LSTM KGE	**353.72**	**93.6**

(b) Performance of jointly learning an LSTM LM and LSTM KGE.

Table 6: We summarize the results from the joint KGE+LM experiments, learned from WikiFacts with a 70k word vocabulary. In 6a we provide results for the architecture shown in Figure 4 (a bi-LSTM KGE, whose forward cells are the cells of a unidirectional LSTM LM). In 6b, we provide results where we replace the bi-LSTM KGE with LSTM LM.

pendently, without any weight sharing, evaluating the LMs on perplexity (lower is better) and KG prediction accuracy (higher is better). We use a vocabulary of the 70k most frequent words.

As Table 6a shows, while there is a very slight decrease in KG prediction accuracy, the distinct improvement in the performance of language model over the baseline LM demonstrates that joint learning is particularly effective for language modeling. This suggests that even simple joint learning can be an effective way of using stated knowledge to improve language modeling.

While joint learning allowed the KG to help the LM, the reverse was not true. We speculate that this is in part because, from a language modeling perspective, the KGE model is able to consider both the forward and backward components. To test this, we replace the KGE bi-LSTM with the same unidirectional LSTM used by the LM. We show these results in Table 6b. Similar to the previous results,

	Sentences
Input sentence	stephen percy steve harris born 12 march 1956 is an english musician and songwriter known as the bassist occasional keyboardist backing vocalist primary songwriter and founder of the british heavy metal band iron maiden he is the only member of iron maiden to have remained in the band since their inception in 1975 and along with guitarist dave murray to have appeared on all of their albums
Output (Joint model)	joseph john james unk born 5 april 1949 is an english musician and actor known as the greatest and guitarist the vocalist guitarist songwriter and guitarist of the band heavy metal band the band he is the founding child of the team band have been by the band until its death in 2003 and toured with unk unk unk they have appeared in one of
Output (baseline)	peter baron dickie unk born 11 august 1943 is an english singer and best and as the most and and and and lead songwriter and member of the heavy rock rock band unk side he is the third singer of the band band have been with the band since its breakup in 1992 while cofounded with with dave tended has have collaborated on hundreds of their films

Table 7: We provide an example of the sentence predicted by the language model jointly learned with knowledge graph embedding and the independently trained language model. Notice how some implicit constraints, learned from the KGE, are transferred to the language model.

KGE allowed LM perplexity to decrease significantly. However, we also see that the LM yielded a 3 point absolute improvement in KG prediction, supporting our hypothesis.

To further demonstrate how our joint learning method improves the semantic understanding of the language, we qualitatively examine the generative capacity of these LMs in Table 7. This provides an example of how joint training a KG and LM can improve output over a singly-trained LM on the same language data, and suggests that joint learning allows transfer of some implicit constraints in the language by learning the underlying relationships between the entities. While both are over-reliant on conjunctive structure, notice how the singly-trained baseline LM starts off alright, but then as the generation continues, loses coherence. Meanwhile, the jointly trained model maintains more coherence for longer. This suggests the KGE training is successfully transferring appropriate thematic/factive knowledge to the LM.

6 Conclusion

This work proposes a joint learning framework for learning real value representations of words, entities, and relations in a shared embedding space. Joint learning of factual representation with contextual understanding shows improvement in the learning of entity types. Learning the language model with knowledge graph embedding simultaneously enhances the performance on both modeling tasks. Our results suggest that language modeling could accelerate the study of schema-free approaches to both KGE and FNER, and strong performance can be obtained with comparatively simpler, resource-starved language models. This has promising implications for low-resource, and few-shot, and/or domain-specific information extraction needs.

Acknowledgements We would like to thank members and affiliates of the UMBC CSEE Department, including Ankur Padia, Tim Finin, and Karuna Joshi. Some experiments were conducted on the UMBC HPCF. We'd also like to thank the reviewers for their comments and suggestions. This material is also based on research that is in part supported by the Air Force Research Laboratory (AFRL), DARPA, for the KAIROS program under agreement number FA8750-19-2-1003. The U.S.Government is authorized to reproduce and distribute reprints for Governmental purposes notwithstanding any copyright notation thereon. The views and conclusions contained herein are those of the authors and should not be interpreted as necessarily representing the official policies or endorsements, either express or implied, of the Air Force Research Laboratory (AFRL), DARPA, or the U.S. Government.

References

Abhishek, Ashish Anand, and Amit Awekar. 2017. Fine-grained entity type classification by jointly learning representations and label embeddings. *ArXiv*, abs/1702.06709.

Sungjin Ahn, Heeyoul Choi, Tanel Pärnamaa, and Yoshua Bengio. 2017. A neural knowledge language model. *ArXiv*, abs/1608.00318.

Bo An, Bo Chen, Xianpei Han, and Le Sun. 2018. Accurate text-enhanced knowledge graph representation learning. In *NAACL-HLT*.

Sören Auer, Christian Bizer, Georgi Kobilarov, Jens Lehmann, Richard Cyganiak, and Zachary G. Ives. 2007. Dbpedia: A nucleus for a web of open data. In *ISWC/ASWC*.

Ivana Balazevic, Carl Allen, and Timothy Hospedales. 2019. Tucker: Tensor factorization for knowledge graph completion. In *EMNLP-IJCNLP*, pages 5188–5197.

Yoshua Bengio, Réjean Ducharme, Pascal Vincent, and Christian Janvin. 2000. A neural probabilistic language model. *J. Mach. Learn. Res.*, 3:1137–1155.

Kurt D. Bollacker, C. J. Evans, Praveen Paritosh, Tim Sturge, and Jamie Taylor. 2008. Freebase: a collaboratively created graph database for structuring human knowledge. In *SIGMOD Conference*.

Antoine Bordes, Nicolas Usunier, Alberto García-Durán, Jason Weston, and Oksana Yakhnenko. 2013. Translating embeddings for modeling multi-relational data. In *NIPS*.

Antoine Bosselut, Hannah Rashkin, Maarten Sap, Chaitanya Malaviya, Asli Celikyilmaz, and Yejin Choi. 2019. COMET: Commonsense transformers for automatic knowledge graph construction. In *Proceedings of the 57th Annual Meeting of the Association for Computational Linguistics*. Association for Computational Linguistics.

Michael Cochez, Petar Ristoski, Simone Paolo Ponzetto, and Heiko Paulheim. 2017. Global rdf vector space embeddings. In *International Semantic Web Conference*, pages 190–207. Springer.

Tim Dettmers, Pasquale Minervini, Pontus Stenetorp, and Sebastian Riedel. 2018. Convolutional 2d knowledge graph wmbeddings. In *AAAI*.

Jacob Devlin, Ming-Wei Chang, Kenton Lee, and Kristina Toutanova. 2019. BERT: Pre-training of deep bidirectional transformers for language understanding. In *NAACL*.

Li Dong, Furu Wei, Hong Sun, Ming Zhou, and Ke Xu. 2015. A hybrid neural model for type classification of entity mentions. In *IJCAI*.

Daniel Gillick, Nevena Lazic, Kuzman Ganchev, Jesse Kirchner, and David Huynh. 2014. Context-dependent fine grained entity type tagging. *ArXiv*, abs/1412.1820.

Sepp Hochreiter and Jürgen Schmidhuber. 1997. Long short-term memory. *Neural Computation*, 9:1735–1780.

Eduard H. Hovy, Mitchell P. Marcus, Martha Palmer, Lance A. Ramshaw, and Ralph M. Weischedel. 2006. Ontonotes: The 90% solution. In *HLT-NAACL*.

Sergey Ioffe and Christian Szegedy. 2015. Batch normalization: Accelerating deep network training by reducing internal covariate shift. *ArXiv*, abs/1502.03167.

Guoliang Ji, Shizhu He, Liheng Xu, Kang Liu, and Jun Zhao. 2015. Knowledge graph embedding via dynamic mapping matrix. In *ACL*.

Guoliang Ji, Kang Liu, Shizhu He, and Jun Zhao. 2016. Knowledge graph completion with adaptive sparse transfer matrix. In *AAAI*.

Diederik P. Kingma and Jimmy Ba. 2014. Adam: A method for stochastic optimization. *CoRR*, abs/1412.6980.

Denis Krompaß, Maximilian Nickel, Xueyan Jiang, and Volker Tresp. 2013. Non-negative tensor factorization with rescal. In *Tensor Methods for Machine Learning, ECML workshop*.

Yankai Lin, Zhiyuan Liu, Maosong Sun, Yang Liu, and Xuan Zhu. 2015. Learning entity and relation embeddings for knowledge graph completion. In *AAAI*.

Xiao Ling and Daniel S. Weld. 2012. Fine-grained entity recognition. In *AAAI*.

Robert L. Logan IV, Nelson F. Liu, Matthew E. Peters, Matt Gardner, and Sameer Singh. 2019. Barack's wife hillary: Using knowledge-graphs for fact-aware language modeling. In *ACL*.

Yukun Ma, Erik Cambria, and Sa Gao. 2016. Label embedding for zero-shot fine-grained named entity typing. In *COLING*.

Tomas Mikolov, Martin Karafiát, Lukás Burget, Jan Černocký, and Sanjeev Khudanpur. 2010. Recurrent neural network based language model. In *INTERSPEECH*.

Pasquale Minervini, Luca Costabello, Emir Muñoz, Vít Novácek, and Pierre-Yves Vandenbussche. 2017. Regularizing knowledge graph embeddings via equivalence and inversion axioms. In *ECML/PKDD*.

Vinod Nair and Geoffrey E. Hinton. 2010. Rectified linear units improve restricted boltzmann machines. In *ICML*.

Dai Quoc Nguyen, Tu Dinh Nguyen, Dat Quoc Nguyen, and Dinh Q. Phung. 2017. A novel embedding model for knowledge base completion based on convolutional neural network. In *NAACL-HLT*.

Maximilian Nickel, Volker Tresp, and Hans-Peter Kriegel. 2011. A three-way model for collective learning on multi-relational data. In *ICML*.

Ankur Padia, Konstantinos Kalpakis, Francis Ferraro, and Timothy W. Finin. 2019. Knowledge graph fact prediction via knowledge-enriched tensor factorization. *J. Web Semant.*, 59.

Jeffrey Pennington, Richard Socher, and Christopher D. Manning. 2014. Glove: Global vectors for word representation. In *EMNLP*.

Matthew Peters, Mark Neumann, Mohit Iyyer, Matt Gardner, Christopher Clark, Kenton Lee, and Luke Zettlemoyer. 2018. Deep contextualized word representations. In *NAACL*.

Matthew E. Peters, Mark Neumann, Robert Logan, Roy Schwartz, Vidur Joshi, Sameer Singh, and Noah A. Smith. 2019. Knowledge enhanced contextual word representations. In *EMNLP-IJCNLP*.

Fabio Petroni, Tim Rocktäschel, Sebastian Riedel, Patrick Lewis, Anton Bakhtin, Yuxiang Wu, and Alexander Miller. 2019. Language models as knowledge bases? In *EMNLP-IJCNLP*.

Xiang Ren, Wenqi He, Meng Qu, Lifu Huang, Heng Ji, and Jiawei Han. 2016a. Afet: Automatic fine-grained entity typing by hierarchical partial-label embedding. In *EMNLP*.

Xiang Ren, Wenqi He, Meng Qu, Clare R. Voss, Heng Ji, and Jiawei Han. 2016b. Label noise reduction in entity typing by heterogeneous partial-label embedding. *ArXiv*, abs/1602.05307.

Petar Ristoski and Heiko Paulheim. 2016. RDF2Vec: RDF graph embeddings for data mining. In *International Semantic Web Conference*, pages 498–514. Springer.

Ronald Rosenfeld. 1994. *Adaptive statistical language modeling: A maximum entropyapproach*. Ph.D. thesis, Computer Science Department, Carnegie Mellon University.

Mike Schuster and Kuldip K. Paliwal. 1997. Bidirectional recurrent neural networks. *IEEE Trans. Signal Processing*, 45:2673–2681.

Sonse Shimaoka, Pontus Stenetorp, Kentaro Inui, and Sebastian Riedel. 2016. An attentive neural architecture for fine-grained entity type classification. In *AKBC@NAACL-HLT*.

Richard Socher, Danqi Chen, Christopher D. Manning, and Andrew Y. Ng. 2013. Reasoning with neural tensor networks for knowledge base completion. In *NIPS*.

Carlo Strapparava and Alessandro Valitutti. 2004. Wordnet affect: an affective extension of wordnet. In *LREC*.

Fabian M. Suchanek, Gjergji Kasneci, and Gerhard Weikum. 2007. Yago: a core of semantic knowledge. In *WWW '07*.

Kristina Toutanova and Danqi Chen. 2015. Observed versus latent features for knowledge base and text inference. In *Proceedings of the 3rd Workshop on Continuous Vector Space Models and their Compositionality*, pages 57–66.

Haoyu Wang, Vivek Kulkarni, and William Yang Wang. 2018. Dolores: Deep contextualized knowledge graph embeddings. *ArXiv*, abs/1811.00147.

Zhen Wang, Jianwen Zhang, Jianlin Feng, and Zhigang Chen. 2014. Knowledge graph embedding by translating on hyperplanes. In *AAAI*.

Zhigang Wang and Juan-Zi Li. 2016. Text-enhanced representation learning for knowledge graph. In *IJCAI*.

Jason Weston, Antoine Bordes, Oksana Yakhnenko, and Nicolas Usunier. 2013. Connecting language and knowledge bases with embedding models for relation extraction. In *EMNLP*.

Han Xiao, Minlie Huang, and Xiaoyan Zhu. 2016. Transg : A generative model for knowledge graph embedding. In *ACL*.

Ji Xin, Yankai Lin, Zhiyuan Liu, and Maosong Sun. 2018a. Improving neural fine-grained entity typing with knowledge attention. In *AAAI*.

Ji Xin, Hao Zhu, Xu Han, Zhiyuan Liu, and Maosong Sun. 2018b. Put it back: Entity typing with language model enhancement. In *EMNLP*.

Peng Xu and Denilson Barbosa. 2018. Neural fine-grained entity type classification with hierarchy-aware loss. In *NAACL-HLT*.

Bishan Yang, Wen tau Yih, Xiaodong He, Jianfeng Gao, and Li Deng. 2014. Embedding entities and relations for learning and inference in knowledge bases. *CoRR*, abs/1412.6575.

Zhilin Yang, Zihang Dai, Yiming Yang, Jaime Carbonell, Russ R Salakhutdinov, and Quoc V Le. 2019. Xlnet: Generalized autoregressive pretraining for language understanding. In *NeurIPS*.

Liang Yao, Chengsheng Mao, and Yuan Luo. 2019. Kgbert: Bert for knowledge graph completion. *ArXiv*, abs/1909.03193.

Sheng Zhang, Kevin Duh, and Benjamin Van Durme. 2018a. Fine-grained entity typing through increased discourse context and adaptive classification thresholds. In **SEM@NAACL-HLT*.

Zhao Zhang, Fuzhen Zhuang, Meng Qu, Fen Lin, and Qing He. 2018b. Knowledge graph embedding with hierarchical relation structure. In *EMNLP*.

Zhengyan Zhang, Xu Han, Zhiyuan Liu, Xin Jiang, Maosong Sun, and Qun Liu. 2019. ERNIE: Enhanced language representation with informative entities. In *ACL*.